PLACE IN RETURN BOX to remove this checkout from your record.
TO AVOID FINES return on or before date due.
MAY BE RECALLED with earlier due date if requested.

DATE DUE	DATE DUE	DATE DUE

5/08 K:/Proj/Acc&Pres/CIRC/DateDue.indd

GOLF GREENS

I hope that you enjoy this book for I believe it is one of the most important and informative ones I have ever written. Sincerely

Michael J. Hurdzan

GOLF COURSE ARCHITECT

NOVEMBER 2010

GOLF GREENS

History, Design, and Construction

By

DR. MICHAEL J. HURDZAN

ASGCA Golf Course Architect

WILEY

JOHN WILEY & SONS, INC.

Published by John Wiley & Sons, Inc., Hoboken, New Jersey
Published simultaneously in Canada

Library of Congress Cataloging-in-Publication Data:

Hurdzan, Michael J., 1943–
    Golf greens: theory, design, and construction / by Michael J.
Hurdzan
        p. cm.
Includes bibliographical references and index.
    ISBN 0-471-45945-3 (Cloth)
    1. Golf courses—Design and construction. 2. Golf
courses—Management. I. Title.
    GV975.H765 2004
    796.352'06'8—dc22

                                        2003023861

Printed in the United States of America

10 9 8 7 6 5 4 3 2 1

CONTENTS

CHAPTER **2**

Golf Green Theories 39

CHAPTER **3**

Design Considerations for Golf Greens 107

CHAPTER **4**

Making Intelligent Compromises in Green Construction . .141

CHAPTER **6**

Rootzone Sampling, Testing, and Evaluation 223

CHAPTER **7**

Selecting Turfgrasses or Artificial Turf for Greens 255

PREFACE

Golf greens are not only the focal point of a golf hole, and often the hallmark of the golf course, but also the center of some heated debates among designers, builders, agronomists, greenkeepers, salespeople, and golfers. Such discussions can be healthy and help advance the art and science of greens, but only if there is a factual point of departure for the differing points of view. As a person with over 45 years of observations, experiences, training, testing, and learning about golf greens, I felt compelled to try to provide that baseline of information. Realize, however, that the baseline has a lot in common with the rhetorical question about whether the glass is half full or half empty: the answer is only in the opinion of the evaluator. Thus, this text, or any text, is only a reflection of the author's biases. I would ask the thoughtful reader not to simply accept my version, but rather to use it as a starting point as you begin or continue your own search for the right answers about greens.

I suspect that one reason such a book has not been written before is because no one ever wanted to endure the proverbial slings and arrows that would accompany opining on such a volatile and subjective topic as greens. I have tried to be as evenhanded and objective as my background would permit, but even so, I expect to recieve a fair share of criticism about some portions of my interpretations.

Another reason that this might be a pioneering text is because the subject is very complex. Simply isolating and studying its various facets, without examining the functional interrelationships involved, seems to me to be counterproductive. For example, one needs to understand the agronomic aspects of greens in the context of the strategic and the marketing aspects, for the topics cannot be fully separated—each affects the others.

Then, too, I have learned, and continue to learn every day, that pure and applied research may conflict, and what works in the lab or on a test plot doesn't always work on a golf course, and vice versa. There are lots of reasons why that is, many not well understood, but nonetheless real. Sometimes it is as simple as the fact that most test plots are flat, and greens are not, and other times it is as complex as the interactions of microclimate, water quality, turf cultivar, pests and stresses, and individual best management practices.

Lastly, I believe that scientists and greenkeepers are both just beginning to understand just how complex greens really are. They are dynamic little islands, each with its own unique chemical, physical, biological, and environmental influences and characteristics, overlaid with an array of inputs and pressures that, too, are unique. The one constant over time, and the master of all of these factors is, and always will be, the greenkeeper, who usually succeeds by being vigilant, intuitive, and dedicated. To those men and women, this book is dedicated.

MICHAEL J. HURDZAN, PH.D.

ACKNOWLEDGMENTS

Although only one name appears as author, there was a team of folks who should be credited for contributing to this book. First among equals is my dear, departed mentor, Jack Kidwell, who was a legendary greenkeeper, an accomplished player, and a skilled golf course designer. Jack could, and did, do it all, and fortunately he guided and shaped my learning for 40 years, starting when I was a 13-year-old greenkeeper for him. Jack understood all of the functional aspects of golf greens, although he never had the benefit of a science based, college background. He knew what worked, and he learned by trial and error on a public golf course that was his principal source of income, where a failure could have been devastating to a small family business. In that context Jack was a bold man who was putting his reputation and livelihood on the line with each new experiment. I trust that the true student will be motivated by Jack Kidwell's courage and will rely on the same skills that he used: questioning, listening, experimenting, observing, and reasoning.

No text on golf greens could possibly be written without acknowledging the United States Golf Association (USGA) for their vision, dedication, and motivation to make golf courses better. They have always sought out and employed or funded smart people who advanced our knowledge and understanding of golf course maintenance, and in particular greens. The Greens Section should be recognized as the world's authority on golf courses and their environments, and their motivation is completely selfless. They defend what they know but they will open-mindedly evaluate new technology and other opinions for the good of the game.

Dr. Norman Hummel and I have been friends and co-instructors of a class on golf greens for many years, a class given by the Golf Course Superintendents Association of American (GCSAA). By repetition Norm has taught the real world of rootzone testing. He not only contributed a great deal to my knowledge bank, he also provided nearly all of the images for Chapter 6, for which I am grateful.

Others who contributed information and pictures or illustrations include Jack Marquart, David Solga, Ed Walsh, Ron Whitten, Matthew Wolf, Ian McQueen, Bert McFadden, Steve Miles, Cole McGinnis, and T. R. Wait.

Last but not least is all of the staff of Hurdzan/Fry Golf Course Design who assisted me, with sincere thanks to P. J. Barton, Chris Hurdzan, and Scott Kinslow. Special thanks to my dear wife Linda, who did all of the word processing and supported this effort.

TIMELINE

1744   First record of payment to a greenkeeper by the Royal Burgess Golfing Society. Payment is six shillings per quarter and a change of clothes, mainly to cut new holes.

1774   Old Musselburgh Golf Club credited with innovating hole cutter.

1780s Old Alick is first recorded greenkeeper by Society of Blackheath Golfers. Cut holes with a knife, started flags.

1823   George Robertson is dismissed as keeper of the green at St. Andrews for being incompetent or incorrigible for his care of the links. Caddy David Pirie is hired to supersede him. First green committee is appointed in 1827 to supervise David Pirie. They too are fired in 1827 for failing to carry out duties imposed upon them.

1828   Edwin Budding invents a machine for cutting nap of wool carpets that becomes a lawn mower and is patented in 1830.

1829   Musselburgh authorizes one pound for an instrument for forming (cutting) holes.

1832   First mention of double putting greens at The Old Course at St. Andrews, Scotland.

1848   Tom Morris is hired by Allan Robertson as a laborer to improve The Old Course by widening fairways and creating the large double greens.

1851   Morris fired by Robertson over using the newly introduced gutty ball. Morris goes to Prestwick to become pro and greenkeeper.

1855   Walter Alexander and Alexander Herd, caddies, are appointed to take charge of The Old Course at a salary of six pounds betwixt them.

1856   A sum of 25 pounds is voted for the improvements of the putting greens at The Old Course, under the superintendence of Allan Robertson.

1863   Alexander Herd resigns custody of the links at St. Andrews and so the green committee looks for a new custodian.

1863   Tom Morris is hired from Prestwick to go back to St. Andrews.

1868   New putting green built at the home hole at St. Andrews so now course can be played both clockwise and counterclockwise. Old Tom also fills in a few sand pits.

1870   Old Tom Morris digs his first well on The Old Course from which to irrigate the sixth green.

1878	Green committee told to submit proposals to a general meeting of the Royal and Ancient Golf Club (R&A) before proceeding to fill up any bunkers, or otherwise materially alter the golf course.
1885	James Olcott establishes turf garden in Connecticut as a hobby.
1887	Old Tom Morris installs the last well at St. Andrews so each green has its own irrigation source.
1888	Golf becomes permanently established in the United States.
1895	Committee appointed to present Tom Morris with a testimonial. The R&A buys an annuity that will pay Old Tom the interest on the annuity, which amounts to an extra 100 pounds a year for the rest of his life.
1895	The New course at St. Andrews is placed under the charge of the green committee.
1895	In America, Worthington Mower Corporation begins producing horse-drawn mowers.
1900	Dr. Charles Vancouver Piper, educated at Washington State College in botany and biology, joins U.S. Department of Agriculture (USDA) staff, becomes interested in turfgrasses.
1902	Old Tom Morris dies.
1910	F. W. Taylor submits for patents for golf green construction methods. Receives them in 1916.
1917	C. V. Piper and Russell A. Oakley publish book, *Turf for Golf Courses* (1923, 1929) which becomes bible of turf care.
1921	U.S. Golf Association (USGA) establishes Green Section, starts publication of the *Bulletin.*
1924	Canadian greenkeepers organize into an association with most members in Ontario.
1925	Self-propelled mowers introduced for golf courses.
1926	Colonel John Morley begins formally the National Association of Greenkeepers of America (later to evolve to GCSAA).
1926	Dr. C. V. (of Piper and Oakley) dies on February 11.
1927	Professor Lawrence Dickinson starts winter program in greenkeeping at University of Massachusetts, while Dr. John Monteith, Jr., a plant pathologist, takes over green section.
1929	Great Depression. British golf union establishes turf research station.
1931	Dr. Russell A. Oakley (of Piper and Oakley) dies August 6.
1932	John Monteith, Jr., and Arnold Dahl publish *Turfgrass Diseases and Their Control* for USGA Green Section.

Evolution of the Golf Green

ORIGINS OF GOLF

The exact origin of the game of golf is unknown, but it is generally accepted that the game has been evolving for more than 600 years. Early evolution was a process of adopting elements of other related activities or games until golf was similar but unique.

By the fifteenth century, the Dutch were playing a game on ice with implements and techniques that closely resemble early golf clubs and golf swings (see Figure 1-1). However, the object was to strike a pole in the ice with the ball in the fewest strokes, and not to put the ball into a hole. It is reasoned that this ice game was also played on dry land and introduced in Scotland by Dutch seamen and merchants who were actively trading with Scotland, and who had time to kill while in harbor waiting for their ships to be refitted. The Scottish linksland was close by, and it was covered by pioneer grasses that were often stunted by the wind, salt air, and heat, or grazed short by wild or domestic animals (see Figure 1-2).

It is not known when the transition was made from striking an object post to putting the ball into an object hole, but it was some time before the first rules of golf were written in 1741. The very first rule of the first rules states: "1. The ball shall be teed no more than one club's length from the hole" (see Figure 1-3). Later the rules were revised to read two club lengths, then four, then ten. Finally, someone somewhere began the profession of golf course architecture by simply separating the teeing ground completely from the area around the object

Figure 1-1: Origins of golf can be traced back to a fifteenth century Dutch game played on the ice, with the target being an upright stake, not a hole. (Painting by Bareno Avercamp, circa 1650)

Figure 1-2: When golf became established in Scotland in the 1600s, it was played on the unimproved and unmaintained linksland, so greens were not distinct from the rest of the golf course, and everything together was called a "fair-green." (Painting by Allan Stewart, 1919)

hole. Some historians believe that this was Allan Robertson or Old Tom Morris in the mid-1800s at the Old Course at St. Andrews. Precisely when and how the teeing ground became distinct from the putting ground is unknown, but it was a critical step in the evolution of the game, as well as in the process of allowing the area we now call greens to begin its own distinct evolution.

In 1857, there were 18 known and established places to play golf in Scotland, which increased to 59 by 1880. While the Dutch game on ice has faded into oblivion, golf had taken root on the earth and is still prospering.

Figure 1-3: The first rule of the first rules dealt with how close together were the object hole and the teeing ground for the next hole, so already greens were becoming the most important golf course feature.

The next 120 years saw rapid changes in all aspects of the game, including demographics, personalities, techniques, rules, equipment, hazards, sites, conditions, golf courses, and not least of all, golf greens. The area around the hole or cup came to be treated with more care and concern than other parts of the golf course and slowly evolved into modern-day putting greens. From then until now, there have been a succession of approaches to constructing and maintaining golf greens, with each having the goal of raising the standard of putting green quality. Many of those old ways are being rediscovered because of today's concern for environment, while others simply formed the foundation from which the art and science of greenkeeping has evolved. Therefore, it seems worthwhile to review this rich history and identify significant advances or discoveries, all the while keeping in perspective the impact of social influences that were prevailing during each of these periods.

FIRST GREENKEEPERS

The earliest verified record of a person being employed to care for a golfing green, or "fairgreen" as golf courses were once called, seems to be a receipt of payment in 1744 to an unnamed boy who was retained as "greenkeeper and caddy" for the sum of 24 shillings per year and a change of clothes by the Royal Burgess Golfing Society. Later, in 1819, a William Ballantyne was paid one

Leith 10 June 1819

£1..1..—

Received from Mr Cundell the sum of one Guinea being in payment of annual allowance by the Thistle Golf Club to me

William Ballantyne

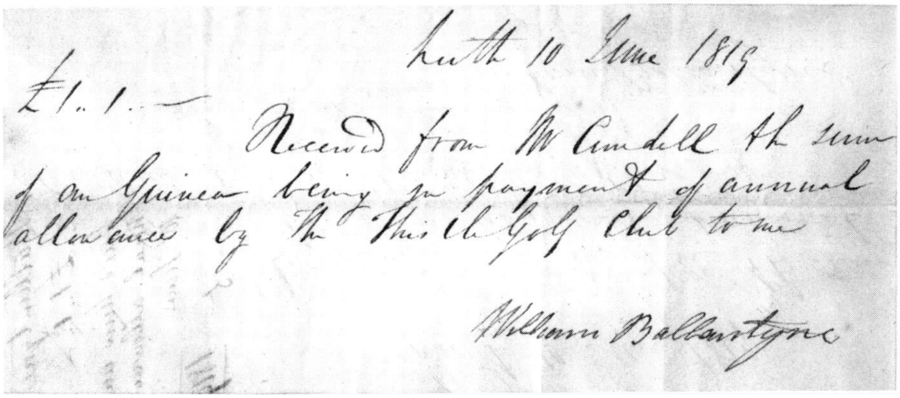

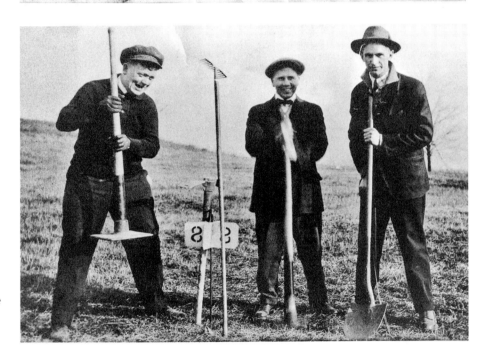

Figure 1-4: An 1819 original receipt for an annual payment to William Ballantyne by the Thistle Golf Club, presumably to perform some greenkeeping duties.

Figure 1-5: Greenkeeping was firmly established as a profession by the mid- to late 1800s, but the crews were small and their equipment was simple.

guinea for the care of grounds for the Thistle Golf Club (see Figure 1-4). What those duties entailed is not clear, but this does show that by this point golfers no longer wanted to simply play the linkslands as they found them, and were willing to pay out some money to preserve or improve them. It is reasonable to assume these early greenkeepers (see Figure 1-5) were not much more than farmhands, employed to be jack-of-all-trades repairmen, whose main golf course duties were to repair minor damage caused by animals, especially burrowing rabbits, and occasionally to change holes and tee markers; they were not necessarily involved with grooming the turf.

THE INFLUENCE OF OLD TOM MORRIS

It is also evident that greenkeeping was not a highly paid or esteemed profession, and hence those early pioneers labored in anonymity, until a person of extraordinary abilities became publicly recognized and respected. That person was Old Tom Morris (see Figure 1-6). In H. S. C. Everard's *A History of the Royal and Ancient Golf Club, St. Andrews 1754–1900* (London: William Blackwood & Sons, 1907), he writes that in 1863, when Old Tom Morris was hired back to St. Andrews from Prestwick after Allan Robertson's death, Tom's duties were listed as follows:

> His duties were explained to him: to keep the putting greens in good order, to repair, where necessary, and to make the holes. For heavy work, carting, &c., he was to be allowed assistance at the rate of one man's labour for two days in the week, and it was understood that he was to work under the Green Committee. Emblems of office were then handed over to him—to wit, a barrow, a spade, and a shovel—in prophetic instinct, belike, that "saund," and ever "mair saund, Honeyman," would be in future ages the watchword of the newly-appointed Chief of the Links. The sum of £50 per annum was voted by the Union Club for payment of the custodian's salary, and £20 for the upkeep of the Links.

Figure 1-6: Although not the first greenkeeper, Old Tom Morris established himself as a leader in the profession as well as in the game of golf, and is still universally known a century after his death.

In the delightful book by G. Witteveen and B. Labbance, titled *Keepers of the Green: A History of Golf Course Management* (Chelsea, MI: Ann Arbor Press, 2002), there is much more detail about the demands and skills of early greenkeepers, and the book is recommended to students of golf course history.

However, the reasons for Old Tom's fame were not only his agronomic skills, but also his proven expertise as a player, club maker, ball maker, teacher, innovator, spokesman, father, and pious man. Every aspect of his personal and professional life earned the respect and endearment of folks in and outside the game of golf. Therefore, he first emerged as a leader and then as a senior practitioner whom colleagues and employers followed because he got favorable results.

Imagine a golf course superintendent of today convincing golfers to reduce their course by four holes, from 22 to 18, as Old Tom did at St. Andrews. Or his closing the course on Sundays to give the golf course a rest. Or alternating the direction the course was played to reduce wear, or building and filling in bunkers as he pleased (see Figure 1-7). Whether legend or fact, Old Tom's role in every one of these decisions seems to have been central. But just as important in establishing Old Tom's stature were the playing conditions at St. Andrews, especially the greens, which became the standard against which every other golf course and all other greens were judged.

HELL BUNKER—OLD COURSE.

[From a photo by J. Patrick & Sons, Edinburgh.

Figure 1-7: This late 1800s photograph of Hell Bunker on the Old Course at St. Andrews shows the sod wall ravetment to stabilize the face against wind and water erosion.

One should not forget that the social climate of Old Tom's era also helped him become even more influential. First, as a result of the Industrial Revolution in northern Europe in the nineteenth century, more people had more time for leisure activities, including golf. Golf equipment also became less expensive because of mass production. Hence there was greater interest in places to play golf, like the vacation town of St. Andrews. Newspaper accounts and golf books were becoming more widely available, and thus making public figures of golf celebrities. Telegraph, then telephone, communications allowed news and sporting results to be reported in a more timely fashion, and exhibition matches were widely promoted and hence of greater public interest. This new interest resulted in town governments acquiring or protecting public land for the growth and playing of golf, and thereby seeking the advice of golf professionals like Morris. Inevitably there developed competition between towns for the recognition of the finest links, and this in turn spawned the collecting and spending of money to improve their links or golfing grounds. This was important, because without money and resources, the greatest greenkeeper in the world could not produce notable results, and that is as true today as then. So in the late nineteenth century, the greenkeepers, course designers, and constructors had some money available with which to advance their crafts and creations. Finally, there developed the social dynamic of forming a committee of concerned golfers to justify and monitor the work and expenditures of the greenkeeping staff, and to advise them on matters of concern to golfers. The Green Committee was born and thus began an even faster upward spiral to obtain and maintain the very best golfing turf, particularly putting surfaces.

Old Tom Morris is credited with accidentally discovering the virtues of routine sand topdressing to improve the density and uniformity of putting turf when he accidentally spilled a wheelbarrow of sand on a green, and the turf thrived. While the benefits of fertilization, lime, sulfates, and compost were well known in other forms of agriculture, it was not until Tom's time that money would be used for such materials to improve the growth of turfgrasses on golf courses. Likewise, the basics of drainage and the advantage of irrigation had long been known in agriculture, but not until Old Tom's era would they be justified to improve linksland golf courses. Old Tom was credited with digging shallow wells at each green for irrigation and with making minor drainage improvements in bunkers. So during the period from about 1850 to 1890, there was the making of "the perfect storm": golfers paying to use golfing grounds; competition between golf courses for income and prestige; formation of green committees whose mission it was to improve the playing conditions; Old Tom Morris gaining recognition as an industry leader and turfgrass innovator; an incredible growth spurt in terms of the number of golfers and golf courses; and recognition of putting greens as being of primary importance to golfers and as a mark of distinction between courses. Golf had money, incentive, and leadership, but limited know-how.

GOLF GREENS AND GREENKEEPING EVOLVE

An excellent glimpse of the state of greenkeeping at the turn of the twentieth century is given in an 1897 letter to the editor of *Golf Magazine* (British), written by an A. H. Pearson of the Notts Golf Club (see Figure 1-8). For purposes of this text, I will summarize a few of his main points, ideas that will become important in shaping the next 100 years of knowledge about golf greens and their evolution.

According to Pearson, earthworms were a major pest. Worms produced casts or small earthen mounds that, unless removed before mowing, would streak and smother the turf beneath them, leaving an imperfect putting surface. Since this was a time before sophisticated pesticides, suggested earthworm control measures included a drench of lime dissolved in water and a topdressing of fine charcoal dust. However, Pearson also recognized the value of earthworms as natural aerifiers, so he further suggested using topdressing of coarse sand broomed into the turf and wormholes to help keep them open for the turfgrass. Rolling of greens was a common practice in the late nineteenth century, but some greenkeepers were beginning to recognize the negative impact of rolling in causing soil compaction on some sites.

Pearson stressed the value of using good clean seed for overseeding and that some grasses are better adapted to some situations than others, but he acknowledged that producing a mature putting surface takes time. Sodding of greens with established turf was not uncommon, so care in cutting and laying the sod was already known to be important in establishment. Amending rootzones with ashes, sand, or other porous material was a practice that was encouraged to gain the benefit of deep rooting by the turf, and improved soil capillarity.

By the 1890s mowing of greens had evolved from using the sickles and scythes of the mid-1800s to using push-type reel mowers (see Figure 1-9). These remained in sporadic use well into the 1930s. However, frequent mowing was thought to impoverish the soil, encourage weeds and mosses, and stress the turf. Fertilization was usually confined to spring with a light application, and Pearson warned of negative effects that can come from either too heavy an application or selecting the wrong nutrient source. And lastly, he conceded that even "Under the best conditions it [putting green turf] cannot withstand the trampling of feet, which it has to endure on anything like a crowded course, unless it has an occasional rest, and where there are a number of daily players, duplicate greens should be provided."

Meanwhile, golf in the United States did not become permanently established until 1888 (see Figure 1-10), and there is no reference basis for greenkeeping in this country until almost 1900. This 10- or 12-year period of golf's infancy in the United States created opportunity for many young Scotsmen who knew something about maintaining a golf course to come to America and work within this now rapidly growing pastime. However, most were experienced on

THE MAINTENANCE OF GOOD PUTTING GREENS.

———

To the Editor of GOLF.

SIR,—I see in last week's "Tee-Shots" a note on the destruction of worms upon putting-greens. The destruction of worms is a very simple matter. A few lumps of unslaked lime placed in a cask of water, and allowed to remain until the lime has settled, will make lime water, which can be poured off, and if the greens are watered with this inexpensive liquid the worms will all come up to the surface and die ; or, again, a dressing of fine charcoal dust will have the effect of destroying the worms. But I would ask the question, "Does one want to destroy the worms?" I dare say the average green-committeeman will think me mad to ask such a question. Well, sir, I am comparatively young (as a golfer), but I have seen and heard of so many foolish things being done upon Golf greens that, even if I be mad I should find plenty of good company upon green-committees. To return to the worms. These are chiefly found upon the heavier soils, and I think they play a most important part in draining and aerating the soil, and if you destroy them you will find the greens become sodden, dead to play upon ; the soil will become sour, and the grass coarse and rank. I would deal with such greens by sanding them well from time to time, and have them well brushed over with a birch broom, lightly applied, to distribute the worm casts. In course of time, as the applications of sand take effect, the grass will become finer and the greens keener, also the worms will be greatly reduced in number, and when the sand acts to keep the soil porous, their services can be dispensed with.

My experience of inland links is that they are not half enough sanded, rarely brushed, and twice too much rolled. I have heard a green-committeeman advocate daily rolling. This would ruin *any* green in the winter, and, with anything like heavy soil, it would be disastrous in any weather. I believe nearly all greens would be better with less rolling and more brushing.

With regard to seaside links, one generally finds the sanding very much overdone and moss rampant, calling in unmistakable tones for manure. I am not going to mention the names of any links, and if you publish my remarks I shall take my niblick to protect myself from the indignation of my own green-committeemen ; so I will continue my criticisms. Some committees sow grass seeds upon their greens ; *cui bono?* They do not grow, and if they did they would ruin the greens, being quite unsuitable. I have seen what are called "hay-seeds," *i.e.*, sweepings from a hay chamber, containing cocksfoot (*Dactylis glomerata*), rye-grass (*Lolium*), and other coarse grasses.

with the ordinary soil ashes, sand, or some other material to make it more porous, and on poor, sandy soil by mixing some better soil with the sand to encourage the roots of the grass. On some sandy links I have seen the turf laid with only an inch or two of poor soil between the roots and a bed of sandstone, with the result that the grass was baked up by a few weeks of hot weather. Again, I have seen such relaid greens beautifully prepared, but raked and rolled as level as a billiard-table, which takes away half the charm of putting upon them. Undoubtedly, natural greens are the best, but if one has to re-lay them a certain amount of roll and inequality of contour should be preserved. I have heard of greens being concreted underneath to prevent their burning up, but this seems to me quite a wrong course, as it altogether prevents the action of capillary attraction which is the action by which Nature keeps sandy soils moist during dry weather, so that unless the concrete is placed so low beneath the surface as to form a reservoir it would be worse than useless, and the cost must be something serious to contemplate. Turf cut for relaying greens is, so far as my observation goes, generally far too thin. Of course thin turf is easy to lay, but if half the roots are cut off it has a poor chance of withstanding dry weather. The turf should be cut at least two inches thick. On established putting-greens, especially on sandy links, constant and continued mowing impoverishes the soil, and the grass becomes poor, weedy, and half smothered with moss. The greens should then be dressed during the early spring with some good chemical manure, properly prepared so that it will not burn the grass ; soluble so that the first shower puts it out of sight and carefully balanced in its ingredients so as to manure the grass without causing a coarse growth. Bones encourage clover, and although I have seen clover sown I cannot imagine anything more undesirable on a putting-green than a carpet of white clover. It bruises to a pulp when much walked upon, and in damp or dew it holds the moisture so that a ball will scarcely travel over it. Basic slag is open to the same objection. Nitrate of soda makes a rank growth of grass, and is far too quickly washed away What one wants is a perfect, plant food, with the lime element kept as low as possible. May I say, in closing, a word on behalf of the poor turf. Even if of the best quality, and under the best conditions it cannot withstand the trampling of feet, which it has to endure on anything like a crowded course, unless it has an occasional rest, and where there are a number of daily players, duplicate greens should be provided. This is done on many links, but on others it is not, and the poor turf comes in for an unmerited amount of abuse.

I am, Sir, &c.,

Notts Golf Club.   A. H. PEARSON.

═══════════════════

ANSWERS TO CORRESPONDENTS.

———

HON. SEC.—The usual practice is to give him a warning, and tell him that next time you will expect a medical certificate ; otherwise he will only be paid for the number of days he has been at work. We should recommend you to pay the full wages this time.

———

MANCHESTER GOLF CLUB.

The annual dinner of the Manchester Golf Club took place on January 30th, at the Grand Hotel, Manchester, the captain, Mr. A. C. Knight, in the chair. It had been arranged that the captain's prize should be played for in the afternoon, but the heavy fall of snow made Golf impossible, and the competition was unavoidably postponed. The disappointment did not prevent a considerable number of members appearing at the dinner, which was in every way a great success. The

Figure 1-8: Early golf magazines like *Golf* (British) often had editorial or question-and-answer columns, which today can give insights into problems and solutions of early golf courses, especially putting greens.

Figure 1-9: By the 1920s in the United States, green-keeping was a recognized profession and golf courses had fairly large staffs because wages were low, maintenance equipment was crude, and maintenance expectations were rising. Notice the large number of push mowers.

Figure 1-10: Just as when golf was introduced into Scotland and was played on unimproved and unmaintained open areas, so, too, was it in 1888 when golf was permanently introduced to the United States. (Lithograph after drawing by Everett Howry, 1931)

sandy linksland golf courses that experienced a climate of fairly moderate and predictable weather. Thus, when employed on U.S. golf courses with conditions similar to those in Europe, such as on sandy soils found along the New England coasts or Long Island, they did well, and many of their golf courses became legendary for the quality of their turf and playing conditions. However, when given a golf course site with conditions uncharacteristic of linksland, they struggled and experimented to find management techniques that were better suited. This need for new and better understanding of how to grow turfgrass comparable in quality to those grown on sandy coastal sites ushered in a whole new emphasis in agriculture, loosely called grassland science or agrostology.

EARLY SOURCES OF INFORMATION ABOUT GOLF GREENS

The very early information sources were seed suppliers such as Sutton's (see Figure 1-11) or Carter's (see Figure 1-12) out of the United Kingdom, or later the O. M. Scott & Company in the United States (see Figure 1-13). Companies selling supplies to the horticulture and agriculture industry made attempts to

Figure 1-11: Early 1900s catalog from Sutton Seed Company of the United Kingdom was a source for information on construction and management of golf greens.

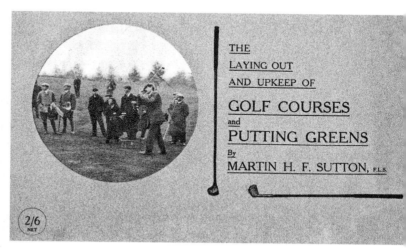

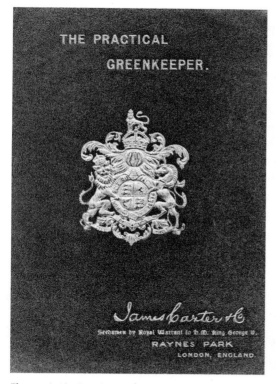

Figure 1-12: One issue of a series of supply catalogs and helpful hints for greenkeepers published by the Carter Seed Company of England.

Figure 1-13: A 1920 booklet published by O. M. Scott & Company to assist greenkeepers in building and establishing golf courses. (Courtesy of O. M. Scott & Co.)

expand their markets by offering products that they believed would benefit turf-grass culture. University research on pastures and/or grasslands was often cited as information sources, and the earliest turf consultants were university professors. Taken together these company publications were important contributors to the body of information that greenkeepers needed, but it was mostly recycled information that had been gathered for other purposes, and it was not based upon research or investigations that were golf course specific. As a result, there was a need for a new science and engineering devoted to golf courses, athletic fields, and lawns. Thus in the early 1900s, Drs. C. V. Piper and Russell A. Oakley were hired by the United States Department of Agriculture (USDA) to begin studying turfgrasses, and their contributions are examined in detail later in this chapter.

By the early twentieth century, the American Industrial Revolution had produced enormous wealth and opportunity for some people. Immigration to America was active and fueled by not only the freedom and potential that our expanding country offered, but also by some severe and oppressive living conditions in other parts of the world. The new immigrants to America brought new energy, skills, and ideas that could blossom and grow and help fuel all aspects of our culture, businesses, and industries, including golf. Donald Ross was one such example (see Figure 1-14).

America in 1900 was still in the mode of the "gay nineties" (1890s, that is), and technology was rapidly changing American lifestyles. One example was the production of the internal combustion engine, which when installed in a chas-

[From a photo by Ewing & Co., Dornoch.

17TH HOLE.
D. J. Ross at " The Witch."

Figure 1-14: A photo of Donald Ross playing golf at Royal Dornoch in his childhood home in Scotland, where he learned all aspects of the golf business before coming to America in 1898.

The late Henry Ford (left) built many experimental tractors before putting one into mass production. This experimental model, which he called an "automobile plow", was built in 1907.

Figure 1-15: 1907 news item showing the state of development of internal combustion engine powered tractors, and why horses and men would remain the primary power source in golf course maintenance for another 20 years.

sis produced the "horseless carriage" or automobile and tractor (see Figure 1-15). This meant a greater freedom of movement, and at a faster pace, so time and space begin to shrink. In 1908, Henry Ford would mass-produce the $800 Model "T," which would make the automobile affordable to the average folks. This, when coupled with high national prosperity and industrial automation that lowered the costs of goods and services, allowed even the common man free time for luxuries such as golf. Although golf in the early 1900s was still somewhat a rich man's sport, mass production began lowering the cost of clubs and balls, and allowed people of more modest means to take up the game. This in turn created a need for new golf courses, and on sites further from towns and cities than previously conventional means of travel, such as walking, bicycles, trains, coaches, and so on, would allow. As golf spread across America, the sites, climates, and problems of producing acceptable golfing turf became even more important and complex, intensifying the need for turf science.

The internal combustion engine soon found all other sorts of applications beyond people movers, such as lawn mowers, tractors, and then bulldozers. This process took another 20 years or so, but without question this mechanical power affected golf courses, and ultimately golf greens (see Figure 1-16).

A documented starting point in the evolution of printed materials on greens and greenkeeping in America is the 1897 book of H. J. Whigham. He was an accomplished player who published one of the first golf books in America, titled *How to Play Golf* (Chicago: Herberts, Stone & Company, 1897). He also

Figure 1-16: By the 1920s, green mowers had become specialized pieces of equipment.

offered many opinions and insights on golf courses and golf greens during these early formative years of 1888 to 1897, and his writing set the standard for much of what would come later. He wrote, "…must your putting greens be flawless," and to obtain that condition he further advised:

> …[t]hat were neither absolutely flat or square. In size they should vary, but they should never have a radius of less than 40 feet [sic, 5,000 square feet].
>
> The excellence of your putting green depends, to a large extent, upon the kind of mowing machine you possess. The ordinary Philadelphia lawn mower of common use does not cut the grass close enough for golfing purposes, and so it is necessary to have a special machine made, with the same width of blade, but with smaller wheels, so that the knife may be brought closer to the ground. This slight change in the implement will make all the difference between good and bad greens.
>
> Finally, you must have a water supply available at each green. The actual amount of water to be used varies, of course, with the difference in climate.

He advocated sodding greens and suggested that one inch of water per week is adequate in most climates, but could be inadequate in extreme ones. Whigham also stressed that sandy loam soils are preferred throughout the golf course, and that a springtime rolling with a three- to five-ton steamroller would help smooth out the turf (see Figure 1-17). So with golf less than a decade old in America, influential golfers were already setting standards for green maintenance.

Some help came from Europe in 1899, when Horace Hutchinson wrote *The Book of Golf and Golfers* (London: Longmans, Green, & Co., 1899), with a chapter on "Laying-out and Up-keep of Greens," written by Messrs. Sutton & Sons, of Reading (see Figure 1-18). Since the Suttons were in the seed business, they naturally recommended more specialized varieties called "golf grasses," consisting of fine fescues, meadow grass, and dwarf perennial rye grass on sandy or chalk soils. Heavy soils, they suggested, require *Poa trivialis* and *Agrostis*.

Prior to planting, the Suttons recommended that greens be given:

> ...a heavy dressing of well-rotted farmyard or stable manure...or on sandy soils, dressing of marl, applied at the time the greens are made, will obviate interminable work in later years, and produce a verdant spot in droughty seasons when surrounding herbage has given up.

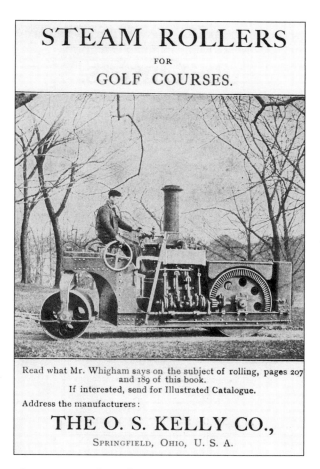

Figure 1-17: Rolling of greens with heavy rollers was espoused as a method of producing smooth putting surfaces.

Figure 1-18: During the end of the nineteenth century and the first quarter of the twentieth, many books were published on golf course and green design, construction, and upkeep.

Later they write: "[T]he principal constituents of plant-food required by grasses, and of which most soils are liable to run short, are nitrogen, phosphoric acid, potash and lime." Of course, they offer to sell some excellent products to answer these needs.

Since the profession of golf course architecture was well established in England, the Suttons remained politically correct and avoided any reference to how to design or build golf greens, or the need for irrigation, again reflecting a philosophical difference between the United States and Europe regarding watering turf.

However, the most authoritative voices on turfgrass management seem to be found in a 1906 book, *Golf Greens and Green-keeping,* also edited by Horace Hutchinson for *Country Life Library of Sport* (London: Country Life, Ltd., 1906) (see Figure 1-18). Fourteen experts contributed their expertise, six or seven of whom were active golf course architects. The book covered a wide range of experiences and observations on various soil types that, taken together, formed some bedrock principles for building and maintaining golf greens, principles that established a baseline for turf science in America.

GOLF GREENS AND GREENKEEPING BECOME MORE SOPHISTICATED

To summarize these experts, they generally agreed that seed should be sown in the fall; thereafter, it takes six to nine months to produce a mature turf strong enough for regular play, and using sod or "turves" works well, but the sod should come from a known and clean seed source. Rootzones were only mod-

Figure 1-19: Topdressing with sand and compost mixes was a popular greenkeeping technique. One person spread the topdressing with a shovel, another brushed it into the turf, and the third person "poled" the green prior to mowing. Note how these golf course workers of the early 1900s are dressed.

Figure 1-20: Horses were a common source of power for constructing and mowing before tractors were developed for golf course use.

ified by working up the soil to a depth of 6 to 12 inches, incorporating in some proven quality organic matter and some natural occurring mineral (chemical manure) or organic fertilizers. Topdressing with light soil or sand was important (see Figure 1-19). Greens were mowed with a scythe for the first couple of mowings, and until "...sufficiently strong to be able to resist the slight snatching movement of a (mowing) machine, which can then be used with safety." Light frequent rolling was encouraged, along with frequent use of "...an iron-toothed rake." Drainage by installed tile lines or gravel filled sumps is done as needed. Irrigation should be light and frequent when the grass is young and tender and infrequent and deep when the green is mature. All simple but good advice.

Back in America, the most common maintenance problems on greens still remains weeds, worms, mosses, worn out or compacted areas, and being able to sufficiently water turf during dry conditions. As in Europe, tools available to greenkeepers were organic fertilizers and a few chemical manures (ammonium nitrate, nitrate of soda, sulfate of ammonia, potash, phosphoric acid, etc.), sulfur, lime, and charcoal along with rakes, shovels, brooms, and wheelbarrows, and sifting screens for compost and topdressing. Greenkeepers might have man- or horse-drawn mowers (see Figure 1-20), carts for hauling, perhaps a water wagon, and a variety of harrows, drags, and farm implements. A crew might consist of the greenkeeper and one or two laborers, supplemented with caddies when needed. Despite these limitations, the golf courses seem quite playable as shown in pictures from that period.

Figure 1-21: Cover of a 1935 catalog for greenkeeping equipment. Studying such catalogs gives insights into the materials and methods used during that period.

Just a few years later, in 1912, Martin H. F. Sutton, F.L.S., edited a book titled *The Book of The Links: A Symposium on Golf* (London: W. H. Smith, 1912) (see Figure 1-18). Here eight different authors, four of whom were golf course designers, offered views on course maintenance and specifically greenkeeping. Drainage was beginning to be emphasized, along with the importance of an irrigation source. Worms remain a big problem but worm killers are available (from Suttons, of course). By now heavy rolling has gone out of fashion and given way to light topdressing and light rolling. Specially selected and blended seeds were advised, along with some weed control materials (both from Suttons, of course), and numerous other tips and insights were offered. But by far the most illuminating feature of the book, for those interested in the history of greenkeeping, is the appendix of tables and useful information. By browsing these pages one can form an appreciation of the state of greenkeeping at the turn of the century. A 1935 catalog of greenkeeping equipment provides similar insights (see Figure 1-21). A comparison of these sources would provide insights into putting green maintenance in the United Kingdom up to the time of World War II.

Although electricity was known about even before Ben Franklin and his famous key and kite episode, and Thomas Edison introduced his electric light bulb in 1880, electricity was never harnessed and made commercially available until almost the 1890s in America, and then only in larger cities closer to the generation source. There were as many different types of electricity with regard to voltage, cycles, and amperages as there were electricity producers and suppliers, with dozens of different types in large cities. Only through President Roosevelt's 1934 Rural Electrification Act did electric power become more standardized as producers figured out how to share transmission lines. But even so, electricity wasn't universally available in the United States until the 1950s. Until then, only 10 percent of the nation's farms had electricity, compared to 70 percent of city dwellers. Therefore, during the early part of the 1900s, power sources available to golf courses located away from metropolitan areas were confined to horses, crude internal combustion engines, and wind or water mills. This lack of a power source and crudeness of electric motors and pumps meant irrigation for most golf courses was impractical. A few places like National Golf Links, Pine Valley, and other wealthier clubs could erect windmills (see Figure 1-22) and water towers, but irrigation was still rare.

Figure 1-22: Electrical service was not available to many golf courses until the early 1950s, leaving wind as the best source of power to pump irrigation water. Consequently, irrigation of golf greens was inconsistent, and volume and pressure were usually low.

GOLF GREENS WITHOUT IRRIGATION

Golf courses without irrigation would simply plant the most drought-tolerant grasses practical, and hope for reasonable rainfall during the golf season. A 1921 USGA *Green Section Bulletin* (see Figure 1-23) stated:

> Eleven years ago there were three grass putting greens in this locality (Southern California) and all of them were failures in every respect.... These three greens disappeared ten years ago and during the next six years no attempt was made to get anything better than oiled sand greens.

Without any irrigation water or power source to pump it, the alternative was to not bother with planting grass on golf greens and instead make putting surfaces of bare soil or oiled sand. Oiled sand greens were developed by simply excavating a green cavity perhaps six to eight inches deep, filling it with a medium to fine sand, then drenching it with used motor oil. The oil kept out the weeds and burrowing insects, as well as helped to bind the sand particles together to resist wind erosion. If the United States Environmental Protection Agency (EPA) had existed back then, it probably would have had strong negative opinions of oiled sand greens. Nonetheless, this was a popular way to build greens in parts of North America, and many still persist today. In the plains states of the United States and prairie provinces of Canada, oiled sand greens still exist, and sand green golf championships are still held. In fact, in Charlottesville, VA, there is still a sand green course.

Since approach shots to sand greens don't hold or check up very well, the technique for playing on a sand green is a bump and run style. Once a golf ball is on the putting surface, it is marked, and the area between the ball mark and the hole is smoothed down of footprints, ball marks, and so on. Smoothing is done with a toothless rake, called a "smoother," or a broom, a piece of carpet, or a drag mat. Then the ball is replaced and putted.

But even without irrigation and turf surfaces, golfers and greenkeepers were trying to find ways to improve playing conditions of greens. Below is a 1923 article from the USGA describing some additional techniques:

Sand Greens on a Sawdust Base

> About two years ago it was reported to the Green Section that a sand green made on sawdust base would provide a resiliency so that balls could pitch to the green. The plan included a base of sawdust, six or eight inches deep, well tamped, then covered with soil, and finally covered with sand. The first sand green of this kind was built on the course of the Ridgewood Country Club, Columbia, S.C., and a second one at Pinehurst, N.C. Mr. Richard S. Tufts reports on his results at Pinehurst as follows:

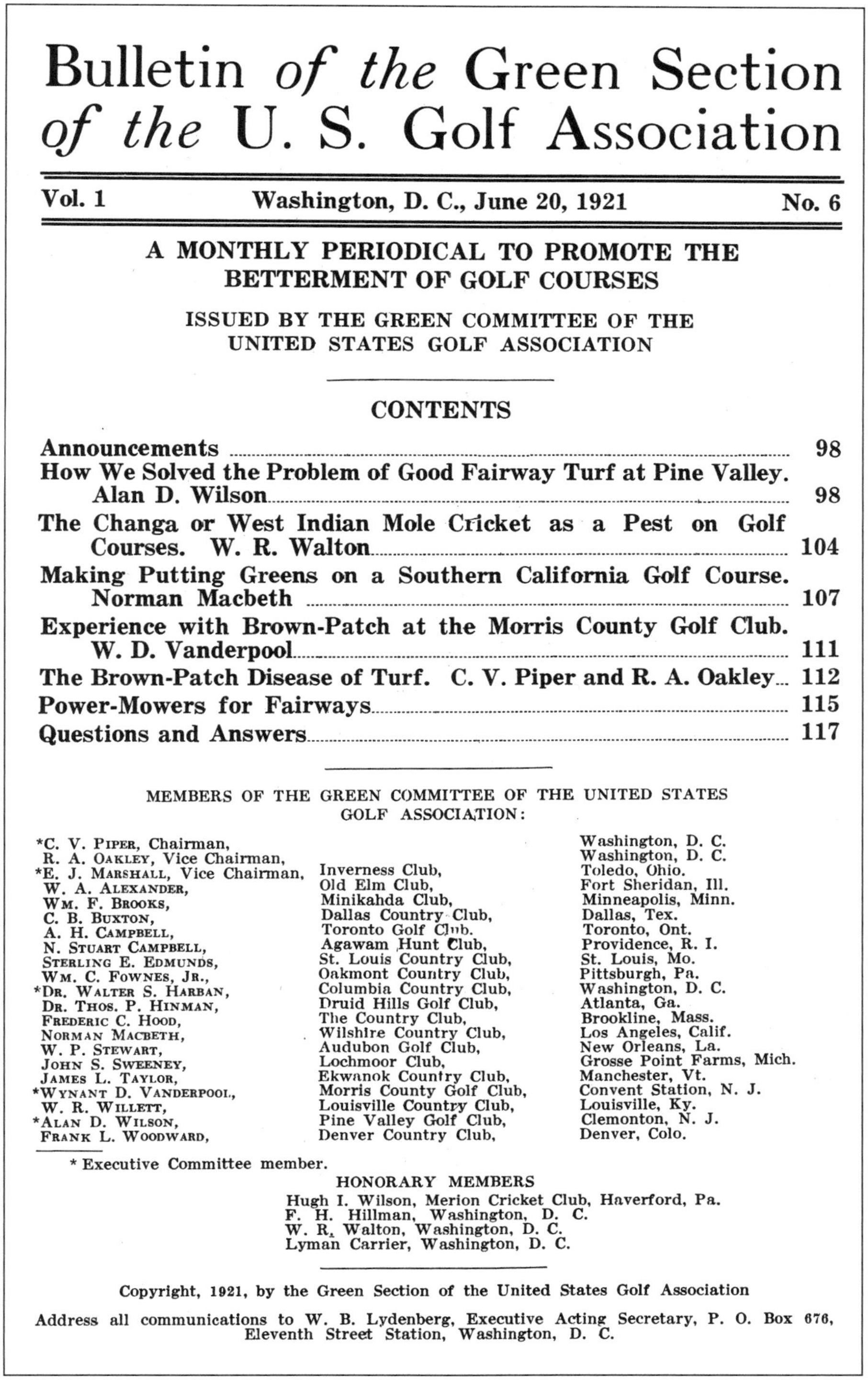

Bulletin *of the* Green Section *of the* U. S. Golf Association

Vol. 1 **Washington, D. C., June 20, 1921** **No. 6**

A MONTHLY PERIODICAL TO PROMOTE THE BETTERMENT OF GOLF COURSES

ISSUED BY THE GREEN COMMITTEE OF THE UNITED STATES GOLF ASSOCIATION

CONTENTS

Address all communications to W. B. Lydenberg, Executive Acting Secretary, P. O. Box 676, Eleventh Street Station, Washington, D. C.

Figure 1-23: In 1921, the USGA began publishing the *Green Section Bulletin,* which was a timely and science based source of information on greenkeeping. (Courtesy of United States Golf Association)

"I have just returned from Columbia and am glad to submit a report on the experience they have had there with their sawdust greens, and also on our own experience.

"I do not believe that these greens have worked out satisfactorily in either case. The main objection to them seems to be excessive maintenance. At Columbia they have been using too much sand and too little soil on top of the sawdust, with the result that the sawdust works up through the sand making the putting very uneven. They have used from one-half inch to one inch of sand, which is too much, as heel-marks are always left in such an amount of sand.

"Our own experience with these greens has been a little more satisfactory. We used about two inches of loam as top-dressing on top of the eight inches of sawdust on one-half of the green, and about three inches on the other half of the green. The half with the thicker top-dressing became too stiff and a ball landing on the green did not receive the deadening effect of the sawdust beneath. The other half of the green has worked out satisfactorily, although we find that the maintenance is about twice what it is with the sand-clay greens.

"The main objection to these greens is that it is impossible to get the surface flat, as it is always slightly rolling and therefore not quite true to putt on. Furthermore, in order to use the greens it would be necessary for us to double the maintenance force that we have in use on the courses, and even then they would not putt as true as our sand greens. We therefore do not consider that it is advisable to replace our sand greens with the sawdust, even though their action can be made satisfactory."

Another problem with any variety of oiled sand green is that, by necessity, they had to be flat, for if they had any slope to them they would erode when they received any significant precipitation. They were usually 20 to 30 feet across with the hole cut right in the middle (see Figure 1-24), so they became a bit monotonous to play. However, to quote the old cliché, "They were better than nothing," and having played on them personally, I believe they are a lot of fun.

Where water for golf greens was sufficient, either as precipitation or through irrigation, fine grass putting surfaces were preferred over oiled sand or greens covered with rough vegetation such as common Bermuda grass or tall fescue. Donald Ross's beloved Pinehurst resort operated for almost 35 years with oiled sand greens, until 1934, when the greens were converted to Bermuda grass. Modern-day information on sand greens can be found on the website for Pasture Golf (www.pasturegolf.com) under the topic of questions and answers about "sand greens."

As an interesting side note, Pete Dye tells the story of meeting Donald Ross often in the mid to late 1940s, when Dye, who was stationed at nearby Fort Bragg, would play golf at Pinehurst. Dye claims the mounded greens on Pinehurst Number Two came about because Ross topdressed the common

A PROFESSIONAL FOUR-BALL MATCH UNDER WAY ON THE LINKS AT CAMDEN, SOUTH CAROLINA ^{Photo by Kirk}

Bermuda grass on the greens with about a quarter inch of sand each week. Dye says Ross often talked about rebuilding those greens to get rid of the crowned effect but died before he could. So then everyone started to believe that was the way Ross wanted them. Now many think those are great greens, but Dye isn't so sure that Donald Ross would think so.

Figure 1-24: Where no irrigation for greens was available, a common method of green construction was to use oil-drenched sand.

NATIVE SOIL GREENS

Some attempts were made by early golf course builders to make the greens rootzones that would support finer turf, but restricted budgets of time or money forced compromises that often were less than ideal. It would be instructive to remember how golf courses were built before the advent of bulldozers and earthmovers in the late 1930s or after World War II.

The best description of how horses and slip scrapers or pans (see Figure 1-25) were used to build golf greens was written by an L. W. Sporlein in about 1920.

> Since golf courses are made in all kinds of soils, the methods of construction will vary somewhat in accordance with their locality. However, there are three principal methods in general use for constructing greens. In this article I shall endeavor to show in a brief manner, from my own experience, how economy in green construction can be attained. The major problem always being to move soil in such a way as to eliminate hand labor as much as possible.
>
> Where the soil is not of a heavy nature one of the most generally used methods is that of employing the five-foot fresnos or dump scrapers. The equipment units required consist of three fresnos each, drawn by four

(a)

(b)

Figure 1-25: (*a*) and (*b*) Until after World War II, the most common sources of power for constructing golf courses was men and horses. As a result, golf greens were generally low profile and built from native soil.

horses, one "railroad" or a sturdy plow with a good team to draw it, four drivers, a loader, a dumper, a plow "shaker" or holder, all under the direction of a superintendent.

In cases where it is desirable or necessary to save the top soil at the green site for replacement on the green after it has been roughly shaped up, the surface soil only is removed, and piled up as near as possible to the green. It is placed either directly in front of, or to the side most convenient for hauling to the green surface, after roughing in with the less fertile soils obtained while building the traps.

After the topsoil has been removed from the green site, the traps are marked off with the plow, and two furrows are plowed along the side nearest the green. The fresnos are now loaded by keeping one runner in the groove left by the plow making the second furrow. A sharp turn towards the green takes a full load of earth directly to the point where needed. The man dumping the fresnos always designates where each load is to be placed and is ready when the load reaches that point. Keeping the trip from the trap to the green and back as short as possible, will enable one to handle much more direct in a day's time. The tendency is for the team drivers to take a much longer route back to the trap after their fresno is emptied than is necessary.

When one plow depth has determined the size and shape of a trap, as many more are removed as is necessary to give the depth required, and by making each succeeding plow depth a foot or two narrower in perimeter gives slope to the sides. Where two or more traps are required, alternate plowing first in one and then in another keeps the fresnos moving and eliminates their waiting for the plow, and the drivers soon learn to switch from one trap to another without loss of time.

In constructing the green, it is best to first build up the entire surface to a more or less uniform height and to place the high slopes or rolls in afterwards, when the approximate shape is obtained. By a single adjustment of the spreader bar on the fresnos, so as to cause the load to spread out to a uniform thickness instead of dumping in one spot, the top soil when ready for replacement can be evenly distributed over the green surface. After the surface has been disced and dragged with a spike tooth harrow, the hand work of raking into final shape is very much simplified.

The second method, making use of the ordinary two horse slip scraper, is practically a repetition of the one just described with the exception of the kind of equipment used. In this procedure the plow is not so essential. I have also found in my experience that it is not as satisfactory or as economical except under some unusual conditions where four horse equipment is not available.

The third method is that in which the greens are rough-stacked with a universal spader or regulation steam or gasoline shovel of one and one-half to two yards capacity, such as is used in excavating the cellar of a small house. One that moves about on its own caterpillar track and can make a complete circle with the shovel is best. This method is most economical in heavy clay or stony soils, or in the fall when an inch or two of frost will stop or handicap other methods.

Three or four horse-drawn dump wagons, depending on the capacity of the shovel, convey the soil taken from the traps to the spot on the green designated by the superintendent. By placing pieces of paper weighted down by a stone or lump of earth at the points where loads are required as many as twenty or thirty can be spotted at one time. The rich surface soils can be first removed and piled conveniently for replacement on the green surface later, in much the same manner as described in the other methods.

The dump-wagons will not give as even a soil distribution as fresnos but if a tractor-driven disc is used before hauling on the top soil as well as afterward, this deficiency is easily overcome. The green is now ready to be loosened up with a spike tooth harrow and the final raking into shape by hand, the sides seeded and stolons planted."

From this description, several things about green construction before 1920 should be clear. Most of it was done by horses using native soil close to the particular green site; no mention of tile drainage is made; and usually the soils deepest in the excavation site ended up in the top layers of the green. Once topsoil was respread, it may have had some organic amendment, but it, too, was as variable as the site. It often took many years of topdressing with good sandy soils to build up a functioning rootzone, just as Donald Ross had done at Pinehurst.

ALTERNATIVE PUTTING SURFACES

In a 1924 *Golf Illustrated* article, Dr. R. A. Oakley quoted one writer as saying, "Good [grass, sic] greens without money, like bricks without straw, are impossible in the absence of miracles." Oakley further observes, "Lack of funds, after all, is largely the cause for the acceptance of sand greens or other substitutes for turf." This would include lack of funds to develop a water source and distribution system as well as the cost of maintaining grass versus alternative putting surfaces. One alternative used in the west for sand greens was magnetic iron sands; these were industrial by-products that would pack tightly together to resist weeds and erosion, without oiling. Another alternative, which seemed to catch Oakley's attention in 1924, was cottonseed hulls, particularly in the south, and specifically at El Paso Country Club. Apparently, when compacted by a wooden roller with a spiked surface, the oily cottonseed hulls would resist being eroded by the hot, high, and dry winds of El Paso. The idea originated in northern Mexico, where total rainfalls of six inches or less per year made oiled sand greens susceptible to wind erosion. But laying down layers of cottonseed hulls and rolling them until the entire mat was about one inch thick worked well, and no weeds would grow in them. Using cottonseed hulls also allowed slight undulations in the putting surface, which were impossible on oiled sand greens.

All design, including golf course design, is a reflection of the technology, knowledge, materials, prosperity, and social values of any given period, as well as the skill of the designers. This holds true even when the discussion is isolated to the narrow focus of golf greens. By now it should be obvious that golf green design and development was limited by several individual factors, including the availability of irrigation water, budget for construction and maintenance, sites, and the available pool of scientific and common knowledge about golf greens. If there was no irrigation water, then oiled sand, bare soil, sawdust, crushed shells, cottonseed hulls, or a myriad of other nonvegetative surfaces were used. Since these could be eroded by wind or water, they had to be dead flat and were usually round so they were easy to drag or smooth down. The hole was cut in the center, and so cupset space was not a factor; neither was any other maintenance consideration. Clearly such greens offered no opportunity for design expression for none was needed, but they permitted the growth of golf where it otherwise could never exist, and at a low cost (see Figure 1-26).

ON THE GOLF LINKS, POLAND SPRINGS, MAINE.

Figure 1-26: As shown in this early twentieth century postcard, golf greens made of oiled sand were small, flat, and featureless. However, these golfers appear to be enjoying themselves.

FORMS OF EARLY GREENS

The earliest and naturally occurring golf greens on linksland courses were in hollows or depressions where the finest grasses were found, because this landform would not only collect surface water, but it also sheltered the greens surface from drying winds (see Figure 1-27). This was also where rabbits and other animals would feel most secure, and they would keep the grass nibbled down short. Occasionally a plateau green was chosen, but it usually had a higher backdrop to protect it from prevailing winds, or it had a readily available and plentiful irrigation source to sustain it. Although sand topdressing seemed to stimulate the fine grasses on such greens, it would also make them droughty unless very fine sand was used, and/or it was mixed with a moisture-holding compost. So with an emphasis on conserving rootzone moisture, the punchbowl or modified punchbowl green became a popular green style, often with the bottom of the "bowl" within the putting surface. Now the greenkeeper could move the hole to take advantage of the natural health of the turf during any given season. Dry hole locations in wet weather, sunny ones in winter, moist ones during drought, and so on.

Perhaps the most dramatic and famous punchbowl green in America, and one of the most fun to play, is the 16th green at National Golf Links (see Figure 1-28). This green epitomizes the concept of surface harvesting water. Oddly

Figure 1-27: Early golf greens on European linksland were generally in hollows or areas of naturally occurring fine-textured grasses. After years of topdressing and close cutting, these greens became well defined but not separated from their natural surroundings.

Figure 1-28: The National Golf Links on the eastern end of Long Island were considered linksland comparable to famous European coastal areas. Not only did the naturally sandy soils support fine-textured golf turf, but also the abundant wind permitted construction of windmills to pump and store water for the golf courses. (Courtesy of Clocktower Press)

enough, right next to it is a windmill that was used to draw water from a well, pump it up to a water tank high in the structure, and then let gravity pressurize it for piping. This tower primarily served the clubhouse needs first, but anything extra could go for irrigation.

So during this pre-1920 period, in both Europe and America, the emphasis on constructing for grass greens was on storing soil water, even to the point of working silts and clays into sandy rootzones, and less thought was given to drainage, other than surface drainage, which, again, limited design expression.

If irrigation water was available, then greens could be planted to turf, and although the designer could now build in strategy and interest with undulation, he or she was still limited by budgets of time and money, so most of the greens were push-up types, which meant the physical and chemical properties of the rootzone usually took on the characteristics of the soil conditions within a few yards of the green. Where irrigation was possible and soils were tight, architects also had to consider drainage issues, and to work at the highest levels of design sophistication and expenditure meant specifying modification of the rootzone, principally with organics or composts, fertilizers and mineral amendments. Even if a water source was available, the methods to pressurize and distribute the water were usually limited to water towers and water wagons. This objective of moisture conservation strongly influenced golf course routings designed by knowledgeable architects as it relates to green site locations and chances of

Figure 1-29: The form of early golf green design attempted to conserve water on the putting surface as well as reduce wind-induced evaporation. However, greens depending on only natural rainfall for moisture often severely dried out in the summer.

maintaining quality turf. The point is that, even with a water source, it behooved the golf course architect to take all available steps to conserve that precious water by developing tight rootzones, for burned-out grass greens were considered worse to play on than oiled sand greens (see Figure 1-29). Design and maintenance were totally integrated.

GOLF GREENS IN THE ROARING TWENTIES

Before looking at golf course construction in the 1920s, it is worth remembering what America was like in the Roaring Twenties. The world had just defeated the Germans in the "war to end all wars," prosperity was at an all-time high, there were many people becoming wealthy in all sorts of industries. Golf was becoming America's game, and no one could imagine that this situation would ever end. There was lots of mass transportation, even as America was becoming a nation of personally owned automobiles, so no place was really remote. This meant suburban communities could develop, elegant resorts were springing up, and country club development was everywhere. As a result, golf courses escalated their competition with one another for egoistical as well as financial reasons. One easy way to distinguish a golf course from its competition was to irrigate it, and with irrigation came new, higher standards of turf care, especially for greens. Power mowers were still in their infancy but were more common, a few pesticides were available, and budgets for manpower were steadily increasing. This period was called the "golden era of golf and of golf course architecture," because it was a time of enormous wealth and a great host of golf course designers and greenkeepers determined to show off their skills by spending it. In addition, there were many sources of mass communications, such as radio, daily newspapers, golf magazines, newsreels, and movies, to sell the message and virtues of golf and golf courses. Golfing celebrities, such as Walter Hagen, Bobby Jones, and Walter Travis, also contributed to the game's popularity.

The 1920s saw increasing use of irrigation for greens, which had a profound but still limiting effect on design concepts. Certainly, being able to have a stable, yearlong turf surface allowed the designer greater freedom of design expression, but the capacity of the irrigation source still set the size of the green that could be irrigated on a frequent basis. Another compounding factor was that, if infiltration rates into the rootzone soils were slow, that fact dictated a gentler slope to avoid runoff waste. Of course, then, as today, designers often ignored these agronomic considerations and left it up to the greenkeeper to figure out how to grow grass on the designer's "masterpiece." Invariably, greens that were too difficult to maintain were ultimately rebuilt to a more manageable and commonsense concept—a practice that has not changed much in the past 80 years. This goes back to the tried and true premise that "form must follow function," and the concept is elaborated upon in Chapter 3, on design.

IRRIGATING GOLF GREENS

The first sprinklers were not much more than rotating nozzles, held up in the air by a stand and supplied by a garden-type hose (see Figure 1-30). There was little or no way to control pressures, and so the precipitation pattern would vary with the rise and fall of available water pressure. Sprinklers had to be set and moved by a workman who, one only hoped, understood how to compensate for wind, variable soil requirements, and pressure fluctuations to get a uniform watering. As a result, most greenkeepers preferred hand watering over sprinklers because it was easier for workmen to see or visualize a uniform water application. Dr. Alister MacKenzie wrote in the June 1931 issue of *Golfdom*, "[T]he greenkeeper at one eastern club recently told me that at times they required as many as 18 men to water the course. This obviously is exceptional. The average would require six men."

This problem of trying to achieve uniform application of water to greens led several researchers to see the value in subirrigation, or applying water at the bottom of the rootzone and allowing upward capillarity to result in a uniform wetting front. This system worked well in small, intensive forms of agriculture and horticulture, and it was reasoned it should work well in golf greens. In fact, it did work well in small, flat test plots, but as soon as the rootzone surface was varied, differential wetting resulted.

(a)

(b)   The Turbo-Irrigator in Operation on a Private Lawn—Price Complete $12.00

Figure 1-30: (a) and (b) 1915 advertisements for golf course sprinklers show that, even if a golf course had a dependable and pressurized source of irrigation water, the means to apply it were crude at best.

Parenthetically, subirrigation still makes good sense, and it is only a matter of time until it becomes a water-conserving approach in the future. Several golf courses are now attempting it, but most are in areas of adequate rainfall where salt accumulation that occurs with subirrigation will be purged by natural drenching precipitation. Where irrigation water is high in salts, or in microclimates where low rainfall is normal, subirrigation may have only limited applicability, if any, unless combined with turfgrasses that have high salt tolerances.

Just as irrigation practices and equipment were being refined, so too was mowing. Early techniques involved skilled workmen with very sharp scythes, who might be able to work within three-quarters of an inch of the soil surface. These workers were supplanted by improved mechanical mowers, which might mow down to just below one-half inch or so. This meant greens putted slow by today's standards, and rolled like a closely cut fairway turf would today. Putters from that era commonly had three to five degrees of loft and were rarely straight-faced, because putts had to be forcibly stroked and would be played as much through the air as rolling on these early grass greens. Slow rolling speeds for golf balls, combined with the need for surface drainage water, meant that slopes on grass greens could and should be accentuated, and so slopes of seven to ten percent were common. As mowing heights began to come down with sophistication in mowers in the 1920s (see Figures 1-31 and 1-32), so did the requirement for slope until now, with ultrafast greens of today resulting from mowing at one-tenth of an inch or less, only one to two percent pitch is usually used. This is barely enough to drain surface water and, again, has limited the designer's ability to build character into putting surfaces. This will be discussed more in later chapters.

THE FIFTH GREEN AT THE ESSEX COUNTY COUNTRY CLUB

Figure 1-31: During the first half of the twentieth century, golf greens were often designed with a good degree of surface slope for drainage, as can be seen in this 1930s advertisement.

Figure 1-32: Through the 1920s and well into the 1930s, green mowers became more refined, capable of mowing to a quarter of an inch or less, but were hand pushed.

While Europe stayed with the old traditional techniques, America after the First World War was not tied to these frugal European approaches. In fact, Reginald Beale, F.L.S., in the 1924 book, *Lawns for Sports: Their Construction and Upkeep* (London: Simpkin, Marshall, Hamilton, Kent & Co., 1924), wrote:

> [N]either the Americans nor the French work on this principle [of economy]; nothing daunts them, they want the best that money can buy, and they see that they get it in spite of their climate, which is thought to cramp any greenkeeper's style, varying as it does from artic to tropical temperatures, so far as America is concerned. If the ground is poor, it is made rich; if it is wet, it is drained; if rocks and stumps stand in the way, steam drills and dynamite soon settle them; water is laid on as a matter of course; the clubhouses are the acme of luxury, and the whole organization goes with a click.

PIPER AND OAKLEY

Beale's view was quite correct and based upon the enormous amount of theoretical and applied research on golf greens in America, which began in 1902 when Dr. Charles Piper was hired by the USDA to work with golf courses and lawn grasses as an agrostologist. Shortly thereafter, Dr. Russell Oakley joined him at USDA as an agronomist, and together (see Figure 1-33) they pioneered noncommercial turfgrass science, not just in America, but also throughout the world. Their work resulted in their classic 1917 book, *Turf for Golf Courses* (New York: The Macmillan Company, 1917), which became the bible for greenkeepers. However, their interests were more on the total scope of golf course maintenance challenges rather than narrowly focused on golf green construction, although they did offer some insights in their book in a section subtitled "Soils for Putting Greens." They wrote:

> For putting greens every effort should be made to secure as nearly perfect soil conditions as possible before seeding the green."...The texture of an ideal turf soil is a loam, which may vary from a sandy loam to a clayey loam ...sandy soils are bettered by the addition of silt or clay, or both, so as to obtain in the surface foot about one-third of these materials. Where clay is used, it should be dry and pulverized, as otherwise a good mixture is not secured. Humus forming materials should be added in large quantity, preferably enough to cover the green to a depth of three to four inches. The thorough mixing of these elements will form a satisfactory sandy loam soil.
>
> In some cases it may be cheaper to carry good soil to cover the proposed green to a depth of at least six inches, but good soil for turf is usually scarce when the prevailing soil is either very clayey or very sandy.

Other suggestions from Piper and Oakley included seeding with a blend of creeping bent and red fescue, having a rootzone depth of 8 to 12 inches, tiling if subsoil is not porous, and using organic fertilizers or well-rotted animal manure. They stressed that irrigation is important and suggested that the moisture-holding capacity of the soil should be higher. They concluded this section by writing:

Figure 1-33: A rare picture from a *USGA Green Section Bulletin* showing Drs. Oakley and Piper, who were hired by the USDA to advance the turfgrass sciences. (Courtesy of United States Golf Association)

...No hard and fast rules can be laid down that will insure the securing of good turf under any conditions, as the factors involved are numerous and far from being thoroughly understood. So far as our knowledge goes, however, all of the factors emphasized are of prime importance, and it is rare that any one of them can be neglected and good results be achieved.

Perhaps the most fascinating chapter of Piper and Oakley's book dealt with "Experimental Work on Golf Courses." Until the work of Piper and Oakley, greenkeepers learned by trial and error, but never really made any bold deviations from the norm because it might cost them their precious job. Piper and Oakley wrote:

> The experience in golf course management has not resulted in much increase of accurate knowledge so far as turf-growing is concerned. Every putting green on a golf course has in most cases been subjected to so many kinds of treatment that it is impossible for any one to determine which factors were good and which were bad.

So true exploratory science was left to researchers in government, universities, or industry, using scientific methods involving check plots, replications, statistics, null hypothesis, and so on. But such investigations take lots of time, money, and energy with no guarantee of any return on investment, or assurance that what is discovered has any utility. However, such searching for truth and principle is what advances a profession. It has been said, "Science is the description of the world as it really is, and proof of that is universally reproducible. Science without proof is philosophy, while art is the creative expression of an idea." Accepting this notion allows one to see that greenkeeping has been and will perhaps always be philosophically both art and science.

Piper and Oakley did set up simple experiments of their own to find "universally reproducible" results, as well as evaluated the work of others as a sort of peer review. One notable investigation they cite was done by J. B. Olcott of South Manchester, CT, at the Connecticut Experiment Station from 1885 until his death in 1910 (see Figure 1-34). Olcott searched localities throughout America, Europe, Hawaii, New Zealand, and Australia for samples of turf that he could propagate and evaluate for superior utilitarian qualities. From among thousands of isolates, he selected over 500 strains of grasses and after many years concluded that, in New England, creeping bent and red fescue were best.

F. W. TAYLOR

When Olcott died, a Philadelphia engineer, F. W. Taylor, purchased the finest turves developed by Olcott and moved them to his home test plots in Highland, PA. Taylor's work was described by Piper and Oakley as follows:

View of the Olcott Turf Garden, South Manchester, Conn., as it appeared about 1910
Courtesy of the Macmillan Company

Figure 1-34: One of the earliest turf gardens to develop improved strains of grasses was Olcott Gardens, started in 1885 as a hobby for an amateur botanist. The garden had as many as 500 different strains of grass and provided valuable information to early turfgrass scientists. (Courtesy of United States Golf Association)

In many ways the most extensive and remarkable series of turf experiments undertaken were conducted by Fred W. Taylor on his home grounds near Philadelphia. These experiments began in 1904 and were continued until Taylor's death in 1915. . . . Purely from the love of the sport, he undertook his experiments with the firm belief that greens could be made in much the same way that an article is manufactured in a machine shop or factory. He believed that careful study would reveal the specific requirements of fine turf, and that these requirements could be met by the use of standardized materials.

Taylor's objectives were to design a standardized rootzone that was a good medium for germination of the seed and the development of the seedlings, and whose fertile soil would have a high water-holding capacity while at the same time providing perfect drainage. Taylor received three patents in 1916, a year after his death, for his method of building golf greens, which are the basis for the USGA recommended method, the PURR-Wick™ system, the California green, and yet to be refined methods of subirrigation for golf greens. Taylor was not so much a genius with profound vision as a keen observer of fundamental principles applied to golf green construction. He recognized and understood capillarity, maintaining proper soil, air, and moisture balance, and site specificity in selecting grasses.

A good description of F. W.'s methodical approach was from Piper and Oakley when they wrote:

> With these conclusions fairly in mind, Taylor sought to construct the ideal green by selecting his grasses and actually building a medium upon which they were to be grown.

What makes this interesting is that the process that Taylor used is precisely the one that we should use today, although with the additional step of factoring in the quality of the irrigation water. It should be a three-step process.

Step 1: Carefully analyze the quality and quantity of any and all irrigation sources.

Step 2: Based upon the water analysis and observed or measured microclimatic factors, select the best adapted putting green turfgrass.

Step 3: Then determine the best method of rootzone and composition architecture for each green site based upon steps 1 and 2.

Although this decision-making process is almost a century old, few have learned to trust it, for most golf course superintendents and turf consultants resist it in favor of some "one size fits all" method. One goal of this book is to help serious students understand the importance of Taylor's approach, so that work is extensively reviewed in Chapter 2 on Golf Green Theories.

From F. W. Taylor's time until now there is nothing really new except *products* (genetic material, soil amendments, fertilizers, pesticides, etc.), but the thought process behind their application remains a constant search for the best balance and control of physical, chemical, and biological factors that influence the health of putting green turf. From this point on, nearly all the history of golf greens is a merger of turfgrass science trying to understand and improve on what is observed on golf courses, and the techniques being used. There is no single best approach, and to optimize performance requires intelligent application, for each particular situation or green site, of proven and evolving science-based knowledge and commonsense.

Currently, there has been a shift in thinking away from emphasizing the conservation of water in the rootzone of greens, as it has been the goal for 150 years or so, to complete and thorough drainage of excess soil moisture, and to directly managing the soil air in the rootzone of greens with vacuums and air pumps.

Golf Green Theories

BACKGROUND

Chances are if one were to mention theories of golf greens to a golf course architect, he or she would have in mind thoughts of size, shape, slope, and strategy of putting surfaces. But an agronomist would probably first think about soil textures, underdrainage, amendments, and plant growth factors. In other words, there are two independent categories of theories about golf greens that are at the same time integral to each other. The best way to understand both theories is to consider them in individual chapters of this book, then see how they relate and affect each other. First, a primer on rootzone construction theories.

Although there are as many ways to construct a green's rootzone as there are greens, for discussion purposes I am going to limit the discussion to four broad types that are sufficiently distinct as to illustrate basic principles; these types are:

1. Native soil or "push-up" greens (see Figure 2-1)
2. The United States Golf Association (USGA) recommendations (see Figure 2-2)
3. The California method (see Figure 2-3)
4. Modified or simplified variations of the above three methods

Native soil or push-up greens (see Figure 2-1) denote areas used for putting surfaces that have little or no modification of naturally occurring soils during

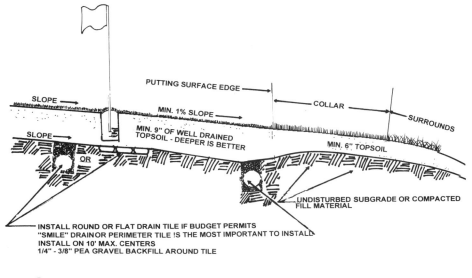

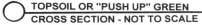

Figure 2-1: Cross section of native soil or "push-up" green. These greens should be made with the best or most well-drained soil available, and may or may not have tile drainage.

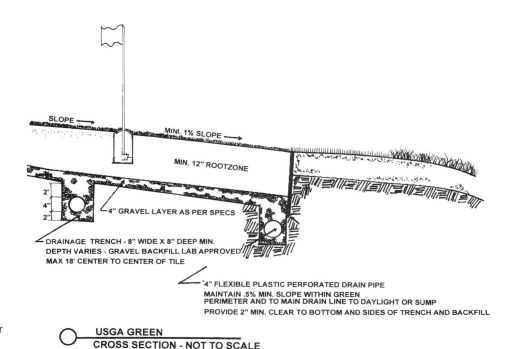

Figure 2-2: Cross section of United States Golf Association (USGA) recommended method of green construction that always has tile drainage, a gravel blanket, and laboratory-approved rootzone material. Perimeter wicking barrier is optional.

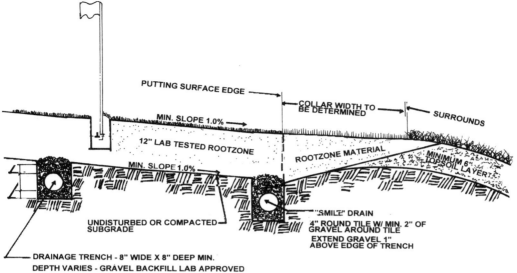

PUTTING SURFACE EDGE

COLLAR WIDTH TO BE DETERMINED

SURROUNDS

MIN. SLOPE 1.0%

12" LAB TESTED ROOTZONE

ROOTZONE MATERIAL

MINIMUM 6" TOPSOIL LAYER

MIN. SLOPE 1.0%

"SMILE" DRAIN
4" ROUND TILE W/ MIN. 2" OF
GRAVEL AROUND TILE
EXTEND GRAVEL 1"
ABOVE EDGE OF TRENCH

UNDISTURBED OR COMPACTED SUBGRADE

DRAINAGE TRENCH - 8" WIDE X 8" DEEP MIN.
DEPTH VARIES - GRAVEL BACKFILL LAB APPROVED
MAX 18' CENTER TO CENTER OF TILE
4" FLEXIBLE PLASTIC PERFORATED DRAIN PIPE
MAINTAIN .5% MIN. SLOPE WITHIN GREEN PERIMETER
AND TO MAIN DRAIN LINE TO DAYLIGHT OR SUMP

"CALIFORNIA" OR IMPROVED GREEN
CROSS SECTION - NOT TO SCALE

Figure 2-3: Cross section of a California method green construction that has tile drainage and a laboratory-approved rootzone material, but usually no gravel blanket or perimeter-wicking barrier.

the construction or planting of the green. Such greens are inexpensive and quick to build, and may prove suitable with well-drained native soils or very low golfer traffic. They are usually good at conserving soil moisture and fertility, and tend to have stable soil microbiology. Their disadvantage is that if the native soils are variable or prone to compaction, then push-up greens can be difficult to maintain. Push-up greens may or may not have tile underdrains.

The USGA recommendation is the most widely researched and documented method in the world (see Figure 2-2). The rootzone is typically a 12-inch-deep blend of laboratory tested and selected sands and organic matter sources that have met rigid criteria for physical and performance standards. Therefore, these greens are very predictable and in theory are easier to grow putting green turf on, but they are also usually more expensive to build and maintain. They are noncompacting, drain well, and are easy to establish. What distinguishes the USGA method is a gravel and tile drainage layer between the rootzone mix and the subsurface of the green.

The California method is so named because of a 1990 publication that summarized 30 years of rootzone trials and testing done at California universities, which concluded that selected pure sand can make the best rootzone for golf putting greens. The California method (see Figure 2-3) utilizes tile underdrains but, unlike the USGA method, it does not have the gravel blanket nor does it recommend that organic matter be part of the rootzone material. These greens are intermediate in cost and complexity to USGA and push-up greens, and so is their maintenance. To be called a California green means that the rootzone sand was laboratory tested and selected to meet the criteria outlined in the 1990 publication. This method is gaining in popularity around the world.

There are hundreds, if not thousands, of modifications or variations of the above three methods, called all sorts of names, and of course, equally variable in cost, complexity, and performance. This should not be taken to mean that any one of these modified methods is inferior to one of the three mentioned standards, for, in fact, such modification may make a superior rootzone. However, making choices about such modifications should be based on hard science more than on intuition. I would speculate that more greens have failed because of ill-advised modifications to standard rootzone concepts than for any other reason. However, if such a modification is done correctly, it can reduce costs and complexity of construction and maintenance.

So which one of these four broad categories of rootzone theory is best? The answer to that rhetorical question is that it depends upon many factors including (1) the quality and quantity of irrigation water, (2) the microclimate of each green site, (3) the availability of construction materials, (4) allowable budgets of time and money, (5) skill and expertise of the contractor and greenkeeper, (6) the vegetative material that will make up the putting surface, and (7) a dozen or more smaller but equally important considerations. The point is that there is no one correct, best method that works every place, every time; and our understanding of what is "best" for a given location is evolving each day because of new research, new materials, new limitations, and new techniques. To understand how to make the most intelligent choices possible will require a more in-depth understanding of each method, which happens to be the purpose of this chapter. After you master the theories and rationale of rootzones, then we will look at design theories in the next chapter to see how they interface.

NATIVE SOIL GREENS

When golf was first played in America, it was on greens of native soils (see Figure 2-4). The native soil or push-up green still has utility in selected situations, namely, if the native soil has some resistance to compaction, low golfer traffic is expected, or construction money is in short supply. The only real downside to a native soil green is compaction, for otherwise most soils have fairly high moisture- and nutrient-holding capacity, can support a rich microbial population, and are easy to grow turf on. The more sandy or loamy a soil naturally is, the better suited it will be for green construction. If possible, it is a good idea to avoid soils high in clay or silt, although there are thousands of such greens in existence that are performing well.

For example, the golf greens on which I was taught the fundamentals of greenkeeping were typical of golf courses built in the 1920s and 1930s, out of native soils high in both silts and clay. To compensate for poor internal drainage, the greens were designed to have between two and seven percent surface drainage. This meant a fairly rapid removal of surface water, which avoided overly soft soils that would result from infiltration. Water would move through these soils at probably one-half inch per hour or less, but my mentor Jack Kidwell, an old-school golf course superintendent, taught us how to manage the soil moisture by carefully watering them only as necessary to sustain the plant. Overwatering could lead to such disasters as wet wilt, sunscald, root drowning, foot printing, or excessive compaction. Although some sprinkler irrigation was used in the form of quick couplers with roller base sprinklers and hoses at each green, the key to success with a native soil green was very careful hand watering of only the places that needed it, and at a rate that the soil could take. Hand watering was an art that usually was done by only the most experienced crewmembers, who had learned to read soil moisture conditions and apply just the right amount of water, for mistakes could be costly. Of course, during wet seasons of slow, continuous rains or when coming out of winter, when soil ice was a factor, these greens would be saturated and very prone to diseases and compaction.

As frequent, light sand topdressing became more popular from the mid-1950s forward, these soil greens became capped with a three- to five-inch layer of good quality rootzone material (see Figure 2-5), and so the greens perform almost as well as if they had been built out of sand in the beginning. The internal drainage of this topdressing layer is perhaps three to five inches per hour. These greens support a mix of bentgrass and *Poa annua* spp., but provide superior putting surfaces that have hosted tens of thousands of rounds of year-round play.

Tile drainage under such native soil greens definitely improved their performance, even when the native soils were tight. Soils have an ability to

Figure 2-4: The first golf courses were not much more than pastureland with crudely dug cross-bunkers and greens built of native soil. Rarely was irrigation or drainage installed, even on greens.

43

Figure 2-5: After many years of topdressing and aerifying, even old clay base greens can develop rootzone capable of supporting strong putting green turf.

"bridge," which means to absorb and distribute a load or force in all directions. When a soil is compacted, there is a limit as to how deep that compaction will take place, and the more compacted a soil becomes, the less the compacting force or load is transferred downwardly. In other words, the most compacted part of a soil profile is typically on the surface or closest to the source of compaction, and deeper areas are less compacted. Ideally, tile is placed about 12 to 14 inches below the surface, on 10-foot centers, and bedded and backfilled in fine stone or coarse sand. Practically speaking, only the top two to three inches of a native soil green really compacts, while areas closer to the tile line are less compacted, and thus are able to percolate water faster than the compacted surface. As a native soil green ages, freezing and thawing, wetting and drying, and other forces that influence soil voids and aggregation will open up channels for air and water flow, and these channels will not close due to bridging until the overly soils are severely compacted or abused when in a plastic state. Hence, by avoiding overwatering and forces that create compaction, as well as by frequent aerification and topdressing of the surface few inches, a native soil or push-up green can be very predictable and manageable, and provide excellent putting surfaces.

FREDRICK W. TAYLOR'S WORK

Up until the early 1900s, development of golf greens continued to be more of an evolutionary process of nurturing turf planted on augmented native soils than a methodical development of rootzones or growing mediums with ideal physical and chemical properties. However, as golf became well established in America and golfers placed a premium on perfect putting greens, research was begun by a Philadelphia golfer and engineer by the name of Frederick W. Taylor (see Figure 2-6). Mr. Taylor is best known for his influential ideas during the late industrial revolution on organizing management practices to increase productivity. Even today, his 1911 book, *The Principles of Scientific Management* (New York: Norton, 1911), is revered and studied as the foundation for industrial management engineering. In 1904, F. W. Taylor began pioneering work in golf greens that led to his subsequent patents for golf green construction, applied for in 1910 and granted in 1916 (see Figure 2-7). But his work was not well understood and remained largely ignored by the golf industry, even forgotten. However, when examined in context of what we know about rootzone architecture a century later, Taylor's research was elegant and his theories foreshadow many theories and practices that are used today. As discussed in Chapter 1, back in Taylor's day, even leaders in turfgrass science questioned the value of his research and conclusions; even Charles Piper and Russell Oakley thought it required too much expense and therefore was not practical. Others simply passed Taylor off as eccentric, and since he died just before his patents

Figure 2-6: Frederick W. Taylor is best known for his revolutionary ideas in industrial management, but he should also be recognized for laying the foundation for all modern theories of green construction.

Figure 2-7: F. W. Taylor received three patents in 1916 for the construction of golf greens. This is one of them.

UNITED STATES PATENT OFFICE

FREDERICK W. TAYLOR, OF PHILADELPHIA, PENNSYLVANIA; EDWARD W. CLARK, 3D, EXECUTOR OF SAID TAYLOR, DECEASED.

PLANT-GROWING APPARATUS.

1,171,558.   Specification of Letters Patent.   **Patented Feb. 15, 1916**
Application filed July 26, 1910.   Serial No. 573,958.

To all whom it may concern:

Be it known that I. FREDERICK .W. TAYLOR, a citizen of the United. States of America, residing in the city and county of Philadelphia. in the State of. Pennsylvania;, have invented a certain new and useful Improvement in Plant-Growing Apparatus, of which the following is a true and exact description, reference being had to the accompanying drawings, which form a part thereof.

My present invention relates primarily to the means employed and steps taken to obtain a growth of grass such as is desired on the putting greens of golf courses and in one aspect my invention may be regarded as consisting in an improved putting green or like grass growing structure.

To obtain a satisfactory growth of grass suitable for the purpose specified, it is essential that the grass roots should receive a proper supply of nourishment, moisture and air, and the latter constituent is no less important than the first two. In rowing grass on putting greens I believe it to be always desirable, and in some cases absolutely essential to, provide conditions which will cause the grass roots to penetrate the soil to a considerable depth below the surface of the ground, I have found that the grass known as red fescue (*Festuca rubra*) which I consider one of the most, if not the, most, desirable grass for putting greens, will not prosper under climatic conditions, such as are experienced in Philadelphia, Pennsylvania, for instance, unless the roots are caused to penetrate the ground for a distance of at least two or three inches, and the, same is true to a greater or less extent with other grasses. This I believe to be due to the fact that, the first two or three inches of ground below the surface vary in temperature rapidly with the temperature conditions at the surface of the ground. In particular this top layer dries out and bakes very rapidly under the direct action of the sun's rays on a hot summer day, with a consequent burning or scalding and deadening the grass roots contained therein, unless vigorous and substantial extensions of the roots lie below this top layer and in contact with a moist and cooler. portion of the ground. It is desirable also to provide conditions which will exclude worms and the consequent annoying worm casts from putting greens.

Conditions should also be such, as to make difficult the propagation of weeds or other foreign vegetation, the seeds of which may blow on to the putting green.

The general object of the invention is to provide a grass growing bed characterized by the presence of the above indicated desirable conditions, and the invention, consists in part in the arrangement and composition of the material actually penetrated by the growing grass roots, and in part in the provisions made for supplying the grass roots with the necessary moisture from a reservoir beneath the material in which the grass roots grow.

A characteristic of the invention is the systematic manner in which the putting green or the like is formed and treated to thereby insure the desired uniformity as well as. excellence in the turf conditions of all parts of the green required to make a first class green.

To a large extent my invention involves an appreciation and utilization of certain characteristics of granular bodies. It is a fact well known to those who have investigated the subject that a mass composed of rigid granules contains spaces or voids which in the aggregate form a considerable percentage of the total volume apparently occupied by the mass. In the case of rigid spherical bodies or granules of uniform size the void volume is about forty percent. of the total apparent volume, and this is independent of the actual size of the individual granules. Of course the smaller the particles the smaller, the individual voids, but as the individual voids decrease in volume they correspondingly increase in number. Where the bodies are not smooth, but are irregular in contour, the void space percentage increases, other things being equal. The percentage of void space in ordinary fine, sand is about the same as the percentage of void space in broken rock, such as is used, for instance, in macadamizing streets, the voids forming about forty to fifty-five per cent. of the total apparent volume. This void space is reduced by ramming about fifteen percent, that is, from an average volume of say forty-seven and a half percent to between forty and forty-one per cent. The void space in a mass of sand or the like may be diminished in a regulated amount, however, by a proper selection and mixture of

were issued, he could not very well defend himself and extend the contributions his research could have made. However, an in-depth look at Taylor's work and patents is worthwhile.

Taylor's objectives were to produce a noncompacting rootzone for golf course putting greens that was well-drained yet conserved moisture, would promote quick germination of the seed, and later permit vigorous growth of putting green grasses. He recognized that sand was more universal and stable than soil and would be the best noncompacting, well-drained medium. But some sands are droughtier than others. Moisture-holding capacity is determined by two forces at work that diametrically oppose one another: (1) gravity, which is trying to pull water downward, and (2) capillarity, which is trying to hold water against gravity. In turn, capillarity is a function of the cohesion of water molecules to each other and the adhesion of water molecules to the surface of objects, in this case sand particles, so that the greater the surface area and the thinner the water film, the more tightly water would be held against gravitational forces.

In fact, most school children have experimented with paper or cloth and have observed the wicking effects of water being lifted by capillarity, against the downward pull of gravity, a process which is a function of the surface tension and amount, and hence weight, of the water. There is also the classic experiment involving straws or tubes of different inside diameters that are placed in water vertically; when the straws are withdrawn from the water, the observer measures the height of the water each contains against gravity. Obviously, the smallest diameter tube can lift the water the highest. Simply put, small pores or spaces between particles are able to hold water more tightly against gravity than larger pores or spaces.

Taylor recognized that, in any given sand, there would be an array of space sizes between the particles (see Figure 2-8 and Taylor's fig. 4) so that, when the sand was saturated and then allowed to drain down by gravity, the amount of water held against gravity was proportional to the size and number of those spaces. Spaces drained of water would naturally be filled with air, thus the terms *air-filled porosity* and *water-filled porosity*. The latter describes those spaces with sufficient capillarity to retain water. The optimum proportion of air and water in the rootzone would permit optimum plant growth. Taylor wanted to find a way to "engineer" such a perfect balance and then maintain it under the putting green. In modern soil-testing labs, these capacities can be easily measured, especially by using a tension table or vacuum to assign a numeric value, and are criteria relied upon to predict the performance characteristics of a sand, or soil, used in modern green construction.

Taylor, however, was satisfied just to experiment with these forces to solve one of greenkeepers' biggest problems, and that was how to provide uniform and controllable moisture to a rootzone. Remember, at this period of time, there were no such things as irrigation systems as we know them, for most irrigation was done by hauling water out to the green in wagons and then applying it by buckets or gravity-fed hoses.

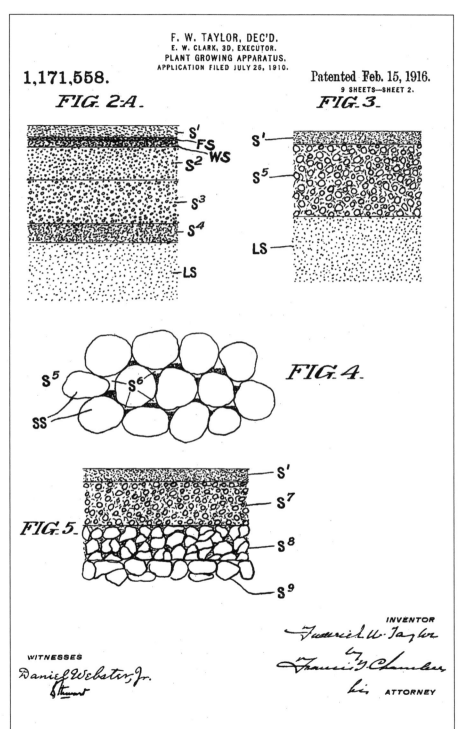

Figure 2-8: Figures taken from F. W. Taylor's patents for golf greens demonstrate his understanding of the two forces working on soil water in a rootzone—capillarity and gravity.

Taylor reasoned that, since fine sands with small voids between particles held water more tightly against gravity than larger particle sand with correspondingly larger voids between particles, it made sense to place coarse or large particles on the bottom of a rootzone profile, with progressively finer materials above them. In fact, one of the cross sections from his patent (figure 2A in Figure 2-8, patent #1,171,558) looks very similar to today's USGA recommended profile of layers of different textural materials (see Figure 2-9). Taylor specifically identified this profile as one he devised to carry off excess water when surface watering or irrigation was used. That principle of rapid drainage is discussed at greater length later when reviewing present-day research on modern green construction methods.

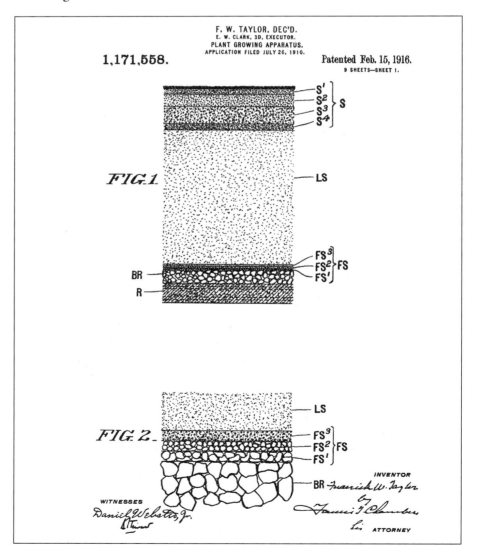

Figure 2-9: Taylor's use of different textural layers is similar to today's USGA rootzone profile, with the same purpose of quick drainage of excess soil water.

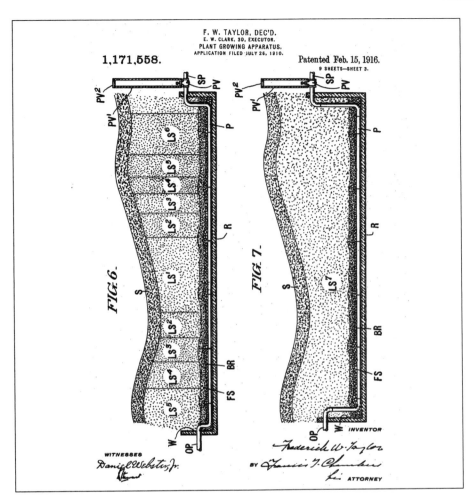

F. W. TAYLOR, DEC'D.
E. W. CLARK, 3D, EXECUTOR.
PLANT GROWING APPARATUS.
APPLICATION FILED JULY 26, 1910.

1,171,558.

Patented Feb. 15, 1916.
9 SHEETS—SHEET 3.

Figure 2-10: Taylor recognized that under high areas of the green, a finer-textured sand was required than under lower areas if a uniform surface moisture content was to be achieved with subirrigation.

Taylor reasoned that, if he constructed a sealed reservoir with clay or concrete and if he could raise or lower the water level in this reservoir by adjusting the heights of inlet and outlet pipes, then he could fill the reservoir with sand and use capillarity to maintain optimum soil moisture supply (see Figure 2-10). Of course, he was correct, but unlike the PURR-Wick green system, or PAT athletic fields, Taylor's system takes into account the fact that golf greens are not flat. In fact, there are areas that are relatively higher or lower than other places, and a sand of uniform capillarity would result in corresponding wet (low) or dry (high) areas. His solution was to simply use finer sands of greater capillarity under high portions of the putting surface and coarser sands under the lower areas (see Figure 2-10). Correctly proportioned sands, he reasoned, would allow for a system to uniformly subirrigate an undulating putting surface. The patent office agreed, and issued patent number 1,171,558 on February 15, 1916.

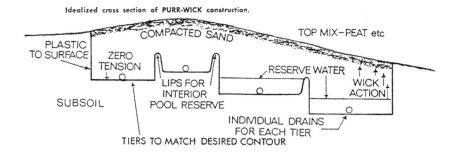

Idealized cross section of PURR-WICK construction.

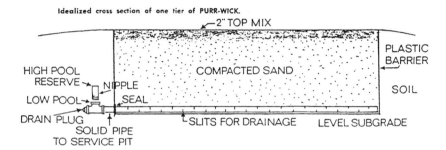

Idealized cross section of one tier of PURR-WICK.

Figure 2-11: The PURR-Wick method of green construction is nearly a mirror image of Taylor's patent for a subirrigated green.

However, Taylor was not trying to improve surface-irrigated greens as much as he was interested in subsurface irrigation. This approach made great sense because subirrigation would require little or no hydraulic pressure to work, it would conserve precious water supplies, and it could provide a controlled and uniform watering of the putting green surface. Fifty years later, Taylor's basic scheme would be reintroduced by the late Dr. Bill Daniel of Purdue University, as the PURR-Wick system (see Figure 2-11), and is still the rootzone construction method of choice for modern natural grass athletic fields, called Prescription Athletic Turf or PAT.

Taylor also experimented with a material that he called M.O., a pure silica that was a by-product of steel-making plants. This material was very stable and consistent, and he used it as an inorganic supplement to alter the performance of the natural sands. This material had high wicking performance characteristics and could be blended in various proportions with a less than perfect sand to achieve the capillarity needed for a particular application (see Figure 2-12). Taylor also experimented with subfeeding of root systems with liquid manures, using layers of cinders or glass fragments to discourage earthworms, as well as amendments of various organic supplements and layers to include leaf mold and various humus sources. Taylor investigated various wicking materials, column profiles, and control mechanisms, all of which led to a total of three patents for golf green construction methods.

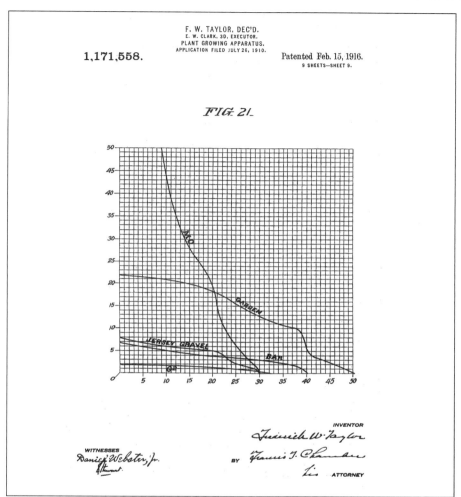

Figure 2-12: F. W. Taylor even experimented with using inorganic materials to amend sands to adjust their performance characteristics.

Taylor's monumental work did not go totally unnoticed, and several golf course architects borrowed ideas from the work he started, most notably, Charles Blair Macdonald and Donald Ross.

CHARLES BLAIR MACDONALD'S SUBIRRIGATED GREENS

In 1914, when Charles Blair Macdonald and Seth Raynor were designing St. Louis Country Club in Missouri, they tried (see Figure 2-13) a variation of Taylor's subirrigation. They installed a complex system of drainage tile in the green cavity, with a control valve at each point where it entered and exited the cavity, which would allow the rootzone of the green to be flooded or drained

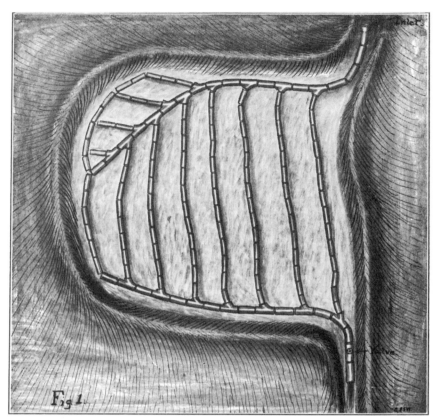

Plan of sub-irrigation system of No. 12 putting green, St. Louis Country Club. The main tile are 6 inches in diameter and the laterals 4 inches

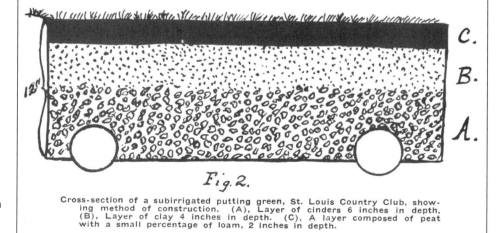

Cross-section of a subirrigated putting green, St. Louis Country Club, showing method of construction. (A), Layer of cinders 6 inches in depth. (B), Layer of clay 4 inches in depth. (C), A layer composed of peat with a small percentage of loam, 2 inches in depth.

Figure 2-13: C. B. Macdonald and Seth Raynor experimented with subirrigating greens at St. Louis Country Club in about 1914.

by opening and closing the valves. Notice their green cross section shown in Figure 2-13, which details four-inch tile, bedded in six inches of cinders, and capped by four inches of clay, and finally two inches of loam and peat blend. The former golf course superintendent from St. Louis Country Club, Jack Litvay, says before the greens were reconstructed in the late 1990s the system was still intact for the most part, and the valves were left open for drainage only, as the greens are now sprinkler irrigated. There is no record of how well or poorly the system worked, but it was considered worthy of mention by the USGA Green Section in their *Turf Bulletin* in 1921.

THE LEWIS SYSTEM FOR AUTOMATIC SUBIRRIGATION

In about 1919, an article appeared in *Golf Illustrated* (USA) magazine explaining a system for automatically subirrigating golf greens. The system was called "The Lewis System," after its engineer innovator, Thomas A. Lewis of New York, a prominent member of St. Andrews Golf Club of Yonkers (see Figure 2-14). The essence of his system was to hook up a constant-pressure water supply source to a float control valve in order to maintain a constant head of

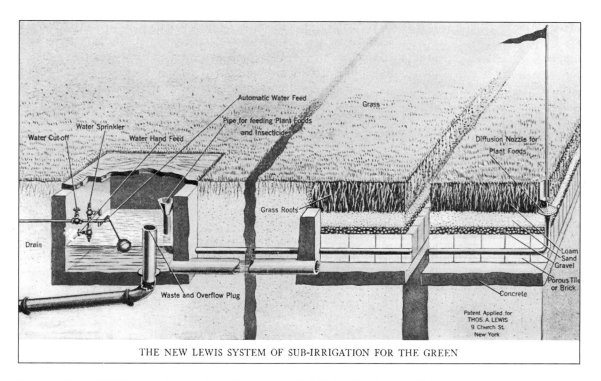

THE NEW LEWIS SYSTEM OF SUB-IRRIGATION FOR THE GREEN

Figure 2-14: In 1919 Thomas Lewis, of the St. Andrews Golf Club of Yonkers, published an article on how to automatically control water levels under subirrigated greens.

water in the under green reservoir. Without question the system would work for growing grass, but notice how even in the illustrations of the system how flat and uninteresting the green must be to use this system. This probably explains why it was never popular.

DONALD ROSS APPROACH TO WELL-DRAINED GREENS

In 1916, Donald Ross worked with a noted Ohio State University professor, Alfred Vivian, to devise a system of rootzone construction for Scioto Country Club in Columbus, which was then under construction. The greens profile (see Figure 2-15) shows a 4-inch clay tile, imbedded in 6 inches of cinders, capped by 12 inches of a blend of 50 percent sand, 30 percent manure, and 20 percent sand, further topped off by 6 inches of rich earth and 4 inches of topdressing of 50 percent rich earth, 20 percent shredded raw horse manure, and 30 percent sand. This layering of finer textured materials over coarser ones again goes back to Taylor's work, and closely resembles the modern-day USGA concept.

Ross and Vivian's rationale was as follows:

> The idea of mixing the sand, earth and manure was to provide (a) satisfactory drainage by breaking up the stiff heavy clay, (b) providing easy means for the grass roots to go down into the subsoil instead of spreading out near the surface, (c) to furnish an ample quantity of organic matter to feed the grass roots for years to come and more efficiently to absorb and retain moisture. This was considered most important since it is obviously impossible to put humus into the body of a green after it is seeded.

Interestingly, the cost to build a green to this standard Ross/Vivian green in 1916 was a little over $1,500, which would amount to $40,000 per green in today's dollars, while a less sophisticated green back then cost about one-half to one-third that amount.

Figure 2-15: Donald Ross and Professor Alfred Vivian, a soil and drainage expert at Ohio State University, devised a multilayer method for green construction at Scioto Country Club in 1916 that resembles the current USGA method.

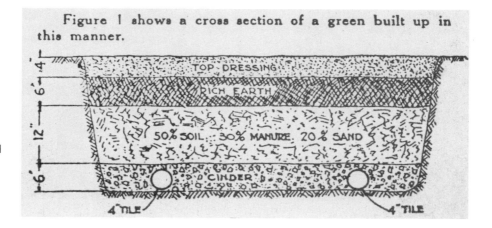

So Taylor's initial work was slightly modified by architects like Macdonald and Ross, but not much advancement was made in the science of rootzones in the 1920s. Of course, the Great Depression came in 1929, and near the end of the Depression, World War II began, and so golf course research slowed down to a trickle between 1929 and 1945. However, during the period leading up to and into the Depression, Piper and Oakley continued to do research involving soil fertility, turfgrass pests and controls, and methods of planting and over-seeding, but not on rootzone materials per se. By 1931, the number of golf courses in the United States is estimated to have been less than 5,000, but that number would later double between 1945 and 1968.

POST–WORLD WAR II TURF RESEARCH

After World War II, the G.I. Bill helped fund college tuition for returning ser-vicemen, the country loved President Ike and he loved golf, and America was ready to relax after a difficult 16 years of Depression and war. Golf grew in pop-ularity and there was a high demand for new golf courses in new suburbs. Personal and mass transportation was easy and cheap, electric power was read-ily available, heavy earthmovers were common construction tools, irrigation pumps, pipe, and sprinklers were abundant, and television was producing golf heroes like Ben Hogan, Sam Sneed, and Arnold Palmer.

With World War II over, the USGA took a strong interest in the deteriorat-ed state of American golf courses, and was financially healthy enough to begin funding research on green rootzones in 1946. Before this time, the most com-mon green rootzone mixes were a 1–1–1 ratio of sand, soil, and organic matter, and with animal manure in shorter supply, various sources of organic and inor-ganic materials were tried with varying success. The USGA sponsored research at Beltsville in Maryland, Oklahoma State University, UCLA, and Texas A&M. Other active research sites were Purdue, Penn State, the University of Rhode Island, and the University of Massachusetts.

Several major turf researchers emerged. One was O. J. Noer of the Milwaukee Sewerage Commission, who authored a series of popular pamphlets for greenkeepers for Milorganite. Later there came Dr. Burt Musser from Penn State University, who wrote the seminal work *Turf Management* (New York: McGraw-Hill, 1950) (see Figure 2-16). Contributing to Musser's book on golf course design were prominent members of the newly founded American Society of Golf Course Architects, Robert Bruce Harris and Robert Trent Jones. Musser's book became the turf management bible for the next 30 years. However, this and other early 1950s text were quiet on the subject of green construction methods. Also coming into prominence at that time were Dr. Fred Grau and Dr. Jesse DeFrance, who studied relationship of soils to turfgrass per-formance but with only vague references to golf greens.

Figure 2-16: Dr. Burt Musser's 1950 *Turf Management* was the first textbook devoted solely to turfgrass management and is still considered by many to be an excellent reference source. (Courtesy of United States Golf Association)

USGA METHOD FOR GREEN CONSTRUCTION

In the June 1949 issue of the *USGA Journal,* R. P. Humbert and Dr. Fred Grau, Director of the Green Section, reported on "Some Studies of the Physical Properties of Putting Green Soils as Related to Turf Maintenance." The study was funded by the USGA in 1947, and the purpose was to evaluate superintendent's "best" and "worst" greens on their golf course based upon core samples submitted to the Saratoga Laboratories and run by Humbert. They found little definitive answers to what makes "best" and "worst" greens, but did see a trend that greens with less compaction did better.

Another early 1950 researcher was R. R. Davis, whose Ph.D. work at Purdue was titled *The Physical Condition of Putting Green Soils and Other Environmental Factors Affecting the Quality of Greens.* The essence of his findings were that the more porous the rootzone, the better the plant growth. He concluded that greens mixes should be at least a 2–1–1 ratio (sand–soil–organic matter) or 50 percent sand content. Typically, he recommended coarse sands that were commonly called "concrete sands."

In addition, in 1950, Dr. Marvin Ferguson authored an article on "Soil Water and Soil Air: Their Relationship to Turf Production" in the July issue of *USGA Journal* (see Figure 2-17). Over the years, Dr. Ferguson would write many such papers for the USGA, for he became a Green Section staff member as well as a noted researcher at Texas A&M, which had an active research program on greens mixes. He concluded that a balance between soil, water, and air is key.

Shortly thereafter, in 1952, W. L. Garman reported in the *USGA Journal and Turf Management* on his research on "Permeability of Various Grades of Sand and Peat and Mixtures of These With Soil and Vermiculite" for golf greens. He found that soil compaction was a key factor in poor green performance. He suggested more of a 7–1–2 (sand–soil–peat) blend. When compacted, this mix had a permeability of 0.8 inches per hour, or four times that of the 1–1–1 standard ratios then in popular use.

Out of Texas A&M came the work of two very important researchers, O. R. Lunt and J. R. Kunze. In 1956, Lunt, P. A. Miller and C. G. Wyckoff reported that they found the best sand for greens rootzones was that having 75 percent of particles in the medium to fine range of 0.2 to 0.4 mm, and less than 10 percent in 0.1-mm range. Their recommendations were more in the 8–1–1 range to 9.0–0.5–0.5. At the same time Kunze was finishing his master's research at Texas A&M on *The Effect of Compaction of Different Golf Green Mixtures on Plant Growth.* Using Bermuda grass as his plant material he found that mixes with 85 to 90 percent of even finer sands, in the range of 0.5 to 1 mm, only 2 to 4 percent clay and 8 to 10 percent seed sedge peat permitted the greatest plant growth.

It was common for most of this research to be done in what was called "pot culture" in a greenhouse or growth chamber, as opposed to "plot culture," which refers to small outside field trials. The reason, of course, is that in a greenhouse or growth chamber, or small plots, conditions were easier to establish, measure, and stabilize to reduce or limit environmental or weather effects, and theoretically obtain clearer research results and conclusions. It could be argued that such research may or may not be a good indicator of what may happen when research findings are tested under the varying conditions of golf courses. Therefore, laboratory research is often termed "pure," while large field research is termed "applied," especially when the field trial is on a golf course. The net result is that what is found to be true in lab research is often internalized as being equally valid in the field, and lack of collaborating field results is blamed on the variability of the conditions. In other words, some observations made in the lab may only be reproducible in the lab and not in the field, which leads to the ingraining of false assumptions.

USGA JOURNAL AND TURF MANAGEMENT: JUNE, 1951

Correspondence pertaining to Green Section matters should be addressed to:
USGA Green Section, Room 307, South Building, Plant Industry Station, Beltsville, Md.

COMPACTION OF TURF SOILS — SOME CAUSES AND EFFECTS

By R. B. ALDERFER

ASSOCIATE PROFESSOR OF SOILS, PENNSYLVANIA STATE COLLEGE

Compaction of turf soils is a condition which has existed for as many years as turf areas have been walked on and driven over.

What is a compacted soil? It is a soil whose particles have been fitted together so closely that the openings or pores which remain between them are of such a size, shape and arrangement that the plumbing, ventilation and heating systems within the soil are out of order. It is within this system of pores, as they occur in the soil, that both water and air are held and through which the soil is warmed or cooled. Soils, as they consist of many different sizes and shapes of particles as well as clusters of particles (called soil aggregates), also have a great many pores of different sizes and shapes.

There are two general types of pores in soils, the large or non-capillary pores and the small or capillary pores. The larger pores serve as drainage conduits. It is through these pores that most of the water enters the soil, and any excess which the smaller capillary pores cannot hold is drained into the substratum. As these pores are unable to hold water against gravity, they not only make up the over-flow system of the soil but also serve as air chambers through which the soil "breathes."

One of the characteristic features of many compacted soils is the way in which the particles assume a flat, platy shape, and are layered together much as bricks are laid in a wall. In this layering, the particles often overlap each other as do shingles on a roof. The pores between these particles not only are small but also offset from one another due to this peculiar particle arrangement. Both air and water movement through these flat, horizontal pores often is very slow. A loose, porous soil has a preponderance of the larger, rounded particles between which there is more likely to be a much more ideal assortment of pores. The larger pores tend to be more or less connected into a pattern of continuous passageways into the substratum. The differences in the physical characteristics of a soil in good and poor structure is illustrated in Figure 1.

Where does compaction occur in turf soils? Water-tight layers, of course, occur everywhere within the soil. Many turf areas are underlain by heavy, natur-

Figure 2-17: The best source of emerging science on golf course turf and greens after World War II was the *USGA Journal.* (Courtesy of United States Golf Association)

Other times things just happen fortuitously, or in 1960s jargon "serendipitously," things that then become part of a situation or finding. One such example might be that it was a common practice to put a stone or gravel layer in the bottom of flower pots to allow for good drainage, while also keeping soil from falling through the big holes normally found in the pot bottom. Kunze may have added a layer of coarse sand between his research mixes and the underlying gravel or stone. However, it was a classmate of Kunze, Leon Howard, who should be credited with seeing the need to build a test green and use the gravel layer. He determined that as long as the average particle size of both the sand and the gravel were within a five to seven times ratio of each other, this would keep the sand–soil–peat blend from mixing with the gravel, it also retained some moisture — less than the topmix but more than the gravel. In 1959, when Leon Howard completed his master's research at Texas A&M on *The Response of Some Putting Green Soil Mixtures to Compaction,* he had established the value of using the gravel layer, but he did not use the intermediate coarse sand layer, so one must assume Dr. Ferguson inserted it into the original specification for use if fine pea gravel could not be found. Why this is important is explained later when discussing revisions to the USGA method.

During the 1950s, Texas A&M was clearly the leading institution doing connected and collaborative research on green rootzone mixes, with Ferguson, Gorman, Kunze, Howard, and Lunt all adding to the information base. They all seem to have agreed that physical properties of sand–soil–peat blends are somewhat predictors of turfgrass performance. Further, they observed that a rootzone should have a high infiltration rate (one and one-half to two inches per hour when compacted), with minimum water retention of 10 percent by volume, and 10 to 15 percent of noncapillary pore space. There was also some agreement that sand-based rootzones are stable and productive growing mediums if there is adequate moisture. In particular, Leon Howard's 1959 work seemed to demonstrate that the optimum performance would result when certain ranges were met:

15–27 percent	Capillary spaces (after 24 hours of drain)
19–22 percent	Noncapillary spaces (after 24 hours of drain)
35–40 percent	Total porosity

and a hydraulic conductivity of 0.2 to 0.75 inches per hour.

FIRST USGA GREENS SPECIFICATIONS

On the basis of this combined research, in 1960, the USGA published a specification for green construction. The principal editor was Dr. Marvin Ferguson, along with Texas A&M professors Lunt, Howard, Morris, and Bloodworth, but the specification was a product of the entire USGA Green Section staff. Their performance guidelines are as follows:

Minimum total porosity	=	33 percent
Non-capillary pores	=	12 percent–18 percent
Capillary pores	=	15–21 percent
Permeability (hydraulic conductivity)	=	0.5–1.5 in./hr.

To come up with these numbers, they did evaluations by mechanical analysis, mineral derivation, aggregation, bulk density, and moisture retention at 40 cm of water tension.

When Dr. Norm Hummel reviewed this early work in 1992 for subsequent revisions to the USGA methods of green construction, he commented:

> It is interesting to note that despite all of the studies identifying a desirable particle size range for sand, the 1960 Specifications did not specify a particular size distribution. Rather, it was stated that "the soil mixture should meet certain physical requirements," presumably, referring to permeability and porosity.
>
> In addition, it should be mentioned that the "hydraulic conductivity" as determined by Howard and Kunze was measured as flux density at a hydraulic head of 6.4 mm (Howard, personal communication) and was calculated as:
>
> $J_w = Q/At$
>
> where
>
> J_w = flux density
>
> Q = quantity of water passing through the core in time
>
> A = cross-sectional area of the core
>
> This equation does not take into account the driving force behind the water movement; the hydraulic potential gradient. Kunze (1956) noted that slight changes in hydraulic head resulted in large changes in permeability. Infiltration rates specified since the 1973 Specifications are measured as saturated hydraulic conductivity. Taking into account the hydraulic potential gradient used in both Howard's and Kunze's thesis, the actual saturated hydraulic conductivity would be about 12 times greater than the flux density. Thus, the permeability of a rootzone mix as specified in the 1960 USGA Specifications would have a saturated conductivity of 15 to 46 cm/hr (6 to 18 in/hour).

So in September 1960, the USGA published a guideline, but the golf course designers and builders of that time asked what is it, what the heck does it mean, and what is its impact on golf green construction? By 1965 the USGA reprinted the guidelines only because, five years after its introduction, it had had time for evaluation and, as Ferguson pointed out, there were "...1,200 greens in existence that have been built by this method."

Basically, building to the earliest USGA Method meant following seven steps:

Step 1:   Establish the green's compacted subgrade.
Step 2:   Install 4-inch tile drains bedded in gravel.
Step 3:   Place gravel blanket and coarse sand layer over green subgrade.
Step 4:   "Ring" or surround the green with topsoil.
Step 5:   Prepare a laboratory selected and blended topsoil mix by offsite mixing.
Step 6:   Place, smooth, and firm 12 inches of topsoil mix over sand and gravel layers.
Step 7:   Sterilize soil and establish turf.

USGA METHOD BEGINS TO EVOLVE

It sure sounded simple enough, but during this boom period of golf course growth, construction techniques were fast and crude. Although there were established standards of workmanship to properly construct USGA greens, very few architects or contractors understood or cared about their importance, for they had used their own methods for years and those methods seemed to work just fine. In addition, because it was commonly and economically imperative to complete a golf course in only a few months in order to make an optimum planting date, emphasis was on speed, not quality, in construction. Coupled to these factors was the fact that after planting no one could see subgrades, drain fields, gravel and sand layers, or percentages of topsoil mixtures. *And* golf course architects were adjusting or changing grades on putting surfaces up to the moment of planting. This series of factors led to some bad mistakes. The most common mistakes included poor soil blending, improper and inconsistent depth of layers, and improper lab testing. The problem got so bad that the Golf Course Superintendents Association of America (GSCAA), in the April 1962 issue of its *Golf Course Reporter* magazine (see Figure 2-18), published the

Figure 2-18: The *Golf Course Reporter* was the official publication of the GCSAA and an excellent source of practical information and applied technology. (Courtesy of United States Golf Association)

results of a "Key Man Series" symposium on putting greens. Dr. Gene Nutter, in his editorial remarks, stated:

Sand, vermiculite, calcined clays, peat, colloidal phosphate, various composted materials and a number of other products—in addition to the great variety of natural soils—are in the limelight today as suggested materials for putting green construction. Yet, there seems to be no definite agreement in the evaluation of these materials, or combinations of these materials. This lack of agreement is not limited to golf course superintendents. Golf course architects, institutional workers, industry technicians, and USGA agronomists—all have their own opinion.

Why, then, the controversy? Why are not evaluations of these materials scientific, objective and final? Why have these inconsistencies and varying opinions not been resolved by the experts?

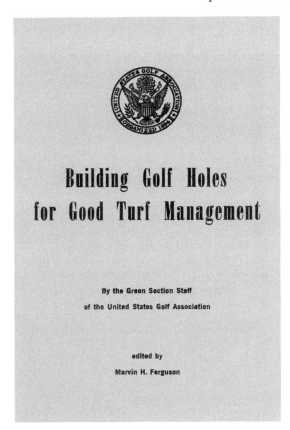

Figure 2-19: In 1968, Dr. Marvin Ferguson edited a seminal text for the USGA that more clearly defined how to properly design and build golf course features, especially greens. (Courtesy of United States Golf Association)

Dr. Nutter could not answer the question he raised about whose responsibility it was, nor could the panel of Robert Dunning, Dr. Ralph Smalley, Dr. W. L. Pritchett, and Professor Emeritus H. B. Musser. The panel did suggest that the problem was probably due to a disjunction between lab results and recommendations that were being improperly interpreted or implemented in the field (the old conflict between "pure" versus "applied" information). However, the "key men" did provide sufficient additional detail to the USGA method that the information helped sensitize architects and contractors to the importance of closely adhering to the guidelines. Apparently not enough, however.

In a 1968 USGA Green Section manual titled *Building Golf Holes for Good Turf Maintenance* (see Figure 2-19), edited by the very mild-mannered Dr. Marvin Ferguson, Ferguson wrote:

The problem of poorly built golf courses usually stems from one of three sources: 1) A number of golf course architects knowledgeable in the field of design have, for one reason or another, generally failed to show a real understanding of fundamental turfgrass requirements. Not once or twice have they failed, but a general pattern of failure is the rule, not the exception. 2) Some totally unqualified individuals have entered the field of golf course architecture. They are superb in salesmanship but basically lacking in an appreciation of design, golfing values, course construction and maintenance. 3) Key men behind the development of new courses, i.e. those with an investment to protect, frequently hold the fallacious belief that, to do anything well, exorbitant costs are required and can never by recovered. They choose to compromise with the future.

Obviously, in the late 1960s and early 1970s, there were still some problems that needed to be solved. Some other changes Dr. Ferguson noted were that, prior to 1960, an 18-hole golf course could get by nicely on a water supply of 500 gallons per minute (gpm) because of water-conserving application techniques discussed earlier; however, since the 1960s, most turf specialists had considered the minimum supply to be 1,000 gpm. This increase was due in part to the crudeness and overuse of the newly introduced automatic irrigation systems, which really got started in about 1960, and in part to the desire for courses to irrigate fairways and tees as well as greens. In addition, USGA greens require more water than old native soil greens, so some adjustments in thinking were also required.

THE PERCHED WATER TABLE CONCEPT DEBATE BEGINS

Summarizing, the theoretical basis of the USGA method evolved from F. W. Taylor's 1916 pure and applied research, which concluded that a properly selected sand, or sand–soil–peat blend, can resist compaction, and by its distribution of spaces or pores between the topsoil mix particles, could provide a plant growth promoting balance of soil, air, and water. However, a huge difference between Taylor's work and the USGA method that appeared a half a century later is that during Taylor's time sprinkler irrigation was virtually unknown, while starting in 1960 automatic irrigation of golf courses became the norm. On the other hand, conserving water in a comparatively droughty sand or topsoil mix was still a concern of the USGA. Hence the concept of the "perched water table" entered into the vernacular associated with the USGA method to describe an effect that was observed in the lab. This concept essentially says that, because of capillarity, water will not flow from a small pore to a large pore until the weight of the water caused by the downward pull of gravity can overcome the capillarity caused by the adhesion of water to the surface that defines the small pore. This is the same principle of the competing forces of capillarity versus gravity that was demonstrated by Taylor in the early 1900s, as well as by soil physicist W. H. Gardner in 1953. Gardner's classic demonstrations, conducted at Washington State University, showed how water moves in soils (see Figure 2-20). In layman's terms, once a rootzone has been saturated and allowed to free drain to gravity for 24 hours or so, there should be a balance between how much water the rootzone can hold and how much it is holding. Theoretically, if one additional drop of water is added to that rootzone, then one additional drop of water should drain out due to gravity. This is an overly simplified explanation but its essence is true. No one is certain, however, how and why it became com-

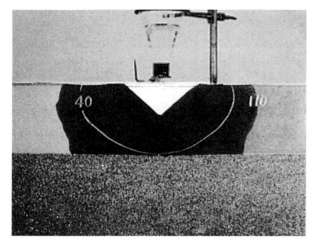

Figure 2-20: The 1953 work of Dr. W. H. Gardner of Washington State University played a large role in supporting the idea of a perching water table by using various textural layers or capillarity breaks. (Courtesy of United States Golf Association)

mon practice to claim that a textural barrier or interface would serve to conserve water, for it is clear that the intended purpose of the coarse sand layers used in early research and called for in the USGA publication was only to keep the finer particles in the topmix from infiltrating into or contaminating the gravel drainage layer, as found by Kunze and Howard in their research. Perhaps it was simply the case that a benign and casual observation became a sales tool to justify installing USGA type greens, an idea that simply grew in importance for the next 20 to 40 years, despite its lack of foundation.

INTERMEDIATE SAND LAYER REEVALUATED

In 1980, Dr. K. W. Brown, J. C. Thomas, and Dr. A. Almodares published in the *USGA Green Section Record* (see Figure 2-21) results of their research into "The Necessity of the Two-Inch Sand Layer in Green Construction." They found that, if the rootzone texture were coarse enough, and if the gravel of the drainage blanket were fine enough, then there would be no migration of rootzone into the gravel. Well, by 1980 it had become institutionalized that the coarse sand layer was important for the perched water table effect, and so there was a lot of confusion and resistance to removing the coarse sand layer. The reason it was even being looked at was because it was so difficult for a contractor to find a proper gradation of coarse sand that met laboratory test criteria, and then it was labor intensive to install it because it had to be done by hand to be perfectly uniform. Furthermore, Brown et al. showed that removing the coarse sand layer apparently had no observable negative impact on the water-holding or drainage capacity of the topmix.

A Publication on
Turfgrass Management by the
United States Golf Association

November/December 1980

USGA Green Section RECORD

Sand Layer
Not Always Necessary

Figure 2-21: A 1980 article in the *USGA Green Section Record* by Brown et al. caused a stir when it questioned the necessity of the intermediate sand layer. (Courtesy of United States Golf Association)

Thus, confusion reigned, and so architects and contractors took extreme liberties with the USGA recommendations and arbitrarily decided when or where to leave out the coarse sand layer. Previously, the USGA had called the coarse sand layer "optional" but had increased its depth from the one and one-half to two inches called for in the original specifications to two to four inches in the 1973 revision, a change intended to make the layer easier to install. They had also raised the saturated hydraulic conductivity (Ksat) from 0.5 to 1.5 inches per hour to 2 to 10 inches per hour. Still, very few architects and contractors understood when and where to include the coarse sand layer.

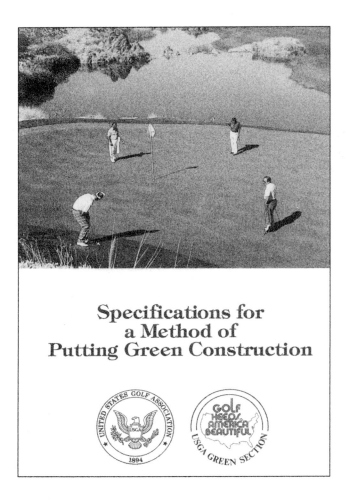

Figure 2-22: The 1989 USGA publication on their recommended method of green construction "...[P]ositively recommends including the intermediate sand layer..." (Courtesy of United States Golf Association)

Then, in 1989, the USGA issued a new revised *Specifications for a Method of Putting Green Construction* (see Figure 2-22) that read in part:

> Note: There are some who vigorously contend that the two to four inch intermediate sand layer is not necessary and is very expensive to install. The Green Section has studied this particular Specification requirement carefully over the years and now definitely concludes and POSITIVELY RECOMMENDS INCLUDING THE INTERMEDIATE SAND LAYER IN ALL USGA GREEN SECTION GREENS. It is an integral part of the perched water table concept. Its function is undeniable, and serious functional consequences may result if it is eliminated. Failure to follow this requirement means you are not building a USGA Green Section green.

Phew—how strong is that? End of discussion, right? Not by a long shot, and now confusion had escalated into chaos, for the 1989 Specification drew a line in the sand that said either put in the coarse sand layer or don't call it the USGA

Method. In addition, the 1989 spec went so far as to say, "...The interface between the coarse sand layer and the 12 inches of upper soil mix acts as a check on the downward movement of non-capillary water." In fact, the caption under their accompanying illustration reads, "Illustration of the perched water table concept, permitting sandy soils to retain adequate moisture" (see Figure 2-20).

For the next three years, the USGA Green Section came under extreme pressure to justify the 1989 recommendations, and it couldn't. Even some of their staff were divided on the issue and the importance of the intermediate coarse sand layer.

In 1991, the USGA asked a Cornell professor of soil physics, Dr. Norm Hummel, to take a sabbatical and review all pertinent research, information, observations, and opinions, and produce a new set of guidelines that would be beyond reasonable questioning. Hummel completed the task and a new revision was released in 1993. Hummel looked not only at the relationship between physical analysis and performance indicators, but also at protocols for laboratory testing, which are much less than uniform.

NEW USGA GUIDELINES

It appears that Hummel's suggestions to revise the USGA guidelines settled all arguments and confusion. Specifically, the new guidelines either spelled out in detail the important requirements, or gave the mathematical and theoretical basis for making decisions about the intermediate coarse sand layer. Hummel clarified that the sand layer's only function is to act as a gradient separation between the topmix and the gravel drainage blanket and not to perch the water table, reversing the 1989 dogma. Further, the 1993 guidelines gave a method of determining when a sand layer is needed based on the particle size distribution between the topmix and gravel, based upon measured percentages. Essentially, the more closely matched in size the topmix is to the gravel, the less need there is for the intermediate sand layer. However, if coarse gravel is used for the drainage blanket, it is probable that the intermediate sand layer will be needed. As a practical matter, golf course architects and contractors try to avoid the need for the intermediate layer because it is expensive and time consuming, and adds nothing to the performance of the green.

Perhaps one of the more interesting issues of the *USGA Green Section Record* is the March/April 1993 issue, with a fold-out cover, featuring recommendations for Putting Green Construction (see Figure 2-23). On one sheet is a profile of the green with the intermediate coarse sand blanket, and on the other sheet is the same profile drawn without it. However, rather than perpetuating confusion and chaos, the 1993 issue resolved the issue by using a classic soil and civil engineering criterion to determine "bridging," or the ability of

USGA Green Section

RECORD

USGA Recommendations for Putting Green Construction

Profile of a green built to USGA Recommendations with the intermediate layer (cover). When the appropriate gravel is used, the intermediate layer can be eliminated (below).

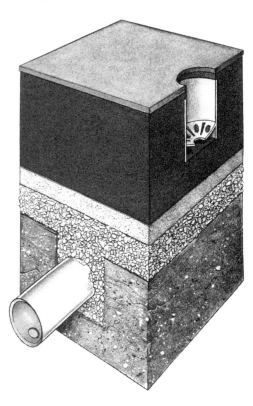 

(a)

Figure 2-23: (a) The fold-out cover of the March/April 1993 *Green Section Record* shows USGA green construction, with and without the intermediate sand layer. (b) Listing of criteria used to determine when sand layer is needed. (Courtesy of United States Golf Association)

two overlying materials to remain physically distinct. Basically, it assumed that 15 percent of the finest particles of the gravel would "bridge," or passively support, the coarsest 15 percent of the rootzone. In other words, the two materials are theoretically close enough in relative size so as not to mix, or to allow the rootzone mix to migrate into the gravel. At last the question of whether or not to use an intermediate coarse sand layer was reduced to a "go, no go" number that could be determined by measurements and calculations. Needless to say, the normal process is to find a good rootzone material, then look for a fine enough gravel to avoid the necessity of the coarse sand layer.

Gravel Layer

When intermediate layer is required:

⇒ Not more than 10% of the particles greater than ½" (12mm)
⇒ At least 65% of the particles between ¼" (6mm) and 3/8" (9mm)
⇒ Not more than 10% of the particles less than 2 mm

Intermediate Layer Material
⇒ At least 90% of the particles between 1 and 4mm

When intermediate layer is not used:

Bridging Factor
⇒ D15 (gravel) less than or equal to 5 X D85 (rootzone)
Permeability Factor
⇒ D15 (gravel) greater than or equal to 5 X D15 (rootzone)
Uniformity Factors
⇒ No particles greater than 12mm
⇒ Not more than 10% less than 2mm
⇒ Not more than 5% less than 1mm

Particle Size Distribution

Fine Gravel (2.0 – 3.4 mm)
Very coarse sand (1.0 – 2.0 mm)
Not more than 10% of the total particles in this range (1.0 – 3.4 mm), including a maximum of 3% fine gravel (preferably none).

Coarse sand (0.5 – 1.0 mm)
Medium sand (0.25 – 0.50 mm)
Minimum of 60% of the particles must fall in this range (0.25 – 1.0 mm)

Fine sand (0.15 – 0.25 mm)
Not more than 20% of the particles may fall within this range.

Very fine sand (0.05 – 0.15 mm)
Not more than 5%.

Silt (0.002 – 0.05 mm)
Not more than 5%.

Clay (less than 0.002 mm)
Not more than 3%

Total Fines (Very fine sand + silt + clay)
Less than or equal to 10%

Physical Properties of the Rootzone Mix

Total Porosity
35% - 55%

Air-filled Porosity
15% - 30%

Capillary Porosity
15% - 25%

Saturated Conductivity

Normal:
6-12 inches/hr (15-30 cm/hr)

Accelerated range:
12-24 inches/hr (30-60 cm/hr)

Conversions

ASTM	mm	inches
12.50	0.5000	1/2
9.50	0.3750	3/8
6.30	0.2500	1/4
4	4.76	0.1870
5	4.00	0.1570
6	3.36	0.1320
7	2.83	0.1110
8	2.38	0.0937
9	2.00	0.0787
10	1.68	0.0661
12	1.41	0.0555
14	1.19	0.0469
18	1.00	0.0394
32	0.50	0.0197
60	0.25	0.0098
65	0.21	0.0083
80	0.18	0.0070
100	0.15	0.0059
140	0.10	0.0042

Useful Info

Per 1000 sq. ft. of green

Gravel	12 cu.yds
Inter. layer	6-12 cu.yds.
Rootzone mix	37 cu. Yds.
Drainage tubing	~ 100 lin. Ft.

Be sure to allow 10-20% waste on all materials

Pounds per yard

Sand (dry)	2700 lbs.
Gravel	3450 lbs.
Peat (compact)	450 lbs.
Peat (loose)	110 lbs.

Slope Equivalents

10%	6°	10:1
18%	10°	6:1
25%	14°	4:1
33%	18°	3:1
50%	26°	2:1
100%	45°	1:1

Confidence Intervals for Quality Control Testing

Parameter	USGA Conf. Interval
Fine Gravel	50%
Very Coarse Sand	50%
Coarse Sand	10%
Medium Sand	10%
Fine Sand	15%
Very Fine Sand	30%
Silt	25%
Clay	25%
Total Porosity	10%
Air-Filled Porosity	10%
Capillary Porosity	10%
Saturated Conductivity	20%
Percent Organic Matter Of mix	0.2*

*The confidence interval for percent organic matter is not represented as a percentage. Thus a reported value of 0.7% organic matter could range from 0.5% to 0.9%

(*b*)

BUT WHAT ABOUT THE PERCHED WATER TABLE?

But the question that remained was: Is there a perched water table that can act as a water reservoir for plants growing in the topmix? The answer is probably "no," or that the effect is not enough to be of any real value. Many will find this shocking because that is not what they were taught, or what they observed with their eyes in the soil lab when they worked with soils of various textures. Then, too, many of us were taught soil water movement by viewing the 1953 film footage of soil physicist W. H. Gardner. The problem is that Gardner's excellent demonstration clearly showed what happens when soil layers are *flat*. Greens are rarely flat (see Figures 2-2 and 2-3), however, so there is a horizontal drainage force as well as a vertical force at work in greens, which was not acknowledged until the 2003 work of Guy Prettyman and Dr. Ed McCoy of The Ohio State University. McCoy concluded that, unless the interface between top-mix and gravel is absolutely level, perched water will run downhill and will not be perfectly distributed, as some would like to believe.

The fact that greens have surface and subsurface undulation means that the real vectors or driving forces to study are not necessarily just perpendicular by gravity. In fact, there are horizontal forces that influence free water laterally, but no one before Prettyman and McCoy had defined or measured that impact against capillarity. Then, too, most of the rootzone research had been done in short duration projects and/or without the confounding influences of turfgrass canopy, stolons, or roots, or naturally occurring channels or pathways called differential fingers of flow. Even ignoring these potential influences, if perched water does exist at, say, eight to ten inches below the turf surface, how meaningful is that free soil water to a plant that has 80 percent or more of its functioning roots at only four or five inches down? It can be argued that there is a continuum of increasing water in the profile down to the perched water, and that this, in fact, provides a reservoir effect, but that has not been shown. Yes, one may even find root growth down at the eight- to ten-inch depth, but there is no evidence that those roots contribute very much to the water balance in the plant. Further research may be able to quantify the value of held water in the rootzone, but at present to accept it as a viable and sustaining resource for putting surface turf is a stretch. There are also questions about the oxygen content of a rootzone at that depth and whether it is enough to allow roots to function at a normal, healthy metabolic rate.

Assuming a flat rootzone, the fact that water may accumulate at a textural interface is without question; however, the dynamics of that water accumulation are unknown, especially over time. For instance, there is evidence from Dr. McCoy's work that hydraulic conductivity immediately after a soaking or drenching event is understandably high, due to the weight of water in the profile being pulled by gravity as a driving force, but once excess water flushes through and out of the rootzone, draining is still taking place, although more slowly, because the driving force has been reduced. At some point capillarity of the soil will be stronger than gravity, and soil water may in theory be held in a static state. However, during the slow draining period when water is accumulating at the interface, it is logical to assume that there could be multiple smaller flushing or pulsing actions taking place with any excess free water. This could lead to a more thorough drainage of the profile depending upon the textural qualities of the rootzone and underlying layers. Whether to encourage the retention of water at the interface or to encourage flushing seems to be a question of how one wants a particular rootzone to behave.

For example, assuming that the quality of the irrigation water is on the salty side, the preference probably should be to err on the side of more thorough drainage to avoid salt accumulation. On the other hand, if the water quality is good and if leachates from under greens are being monitored due to environmental concerns, and especially if this is an important issue, having slugs of water draining out from under a green may show higher leachate levels than slower continuous drainage. There are probably dozens of other site-specific concerns that should be considered before final selection of rootzone materials and under drainage layers, and their interfaces, is decided. Again, here is where concepts derived from research may collide with applied research results.

USGA GREENS AND ENVIRONMENTAL IMPACT

One often hears that USGA recommended method greens are environmentally more correct than other methods, because with a small amount of cation exchange capacity (CEC) conferred by the incorporation of organic matter, nutrients are held against leaching in the rootzone. Despite the years of research, this "better environmental quality" has never been proven. In fact, if anything, the speed and completeness of drainage of a USGA green after a soaking event, as demonstrated by McCoy's work, would lead one to speculate that USGA greens may result in worse leaching than methods that drain more slowly over a longer period. Until this research has been done and tested on golf courses, however, I believe it is wrong to speculate either way.

BLENDING TOPMIX

The USGA recommended method does not require any organic or inorganic amendment be added to the sand selected for the rootzone. But the Green Section staff highly recommends organic amendments, and has no opinion about inorganic amendments other than to warn that some of these amendments may add value to the rootzone while others may be a total waste of money.

Assuming a cost-to-benefit ratio has determined that a push-up or native soil green or a pure sand California green are impractical for a particular project or sand or soil source, then blending should be considered. The theory of blending materials into a rootzone sand is that sands for the most part are nearly inert, being either of silica (quartz) or calcareous base materials, and therefore that blending will improve growth-promoting characteristics. Sand by its simplest definition is ground-up parent material, and so it is the parent material that gives the sand its chemical and structural properties, and it is the fineness of sand that mainly confers its physical qualities. Chemical properties can be measured by chemical composition of the sand particles along with its pH, buffer pH, and cation exchange capacity. Structural determinations are for hardness and resistance to weathering, while physical analysis looks at soil particle size, shape, uniformity, and distribution of particle sizes, as well as aggregation of particles. These physical properties are of interest to golf green construction because they have been shown to influence the performance measures of total porosity, capillary and noncapillary pore space, saturate hydraulic conductivity (Ksat), bulk density, and moisture retention at various levels of tension. Thus blending is a way to mitigate or improve these chemical, physical, and performance characteristics. The key, however, is to avoid the tendency to believe that if "a little is good, a lot is better," and thus to blend in more amendments than necessary. Such overblending may not only defeat the original purpose for blending, but also waste money.

In an article titled "How Do Soils Breathe?" by She-Kong Chong et al. in the January 2003 issue of *Golf Course Management* magazine, the researchers looked at the effect of increasing amounts of blended-in organic matter on soil, air, and water conductivity. Their data showed that conductivity of soil, air, and water was negatively impacted by incorporation of organic matter, with the rate of three percent organic matter being about five times slower for water and three times slower for air than pure sand. Again, the question of whether to blend or not to blend depends upon how one wants the rootzone mix to perform.

Forty years ago, rootzone blending methods were extremely crude, and so were the results. Typical methods involved dumping the rootzone constituents into separate stock piles, then using a front-end loader to take so many scoops from each pile to create a new pile, then mixing the new pile by lifting and dumping it until it looked homogeneous. Obviously, this was a volume-to-volume ratio, which was expressed as a 6–2–2 (sand, soil, organic matter, respectively) or a 60–20–20 blend, which meant six scoops of sand, two scoops of soil, and two scoops of organic matter. Typically, the soil and organic matter sources were local and highly variable, even from truckload to truckload, and the sand was graded only to the precision required for the cement and concrete industry, and not to the higher standards needed for golf greens. Further, this blending took so long that the materials often varied in moisture content over the blending period, resulting in different actual percentages of materials, and/or a different operator or machine might be used, which further confounded the accuracy of blending. Once this "blend" was "mixed," the whole thing was put through a soil shredder or hammer mill, which by the abrasive nature of the operation further altered the structure, and hence performance, of the rootzone (see Figures 2-24 and 2-25). This definitely was not rocket science, and it definitely was not soil science either.

Other methods that were tried in attempts to get greater consistency of a blend included mixing with scoop shovel and men, readaptive use of old cement mixer tumblers, and placing the material out in layers on soil or cement and using various types of mixing machines ranging from paddle pans to rotovators. But these methods were not much more accurate than "on-site" mixing where sand was delivered and placed in a green well, amendments were placed in a uniform layer on top, and then mixed with rotovator, disc, or roterra-type farm tools (see Figures 2-26, 2-27, 2-28, and 2-29).

Figure 2-24: 1970s-style green mix blending was done by using a bucket loader and scoop count method that was far from accurate.

Figure 2-25: Early off-site soil blending, 1960s style, was based on volume-to-volume, or more precisely bucket-to-bucket mixing, and then soil shredding before being hauled to the green. Note clay soil base under the pile and scraper marks from when "mix" is picked up.

Figure 2-26: Another method called "on-site" blending meant laying out bales of compressed peat on sand in green well, opening and evenly spreading the peat, then using a rototiller to mix the peat into the sand. This was not accurate, but it seemed to work in the 1960s and 1970s.

Figure 2-27: Baled peat is split open and spread evenly over sand in green in preparation for on-site mixing.

Figure 2-28: Often loose or mined peat, compost, well-aged sawdust, as shown, or other organic source was bulk hauled, dumped on green, and spread to grade stakes for on-site mixing.

Figure 2-29: A 40- or 50-hp tractor with a rotovator was the method of choice for on-site mixing of organic matter into green sand. Two inches of organic mixed into eight inches of sand gave a standard 80–20 mix.

INTRODUCTION OF MODERN SOIL BLENDING

Despite all of these inaccuracies in blending, it seemed like all of these greens would grow good grass when management techniques were properly adapted. That was how it was done until about 1980, when the first precision soil blender was introduced by a Texas fellow, Troy MacNeil, who invented an auger-type mixing machine that could accurately feed materials out of hoppers onto a belt or belts (see Figure 2-30). These accurately measured amounts of materials were then augured together before being dumped into a pile ready for movement to the green cavity. Suddenly, with this accuracy in blending came also greater consistency in the blend, but still there remained the same old problems of materials being too wet or too dry for blending, operator error, inconsistent materials or amendments, variations between machines, and dozens of other variables. Further, since these auger-type machines were custom built, there weren't very many of them, and only a few golf course contractors could afford to own one, and only work it for the week or two it took to do all of the blending they needed, so they subcontracted for the machine and operator. Soon there were 10 or 20 soil blenders crisscrossing the nation offering blending services to golf course contractors, usually using some variation of Troy's machine. Some ended up being only slightly better then the old ways of mixing.

So in the early 1980s, the idea of quality control (q.c.) to monitor this blending came into vogue, but by the time a blender had, say, 1,000 to 1,500 tons blended, and a q.c. sample was taken and sent to the lab and results returned,

Figure 2-30: A major advance in soil blending was the auger-type machines that were accurate to within a few percent of the goal. A front-end loader filled the hoppers with sand, peat, and/or soil, and then they were proportioned together before being dropped onto the elevator, which further blended them.

either the blender had almost finished, or he had finished and had been waiting for two to three days to see if he had mixed correctly. Since golf course construction is usually done over a short season, working seven days from sunup to sunset to get done, no one wanted to wait for lab results. So the blenders started running their own on-the-job tests for consistency, while lab results were being done for comparison purposes, and the blenders' methods were fast but hardly precise. Inevitably, the blender was done and gone before any problem was detected, at which point there would be a 6,000- to 7,000-ton pile of mix that did not meet the specification. To further complicate the mess, another sample of the nonconforming blend could be sent to a different lab—and *pass*! So now there would be a pile of topmix the size of a large house that one lab said was "no good" while another lab said "good." The owner and contractor couldn't know who or what to believe, the blender would be gone, and the golf course would still be under tight time constraints for completion. As a result, all sorts of compromises were worked out—and a lot of lawsuits were filed. Even the lawsuits were wacky because no one knew who to believe. Somehow golf course superintendents usually managed to solve the problems well enough to produce excellent greens. Needless to say, the whole issue of blending came under criticism and review.

Even though blending methods have greatly improved, it has been discovered that the methods for testing saturated hydraulic conductivity can be highly variable, with results varying by as much as 200 percent, even between certified labs using essentially identical protocols. This has led to new confusion and a movement to eliminate or discount using Ksat as an indicator. This issue is discussed further in Chapter 6.

Blending anything into a rootzone should be evaluated by adding together the cost of the material, the blending activity, the rehandling of the blended material, and associated material losses from handling. Total cost of blending can be as low as $12 per ton or as high as $40 per ton, depending upon the specific materials and circumstances. This may sound like a small cost, but when multiplied by the 6,000 to 7,000 tons of rootzones required by an average 18-hole golf course, the cost can be between $72,000 and $280,000.

COST-TO-BENEFIT RATIO

Since blending is expensive it should be carefully evaluated using a cost-to-benefit ratio. In essence this means that if, say, one alternative method of green construction would cost $100,000 for a rootzone material installed, and another would cost $400,000, someone should be able to demonstrate if and how that greater expenditure would provide benefits commensurate with the increased cost. Will it save that amount in water, fertilizer, pesticides, and labor? And if so, over how long of a period of time? Further, this assumes that the value of money is free, but any businessperson knows it is not, and if the value of using the $100,000 is at the prime lending rate plus two percent over 10 to 15 years, the actual payback of that blending cost may be $150,000 to $200,000. So just as there is no question that the recommended blending of materials into a rootzone may improve its plant-growing qualities, there is also no question that it is expensive, and someone should question if the benefits justify the cost, or if that money would be better spent to improve the total golf course project with more sod, better irrigation system, better maintenance equipment, and so on.

The USGA Green Section, however, still recommends blending, for they believe the benefits outweigh the cost and problems. The Green Section staff believes that adding a proper amount of organic matter to a blend will (1) increase the moisture retention with only a slight effect on permeability, (2) increase the cation exchange capacity, and (3) provide an organic substrate for soil biological activity. They feel there are also a few lesser reasons. Although the minimum amount they recommend is zero, the maximum is 20 percent by volume, but since volume measures are very inaccurate because of the variability in the bulk density of various organic materials, they recommend 2 to 3 percent by weight. Now there are those who debate the value of adding amendments to properly selected sands, and that brings this discussion to California greens.

CALIFORNIA GREENS

Way back in the beginning of this chapter, California greens were defined as being built of laboratory-selected sands, without any amendments blended into them to alter their basic properties, and built without underlying drainage blankets or layers of sand or gravel. In essence, to build a California green one simply excavates a cavity below the putting surface, installs tile drainage bedded in one-quarter to three-eighths inch of pea stone, and then places a uniform 12-

inch layer of laboratory-selected sand directly over the drainage. Obviously, with no associated cost for blending or gravel layers, and no repeated handling of the rootzone, California greens are much less expensive to build. But do they work well? The *University of California Cooperative Extension Publication 21448* (see Figure 2-31), released in 1990, says:

> In the mid-1960s, researchers at the University of California explored the possible use of sand and amended sands that could resist compaction and provide a growing medium for grass. This research, combined with field observations, led to the conclusion that unamended sand was the best and most practical foundation for putting-green turf. The sand that is used, however, must be the "right" sand; not all sands are suitable as a growing medium for putting greens. The right sand will need no amending and will meet all the requirements to produce an easily managed, high-quality putting surface.

Before discussing the theory of the California concept and how to select the "right" sand, it is worthwhile to look at how the researchers reached this conclusion for the "...best and most practical foundation for putting green turf," which is different than the USGA concept.

Figure 2-31: This 1990 publication is still considered the sole source document on California green construction, so named because the University of California published this booklet. (Courtesy of University of California)

DAVIS AND MADISON

In 1970, Drs. John Davis and J. H. Madison authored the *University of California Agricultural Extension Publication AXT-N-113, A Guide to Evaluating Sands and Amendments Used for High Trafficked Turfgrass* (see Figure 2-32). Davis and Madison took five different sands, ranging from texturally coarse to fine, tested each blended with one of 16 different popular organic and inorganic amendments, in percentages ranging from 0 to 60 percent volume of amendments. Davis and Madison measured four performance indicators for (1) total water, (2) unavailable water, (3) infiltration rate, and (4) air-filled porosity for various depths of mixes ranging from 3½ to 24 inches (see Figure 2-33). By any measure, this was a monumental work on a monumental scale. They published their results in the aforementioned booklet, which was generally overlooked by everyone except researchers and a few field agronomists. The work was intended to provide baseline information to help the turfgrass manager to make better-informed decisions about materials for constructing putting and bowling greens. This was an excellent piece of work that wasn't very practical at a time when the prevailing method of rootzone

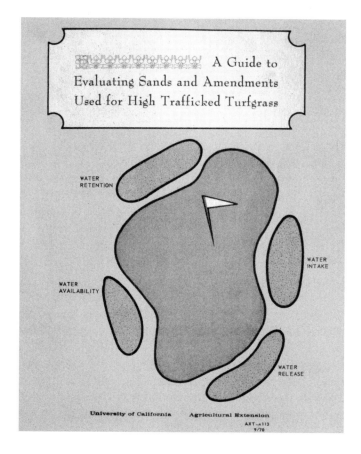

Figure 2-32: Drs. Davis and Madison laid the foundation for the California method of green construction with this 1970s research summary. (Courtesy of University of California)

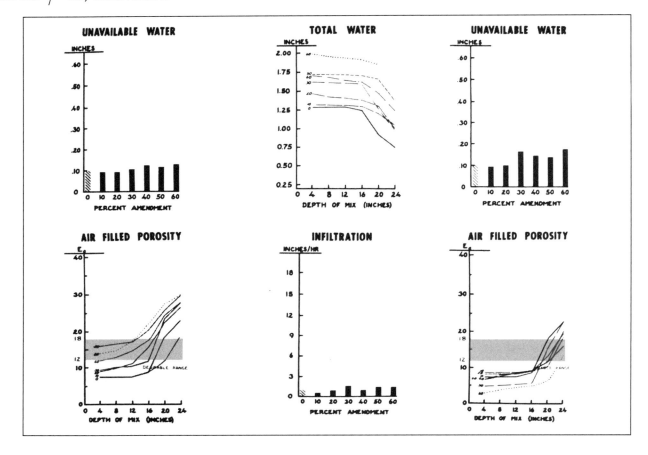

Figure 2-33: A typical page from Davis and Madison's work on evaluating sands. Their monumental effort was for five sands, with 16 different organic and inorganic amendments, in 10 percent increments. (Courtesy of University of California)

material selection was to put some of each possible constituent in a bucket, mix them up by hand, feel the texture of the combined materials by squeezing a handful or two, maybe even adding a little water to see if it thickened up, then finally put some in a mason jar, fill the jar with water, vigorously shake it, and let it settle for a day or two. After allowing the jar to sit undisturbed for a day or so, the "expert" would "read" the rings, or layers of settled material, to ensure that there was not too much silt or clay in the mix. Given this prevailing attitude, it was easy to see why any specified method of green construction was not taken too seriously in the early 1970s.

Just after the USGA released its 1989 version of their green construction recommendation that caused so much confusion and chaos, the 1990 booklet on California greens was made available. Here was an easy-to-build method that costs less, worked well, and in which little or nothing could go wrong with blending because there was no blending. Several golf course architects and agronomists had been working with pure sand greens clear back into the mid 1950s, so for them this California publication was a vindication, while for others it was an abomination.

The notion that pure sand had to be amended was taught for years in schools, stressed at turf conferences, and generally filled popular and scientific publications. People involved in green construction were generally slow to change their attitude because what they were taught made sense to them, and it was comfortable to believe. But the reality was that there were many 100 percent, laboratory-selected sand greens that were doing well with no more, and perhaps fewer, problems than greens with amended rootzones. For some reason, there is a resistance to believing that simple concepts can be equal to or better than complex ones, especially when the simple one costs less. It is fair to say that the majority of turf folks believed that the USGA method was superior, and defended their beliefs with false rationalizations, such as claiming that California greens use more water, fertilizer, and pesticides, California greens are environmentally irresponsible, and California greens are doomed to long-term failure. All of these assumptions either have already been proven incorrect, or will be in future years as more comparative studies are fairly done. A thorough understanding of the method may help convince you of this.

THEORETICAL BASIS OF CALIFORNIA GREENS

Again, the basis of the California concepts can be traced back to the work of F. W. Taylor. Taylor was looking for a soilless green using pure sand, one that he could subirrigate and that would involve, in his words, "...[A]n appreciation and utilization of certain characteristics of granular bodies." He contended the total percentage of pore volume in any sand of uniform size will be about 40 percent, and that the finer sand, the smaller the pores, and the larger the sand, the larger the pores. Similarly, the California method relies on using sand that is much more uniform in particle size, and hence has more uniform voids or pores than is recommended for a USGA rootzone.

The graphic illustration or mental image most often used for explaining the differences between the USGA and California greens is to start with a large room, and in that room place as many inflated weather balloons as would comfortably fit. These balloons represent large size sand particles. Then to this room add, in sequence, particles of progressively smaller size, such as the size of bowling balls, then baseballs, next golf balls, and then marbles, and finally fine buckshot. As each different size "particle" is added, suppose the room could be shaken to help smaller particles fill the voids between larger particles. In theory, by adding finer and finer particles, it may be possible to nearly fill all voids between all particles, thus leaving little or no pore space. The California green concept therefore would be most analogous to having only a few different sized particles that are fairly close in size (see Figure 2-34). The USGA concept is based upon a broader distribution of particle sizes because it is more inclined to perch or hold water than drain it. The more uniform particle size makes the sand more predictable in its physical properties, and hence will have more distinct performance characteristics.

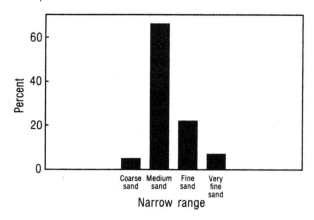

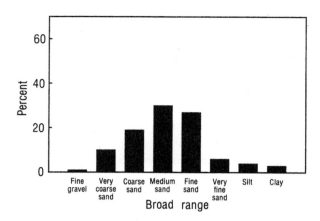

Figure 2-34: The ideal range of particle sizes for building California greens is quite narrow (left) compared to ideal sands for USGA greens (right). California green construction requires the same amount of lab analysis as USGA construction. (Courtesy of University of California)

In Davis and Madison's work, the authors found that the range of particle sizes that gave the best performance, when unamended, were in the narrowest range bracketed near a medium sand defined as 0.25- to 0.50-mm particle size. Therefore, the California recommendation is for 82 to 100 percent of any potential rootzone sand to be in the total range of 1.00 mm (coarse sand) to 0.1 mm (fine sand), with at least 50 to 70 percent in the 0.25- to 0.50-mm range (see Figure 2-34, top). Where within that range the majority of particles fall will determine such performance properties as infiltration rate, saturated hydraulic conductivity, and water to air porosity. Since the sand is so uniform, it is not expected to experience any migration of finer materials and hence change drainage characteristics. However, like all sand selection criteria, this ignores the impact of plant organic layers and roots growing into these pores or spaces, and hence altering the original balance of air and water available as well as hydraulic conductivity (Ksat), commonly called infiltration rate. So although all rootzone materials are selected on a basis of numbers, those numbers will change dramatically once plant parts start occupying available pore spaces.

Therefore, when choosing between laboratory approved sands, one deciding criterion is, again, the irrigation water quality. If the water quality is high and the water is low in salts, then selecting sand with a lower Ksat makes more sense than if the irrigation water may at times be salty, when a much higher percolation rate is desirable.

NATURAL ORGANIC MATTER ACCUMULATION

Although a California green starts out with little or no organic matter, experience has shown that within 12 to 18 months it reaches an equilibrium of two to three percent of soil organic matter, almost identical to what is built into a USGA type green. A couple of logical questions might be: what is the source of this organic constituent and why not just put it in to begin with?

The soil organic matter comes from the early application of organic fertilizers, a topic discussed later under grow-in procedures in Chapter 7, as well as from sloughed-off roots and the accumulation of some organic debris such as leaf clippings. In March 2001, Andrew Curtis and Matthew Pulis of the International Sports Turf Research Center in Olathe, KS, published an article titled "Evolution of a Sand-Based Root Zone" in *Golf Course Management* magazine. In it they measure performance changes of a green rootzone by age. Most dramatically, infiltration rate (inches per hour) fell from 36.92 to 4.42 in one year and to 1.20 by the third year. Water-holding capacity nearly doubled over that period, and air porosity fell by nearly a third as organic matter in the top one inch naturally increased from 0.08 percent to 2.40 percent. Below three inches, the topmix was not significantly altered.

At Widow's Walk Golf Course in Scituate, MA, America's First Environmental Demonstration Golf Course, the decision was made to build six USGA, six California, and six native sandy loam greens (see Figure 2-35). The objective was simply to observe any differences in grow-in, long-term performance, or playing qualities. Investigations included lysimeters in greens to meas-

Widow's Walk Golf Course
Greens Matrix

Hole No:	Push-up	California	U.S.G.A	4" Perfer.	12" Flat	No Drains	Shphagnus	Shamrock	C-nut Coir	Axis	Profile
		Soil			Drainage			Peat		Soil Amendments	
1	XXXXX					XXXXX					
2			XXXXX		XXXXX				XXXXX		
3			XXXXX			XXXXX		XXXXX			
4			XXXXX			XXXXX		XXXXX			
5		XXXXX			XXXXX						
6	XXXXX			XXXXX						2.4 lbs/sq.ft	
7	XXXXX				XXXXX					1.25lbs/sq.tf	
8	XXXXX					XXXXX					
9			XXXXX	XXXXX					XXXXX		
10			XXXXX		XXXXX		XXXXX				
11		XXXXX			XXXXX						8 tons/GF
12	XXXXX			XXXXX							10 tons/GF
13			XXXXX	XXXXX			XXXXX				
14	XXXXX				XXXXX						
15		XXXXX		XXXXX						1.25lbs/sq.ft	
16		XXXXX		XXXXX							9 tons/GF
17		XXXXX				XXXXX				2.4lbs/sq.ft	
18		XXXXX				XXXXX					
P.G.	XXXXX					XXXXX					4 tons/GF
P.G.-R	XXXXX			XXXXX							
Note: All greens were seed with "G1" except for the practice green at the range which was "L93"											
Note: All greens containg Profile also contain 500lbs of Humates/green											

Figure 2-35: Chart showing the various methods and variations of greens constructed at Widow's Walk, America's first environmental demonstration project golf course. Basically there are six USGA, six California, and six native soil greens, with round, flat and no tile, and various organic and inorganic amendments.

ure leachate, temperature and moisture sensors, detailed record keeping by the golf course superintendent, and general observations. Furthermore, two of each of the six greens had either no drainage, conventional round tile, or flat tile drains. In a nutshell, other than the native soil greens growing in faster, nothing of significance was noted. This null result could be the result of the already naturally well-drained soils of the site, its mild New England seashore climate, or that there were no observable differences. Again, when a cost-to-benefit ratio is applied and one finds that the construction cost for native soil greens was $0.50 per square foot, compared to $1.70 for California and $4.50 for USGA, one has to ask if such investment is necessary. At Widows Walk, it was not, but under different site conditions, the answer could be an emphatic "yes."

The six USGA greens had two percent organic matter from three different sources blended into the rootzone, giving two greens of sand and Shamrock Irish peat, two greens of sand and coconut coir, and two greens of sand plus composted sewage sludge. Eighteen months after planting, laboratory tests showed the mature California rootzone also had developed two percent soil organic matter. Even during initial grow-in, the concept for differential water requirements based upon rootzone composition seemed to be anecdotal. At Widow's Walk, each green was equipped with its own water meter to answer the question, but the data was either lost or not properly collected, so speculation continues. It would be such an easy experiment to properly build greens of different theoretical bases, install a water meter at each green, and then link them back to a computer to accumulate data on water usage for an hour, day, week, month, year. Observations in the field show that there is no significant difference in water requirement during germination or early establishment. Long-term requirements remain a mystery, but an easily solvable one.

SIMILARITIES BETWEEN USGA AND CALIFORNIA CONCEPTS

The only significant differences between a California and a USGA recommended method (see Table 2-1) is whether the selected rootzone sand is amended and the existence of a gravel drainage layer. Both concepts require clean sand with very small percentages of silt and clay and/or coarse sand particles. Both concepts shoot for a total porosity of 35 to 55 percent, with a balance between air- and water-filled pores, although California sets a higher and broader range for hydraulic conductivity (Ksat). It really does not matter whether those numbers are a result of sand and organic amendment, or pure sand alone, although it is expected that more of the water held by organic sources will be unavailable for plants than that held by pure sand. Besides, these values are laboratory numbers only, and don't reflect the changing nature of these performance indicators once a mat layer develops on the surface of the rootzone, and roots begin to fill the macro pores. Likewise, in both USGA and

California greens, the hydraulic conductivity (Ksat) falls from around 25 inches per hour to less than 3 inches per hour. At Widow's Walk, after one year, there were no noticeable differences in performance between any of the greens, push-up, USGA, or California. Seemingly 2 to 3 percent organic matter is the range of stable and healthy rootzones, regardless of age.

Table 2-1 COMPARISON OF USGA & CALIFORNIA TEST CRITERIA

| Particle Classification | SIEVE | | ALLOWABLE RANGE (% RETAINED) | |
	Mesh	Diameter	USGA	California
Gravel	10	2.00 mm	0–3%	0–10%
Very coarse sand	18	1.00	0–10% w/gravel	w/gravel
Coarse sand	35	0.50	min. 60% in this range	82% min. with 50–70% medium sand
Medium sand	60	0.25	min. 60% in this range	82% min. with 50–70% medium sand
Fine sand	140	0.15	20%	82% min. with 50–70% medium sand
Very fine sand	270	0.05	5% max.	0–8% total in this range
Silt	—	0.002	5% max.	0–8% total in this range
Clay	—	<0.002	3% max.	0–8% total in this range
Bulk density (gm/cc)			1.3–1.65	1.4–1.65
Particle density (gm/ec)				
Coefficient of uniformity			2–3	2–3

| Performance Measure | ALLOWANCE RANGE | |
	USGA	California
Saturated hydraulic conductivity (inches/hour)	6–24	15–50
Total porosity (percent)	35–55	35–55
Aeration porosity (percent) [a]	15–30	15–30
Capillary porosity (percent) [a]	15–25	10–20
Saturation percentage [a]	40–55	25–55
OTHER		
Organic matter amendment (by weight)	0–3%	0%
Inorganic amendment (by weight)	0%	0–3%
Gravel drainage blanket	Yes	No
Tile drainage	Yes	Yes
Rootzone depth [a]	12 in.	10–18 in.

[a]Determined at 30-cm tension (or tension corresponding to profile).

MISCONCEPTIONS BETWEEN USGA AND CALIFORNIA GREENS

This idea of the USGA concept acting as a reservoir for water, whether available for plant use or not, also may have spawned the notion that, since California greens are pure sand, they must be droughty and hence use more water on a daily basis, which would extrapolate to more leaching of rootzone solutes, and hence a greater risk to the environment. For years a number of intelligent people bought into this concept, despite there being no proof to back it up. Then, in the late 1990s, Dr. Ed McCoy set up some rootzone plots, built aboveground in troughs and angled or tilted like a real green's surface and subsurface would be, and studied water movement in the soil profile, with and without a gravel underlayer (see Figure 2-36). He gathered his data by using a system of soil moisture probes set at incremental distances and depths away from an outlet drainage tile, and he recorded the amount of water drained over a period of time after total saturization of the rootzone. To most people's surprise, the USGA design drained water much faster—three to four times faster—and more thoroughly over a 72-hour period. This means that the USGA green would require supplemental irrigation sooner then a California concept green, and the USGA would leach the solutes in the rootzone as fast as it did drainage water. McCoy's explanation for these measurements is that the excess water in the saturated USGA rootzone only had to travel vertically 1 foot down in a 12-inch-deep rootzone to get to the drainage layer, while the same profile without gravel had to drain as much as 15 feet to reach a tile drain. A perfectly logical explanation for what superintendents have observed for years—for any given sands California greens need less water than USGA greens. Assuming the putting surface plants never went into wilt or moisture deficiency, the USGA perched water may be of value in the long-term sustainment, but not necessarily in situations of everyday irrigation.

Of course, critics would cite a major fault in McCoy's research in that he used an amended rootzone in both systems as opposed to pure sand in a true California system. However, if one is to assume that his research was run over such a short time interval that the performance characteristics of the rootzone would be indicative of pure sand, then his results are illuminating.

MODIFIED OR SIMPLIFIED GREEN CONSTRUCTION METHODS

Folks familiar with green construction usually wince when a construction method is described as "modified" or "simplified," for it implies someone has taken liberties with the original concept. Usually modification means something else was added and simplification implies something was left out. Obviously what that "something" is, and to what degree the method was modified or simplified can determine success or failure of the rootzone.

Figure 2-36: Dr. Ed McCoy's green research plots in Wooster, OH, for The Ohio State University, to assess the effect of slope on water content in golf green rootzone soils. (Courtesy of Dr. Ed McCoy)

Starting with the simplest example of a native soil green, modified push-up usually connotes something was added to the soil, be it a sand, organic or inorganic material, or any combination of the above. This seems innocuous enough for, intuitively, anything added to a soil, especially a clay soil, should improve its performance. This often is not the case. For instance, it would seem reasonable that adding 40 to 50 percent coarse sand to a slow-draining clay soil would improve its porosity, especially the air-filled pores. In fact, what may happen is that the soil will lose much of its structure and the clay particles will fill the voids between the sand particles, resulting in low-grade concrete with no measurable porosity. Remember the example of the various size balls in a confined space used to explain the California system, and that the more uniform the particle or ball sizes, the more uniform the spaces between them. Mixing coarse sand with a clay soil is like mixing weather balloons with buckshot, with the buckshot filling all of the spaces between the balloons.

Dr. McCoy reported in the May–June 1998 issue of *Agronomy Journal* on research he conducted amending a native loam soil with peat humus and spent foundry sand. The article, titled "Sand and Organic Amendment Influences on Soil Physical Properties Related to Turf Establishment," described making 28 individual soil mixes and seeding them with perennial ryegrass and measuring their growth after four weeks in a growth chamber. McCoy concluded that a high-quality, general use soil should texturally be a sandy loam or sandy clay loam of 65 percent sand and 8 percent organic matter by volume, which means only about 27 percent or less would be silt and/or clay. In other words, to properly modify a clay soil would require at least 73 percent sand, and 80 percent or more would be better. The reality is that it is usually better to not amend a native soil if push-up greens are to be built.

Back in the early 1900s, efforts were made to blend organic matter and manures into native soil greens, and with good success (see Figure 2-37). Although the organic would be expected to decompose and ultimately mineralize, it would provide a short-term (a year or two) deterrent to compaction until the greens developed a mat layer, as well as channels for drainage that stayed open due to shrink-swell drying cycles. Presumably, the plant roots would become established in spaces as the organics decomposed, and the original structure and texture of the soil would be unaltered so it could establish its own drainage channels.

In the 1930s or so, there was good evidence that compacted greens could be improved by aerifying and backfilling with sand or a sand and compost. The earliest machines were Turferators (see Figure 2-38), which were nothing more than a series of drill bits mounted on heavy frames that would drill down into the compacted soil surface. This was the original drill and fill, which gave good results. Later, a series of horticultural materials were also promoted as backfill materials; the most notable was Turface, a calcined clay material that was basically kitty litter. Initially it produced dramatic improvements, but with continued use caused layering, and later was found to deflocculate into a dense clay layer. Equally unsuccessful was incorporation of perlite, vermiculite, and other products used in greenhouse potting culture. Slowly these materials fell out of favor, as did the notion of push-up greens.

It would not be until the 1990s that new and improved inorganic materials were experimented with, and developers considered building native soil greens to keep total construction costs down. Today, modified native soil greens are being built by first testing the native soil for textural characteristics, then blending various amounts of soil and amendments, and finally running performance evaluations much like for a sand green. This laboratory work cannot guarantee results as much as it can help avoid failure.

VARYING DEPTH OF ROOTZONE

There is not much latitude for modifying or simplifying USGA or California construction methods except to vary the depth of the rootzone to achieve a target balance of capillary versus noncapillary pores or to add a stable inorganic amendment. Although most green construction recommendations and testing are developed around a 12-inch-deep rootzone, this is not a hard and fast requirement. The minimum depth of rootzone could be 8 inches or so, or just deep enough to set a cup, and the maximum is limited only by budget and performance curves of rootzone material. As explained earlier, the deeper the profile, the greater the pull of gravity on the water column in that profile. Deep profiles will be drier on the top surface than more shallow profiles.

Research at Michigan State University by B. Leinauer, J. Crum, and P. Reike experimented with varying the depths of rootzone profiled in a USGA green to help reduce differential drying, or said another way, watering requirements (see Figure 2-39). The logic was to make the profile shallow on high places and

Figure 2-37: Blending organic matter into greens and topdressing has been the stock-in-trade of greenkeepers for over 150 years. This is one example of how it was prepared and blended in the early twentieth century.

Figure 2-38: The first aerifiers were a set of drill bits or augers that actually bored holes down into the green. The machines were heavy, slow, and made a mess, but they did improve compacted greens, especially when holes were topdressed and filled with sand.

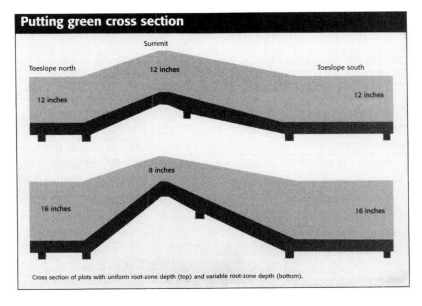

Putting green cross section

Summit

Toeslope north   12 inches   Toeslope south

12 inches   12 inches

8 inches

16 inches   16 inches

Cross section of plots with uniform root-zone depth (top) and variable root-zone depth (bottom).

Figure 2-39: B. Leinauer, J. Crum, and P. Reike at Michigan State University evaluated the possibility of varying depths of the rootzone within a green, to produce a uniform surface water content, with good results. (Courtesy of Golf Course Superintendents Association of America)

deeper in low places on a green to equalize the water availability in the profile. They found that an 8-inch-deep profile on top of a slope and a 14-inch-deep profile at the base gave rather acceptable results.

This brings up an interesting point of how much leeway there is in depth of any profile and how practical it would be to try to vary profiles to achieve a more uniform water balance. From the golf course contractor's point of view, such profile manipulation would be seen as a nightmare that would greatly add to the labor cost of building a green. From the golf course architect's point of view, this would be seen as one more concern or limitation to artistic expression in putting surfaces for which he or she would not want to assume responsibility. Actually all of this is reminiscent of remarks made when F. W. Taylor introduced his idea of using various lifting sands for surface moisture balance in his subirrigated greens. However, it does make some sense to do the performance evaluation of rootzone mixes in the laboratory at 10-, 12-, and 14-inch depths, just to see what impact a variable profile might make.

A more frequently used profile depth modification of the California green is when the right sand cannot be found or afforded, and a sand of marginal quality may work if it is placed at a depth of other than the standard 12 inches. For example, at the Bully Pulpit Golf Course in Medora, ND (see Figure 2-40), there was no room in the construction budget for building greens with rootzone materials that would meet either USGA or California standards. Fortuitously the native soils were fairly sandy coming from the outwash floodplain of the Little Missouri River. After laboratory testing it was found that if the native sandy soil was placed 16 inches deep, it would have a reasonable porosity and balance of air and water-filled pores. Placing an extra 4 inches of native sand would fit the budget, and so that was how the greens were built. In fact, where subsoil beneath the greens was equally sandy, no tile drainage was installed, resulting in a further savings in an already modest budget.

INORGANIC AMENDMENTS

The other area where modifications or simplifications of standard construction methods can be seen as either benign or acceptable is in the addition of a stable, inorganic amendment. Here it is simply a case of doing a good cost-to-benefit ratio analysis and being able to justify the added expense. Without question, some of these materials offer enormous benefits but can add $250,000 or more to the cost of an already laboratory-approved rootzone material. If cost is a factor, then consideration for partial incorporation may be considered. For instance, using the Bully Pulpit golf greens again as an example, the golf course superintendent, David Solga, did some research on various materials and found that, for an investment of under $20,000, he could incorporate 12 percent of one particular product ($PermO_2Pore^{TM}$) into the top two inches of the profile and greatly improve the germination of seed and establishment of the greens.

The USGA Green Section neither recommends nor condemns the inorganic materials but does issue the age-old warning "buyer beware." Any thought of modifying or simplifying a standard construction method should be considered carefully, and in consultation with an independent party knowledgeable about golf greens. Do not rely on intuition or sales pitches, but rather go for peer reviewed, hard data if at all possible.

No complete discussion of the theory and agronomics of golf green design should ignore flat tile or rootzone gas exchangers. Although these systems have been around for a decade or more and have proven to be of great benefit when properly used, some still consider them to be new technology.

Figure 2-40: The Bully Pulpit Golf Course in Medora, ND, has greens built of native sandy soils deposited by the Little Missouri River, which created the valley floodplain on which the course is built. (Courtesy of Jack Marquart)

FLAT PIPE

The author first used flat pipe in green construction in 1992, although the product had been available since the mid 1980s. The material has been called flat tile, flat pipe, panel pipe, waffle drain, AdvanEdge®, and a few other things, but it is basically a perforated, extruded, polyethylene drainage tubing that is made with flat sides. AdvanEdge®, made by A.D.S. in the United States, measures 2 inches by 12 inches wide or 2 inches by 18 inches wide. There are also two widths of openings into the pipe, a narrow sand slit and a wider, standard opening. It has been found that it is best to use the wide slit 12-inch width pipe with either a white (not gray) geotextile sock covering, or to use no sock but to cover the tile slightly with one-quarter to three-eighths of an inch of pea gravel (see Figure 2-41, color insert).

The flat pipe was first used at Westwood Plateau Golf Club in Vancouver, Canada, when installing conventional round tile into extremely rocky soils was deemed cost prohibitive. A logical alternative was to install a drainage material that required no trenching and could be laid right on the subgrade cavity of the green. After some experimentation and extensive testing of the sand rootzone material, it was decided to install the pipe without any geotextile or gravel (see Figures 2-42, 2-43, 2-44, 2-45, 2-46, and 2-47 in color insert). The installation went well and is more fully described in Chapter 5 on construction, but fortuitously we found a flaw in the concept early on that was easily and quickly corrected.

Immediately after seeding a green that had flat tile, a pretty strong, prolonged rainstorm hit the site. It was observed that the flat pipe was working so well that it actually sucked sand down into the tile. Had any turfgrass been growing on the green, this may not have been discovered for years, for the turf would have slowed down the water infiltration and the effect would have been less obvious. So initially the flat tile idea appeared to be a disaster, but the clogged tile was replaced with more flat pipe, a layer of very coarse geotextile was laid over the top of the pipe to keep the rootzone in place, and the California greens were successfully grown in. Today that system is functioning well, and better than round tile installed in other greens on the course. The director of golf course maintenance, Bruce Thrasher, has been at the course from during construction to present, and he has remarked that he wishes we had done all of the greens in flat tile, but with a shallow gravel layer between them. Remember, this area gets 120 inches of rain per year, and nearly all of it in only eight months, so this is a very wet site. Because of Bruce's observations, we currently recommend that if rapid drainage is an issue, then a two-inch layer of fine pea gravel (one-quarter to three-eighths inch) layer between the tile lines works best.

The reasons for considering flat tile instead of round tile are cost savings, faster, cleaner installation, and equivalent drainage capability. The cost savings

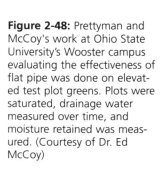

Figure 2-48: Prettyman and McCoy's work at Ohio State University's Wooster campus evaluating the effectiveness of flat pipe was done on elevated test plot greens. Plots were saturated, drainage water measured over time, and moisture retained was measured. (Courtesy of Dr. Ed McCoy)

observed in competitive bid analysis is about $2 to $3 less per foot for flat tile over conventional trenched in round tile. No trencher is required, there is no spoil to deal with, and a smaller crew is needed to install it. These are the sources of the cost reduction. However, the best reason to install flat tile is that it gives good performance.

Research evaluating flat pipe was conducted by Guy Prettyman and Ed McCoy at the Ohio State University, and reported in the *Ohio Turfgrass Foundation News* in 2002, as "An Evaluation of Trenchless, 2-Tier Greens Construction" (see Figure 2-48). Their purpose was to "…[A]ddress whether panel pipe laid flat in a two-tier (USGA type) green is equally effective as a conventional trench design in intercepting flow through the gravel layer." They concluded, "Both the drainage discharge and ponding depth data showed equivalent water interception for a two-tier soil profile when employing a trenchless or conventional subsurface drainage system." In other research, they found flat pipe to be superior to the round stuff, which is logical based upon the exposed surface area able to accept drainage.

ROOTZONE GAS EXCHANGERS

The idea of exchanging or controlling the soil air or soil gases has been known for a long time, to the point that even F. W. Taylor touted that as one of the benefits of his approach to subirrigation. The concept is that plant roots and soil organisms use oxygen for respiration and produce carbon dioxide. An imbalance between oxygen and carbon dioxide found in soil air as compared to atmospheric air is believed to be a critical growth factor, and levels in soil air can be quickly restored to those of atmospheric air by simply exchanging gases between atmosphere and soil. This happens naturally when drenching rainfalls saturate the soil and displace all of the gases, as atmospheric air is then drawn in when the water drains out. Without this method of water displacement, there can occur a diffusion of gases based upon concentration gradients between soil and air, especially when the soil dries, shrinks, and creates cracks. Artificially this exchange of gas can be very difficult to achieve through just irrigating the soil, unless it is saturated, which is not a best management technique. However, gas exchange can be accelerated by either forcing air into or under, or sucking gases and water out of, the rootzone by means of a pump system.

The earliest patent related to this idea was issued in 1913, and since then there have been a couple of dozen other patents approved for devices to exchange or manipulate soil air. The current trend of using this as a management tool for turfgrasses on greens began in the late 1980s, when Marsh Benson, CGCS, began experimenting with it at Augusta National. By the mid-1990s, a pump system was marketed under the trademark name of SubAir™ (see Figure 2-49). Since then, several other machines have become available to the market, each with its own improvements (see Figure 2-50).

SubAir™—The Next Generation

OXYGENATION

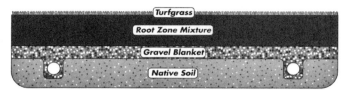

▲ **Existing perforated pipe spaced 10'-15' apart** ▲

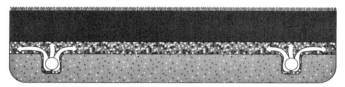

Air is pumped into perforated pipe and begins to move into gravel blanket

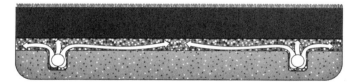

Air completely fills the gravel blanket before moving up into the root zone mixture.

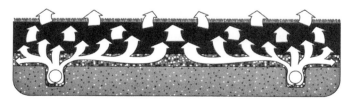

Air fills root zone mixture in just 15 minutes before it releases into the atmosphere.

Note: in all illustrations, the choker layer has been omitted for visual simplification only; the choker layer and the SubAir™ System are entirely compatible.

The revolutionary SubAir™ System, developed by Golf Course Superintendent Marsh Benson, produces a stronger, healthier, more resilient turfgrass community which will therefore better utilize the components of the complete root zone, leading to less requirements of fertilizer, pesticides, water, labor and stress.

HOW SUBAIR WORKS. SubAir is an environmentally friendly system that uses your USGA — spec. greens' existing drainage. The SubAir™ System features a blower which distributes positive air flow into the integral drainage system below the root zone of a USGA green. In addition, the blower can create negative air flow in the same drainage system. The blower is situated either permanently below the surface in a custom plastic vault or on a portable trailer located near the use area.

OXYGENATION. When the blower distributes positive air flow in the "Oxygenation Mode", positive air flow through the soil profile allows:
• Oxygenation of the root zone to increase root zone vigor.
• Transference of water vapor to the root zone from the perched water table.

SUCTION OF

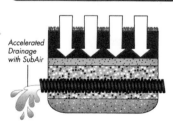

Accelerated Drainage with SubAir

Upon turning on the SubAir™ System in the removal mode-water, salt and gases begin drawing down into perforated pipe at an accelerated rate.

Figure 2-49: The SubAir concept is to either use an air blower to pump air under the green rootzone or use a vacuum to remove excess soil water. (Courtesy of SubAir™ Systems)

in Healthier Turfgrass

TEMPERATURE MODERATION.
The outside air temperature becomes moderated by the consistent temperature within the gravel blanket so that an unlimited supply of moderated temperature is passed upward, eventually adjusting the soil temperature of the root zone mix and turfgrass surface.

Part of the cooling effect comes from the transference of water vapor from the perched water table that is carried upward with the upward air flow.

As an option, SubAir provides a supplemental heating/cooling heat exchanger which is installed at a lower level than the gravel blanket. (At a depth of 4 1/2' to 5', the temperature of the native soil is approximately 55 degrees in summer and winter.) This allows the SubAir™ System to provide more heating or cooling and at a faster rate.

REMOVAL OF WATER, GASES AND SALT.
When the blower is in the "Removal Mode", negative air flow through the soil profile allows:
• Removal of excess water
• Removal of trapped gasses
• Removal of excess salt buildups in the soil profile.

TEMPERATURE MODERATION

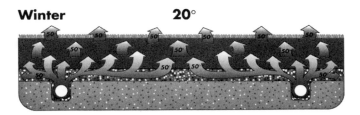

Summer   **95°**

In summer, the temperature within the gravel blanket is approximately 65-70 degrees — which cools the outside air and eventually the root zone mix and turfgrass surface.

Winter   **20°**

In winter, the temperature within the gravel blanket is approximately 45-50 degrees — which warms the outside air and eventually the root zone mix and turfgrass surface.

WATER/SALT/GASES

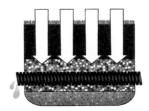

After 2-4 hours in the suction mode, the water is replaced by air in the entire root zone. (Note: This includes a draw-down of the perched water-table which is beneficial to the removal of salt buildups.)

SUBAIR — A WISE INVESTMENT.
Oxygenation, suction of water and gases, and temperature moderation produce roots that are whiter and larger in diameter with easily twice the total mass of roots maintained by conventional methods. In fact, the bottom profile of the root system "re-explodes" with new growth. Healthier turfgrass requiring fewer chemicals, water and labor produces the cost savings that make SubAir a wise investment. The SubAir™ System gives turfgrass managers the tool to utilize their talents to provide new standards in turf quality against which all others will be measured and compared for years to come.

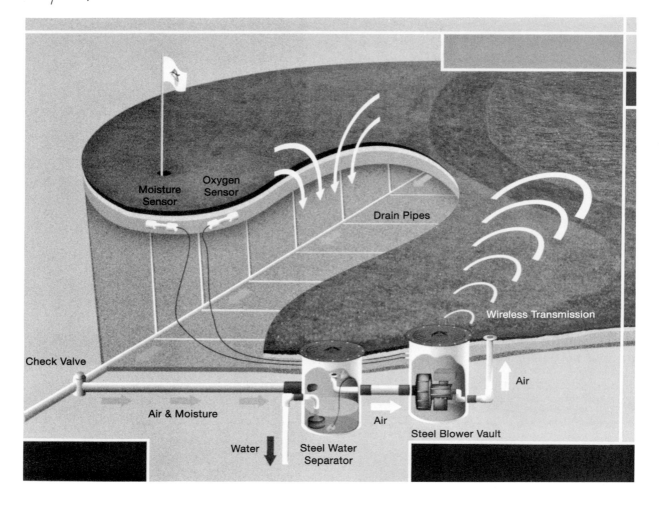

Figure 2-50: Advanced Aeration Systems™ offers a vacuum/blower system that senses and is controlled by soil moisture and oxygen levels, as well as by remote transmission. (Courtesy of Advanced Aeration Systems)

Basically, these machines are very large efficient air pumps that, when running, create a vacuum at one end of the pump and produce forced or pressurized air at the other end. By hooking up a six-inch hose to the air pump that also connects to the subdrainage of the green, one can either force air under the green or put a vacuum on it and suck air and water out. It has been my observation that the forced air approach is much less efficient because the air will travel in preferential fingers of flow, or channels of the least resistance. Vacuum, on the other hand, occurs on the saturated portions of the rootzone where the water tends to act as a capillary seal and thus permits more uniform action and efficiency across the bottom of the rootzone. Once that free water is drawn off, then the vacuum will also draw air in. In this case, too, the air will take the path of least resistance, but this will still result in better distribution than the forced-air method.

ROOTZONE GAS ANALYZERS

Similarly, these companies also offer handheld soil gas analyzers that can measure concentrations of carbon dioxide, oxygen, methane, and hydrogen sulfide, with optional capabilities to measure ammonia and ozone. Soil gas measurement can be made by making a small hole in the putting surface and rootzone with a soil probe, inserting a gas pickup receiver, turning on the machine, and getting readings within seconds. This is not only an inexpensive way to monitor or correlate soil gas content to green performance but also a way to measure the speed and efficiency of the gas exchanger (see Figure 2-51, color insert).

ROOTZONES FOR GAS EXCHANGERS

The best gas exchange, in either the blower or vacuum mode, will occur if the substructure of the green was constructed to permit good gas flow. A USGA green's gravel blanket is an excellent medium for flowing gases and will work more effectively than a soil green or a California system that does not have that layer. To attach the air pump to the green's substructure means attaching it to the tile line outflow pipes. Of course, this must be a closed system, or the air will follow the path of least resistance, which would be out of a "clean out" surface drain inlet connected to the green's tile or through a sand bunker if it is connected to the green drainage. Since the introduction of air pump systems, forward-thinking golf course designers have specified closed-loop tile drainage systems under greens to accommodate these tools. Early green construction methods never considered this aspect and hence may not work well without shutting off air leaks.

The air pump itself can be portable and taken from green to green for short-term operations of 15 to 20 minutes, or the pumps can be more permanently installed in either above- or below-ground vaults near the problem greens and connected to either moisture or gas sensors to automatically control the pump operation. Recently, one golf course permanently installed one pump per green, which is a bit of overkill since one pump is capable of treating several greens, if it is strategically placed within 100 yards of the greens. This approach does require some valving, but the overall cost savings makes it well worth it.

For the past several years, I have designed greens to get maximum efficiency from these air pumps by using the California concept (see Figures 2-52 and 2-41), with flat tile, with the white sock, placing one-quarter– to three-eighths–inch pea gravel between the tile lines, which are on 15-foot centers, and connecting them to a valve box outside the green with six-inch round tile (see Figure 2-53). In the valve box is placed a manual valve to allow the downstream flow of the tile to be closed off, and the air pump to be hooked in for treatment. After the treatment, the gas exchanger is disconnected and the valve is opened to allow the drainage system to flow. It has been found that it is best

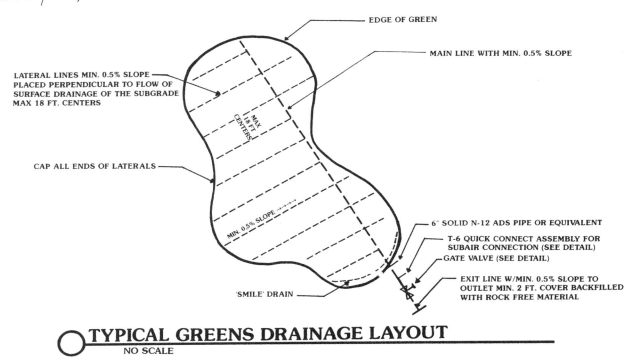

EDGE OF GREEN

MAIN LINE WITH MIN. 0.5% SLOPE

LATERAL LINES MIN. 0.5% SLOPE
PLACED PERPENDICULAR TO FLOW OF
SURFACE DRAINAGE OF THE SUBGRADE
MAX 18 FT. CENTERS

MAX 18 FT CENTERS

CAP ALL ENDS OF LATERALS

MIN. 0.5% SLOPE

6″ SOLID N-12 ADS PIPE OR EQUIVALENT

T-6 QUICK CONNECT ASSEMBLY FOR
SUBAIR CONNECTION (SEE DETAIL)

GATE VALVE (SEE DETAIL)

EXIT LINE W/MIN. 0.5% SLOPE TO
OUTLET MIN. 2 FT. COVER BACKFILLED
WITH ROCK FREE MATERIAL

'SMILE' DRAIN

⊙ TYPICAL GREENS DRAINAGE LAYOUT
NO SCALE

Figure 2-52: Typical green drainage layout to maximize efficiency of vacuum/blower-assisted drainage with six-inch main line and T-6 isolation or slicer valve.

Figure 2-53: Drainage installation of round and flat tile under newly reconstructed greens at Tucson Country Club maximize the effectiveness of a vacuum/blower pump system. The greens will be seeded to a blend of A-1 and A-4 bentgrass. (Courtesy of Karl Olson)

to divide the green into two halves and to hook each half into a separate valve pit. Sometimes it makes sense to separate the green front and back, or left and right, or sun and shade, and so on. The cost is about $350 to $500 per valve pit installed, but it does provide the superintendent with the option of using a gas exchanger when needed.

Dr. Ed McCoy and Guy Prettyman ran some research on the comparative effectiveness of round and flat tile when vacuum-assisted drainage is used. This work was published in the April 1999 issue of *SportsTurf* magazine under the title of "Vacuum Assisted Drainage" (see Figure 2-48). (By the way, Dr. McCoy was issued a patent in 1993 for a vacuum-assist technique called "Method and Apparatus for the Hydrologic Regulation of Turf Soil Profiles.") What they found was that not only did the flat tile drain water faster than a round tile, with and without vacuum assist, but also the zone of influence of the flat tile was wider and less isolated directly over the tile than in a conventional trenched in 4-inch round pipe. They theorized, "Perhaps the 12-inch AdvanEdge® pipe laid flat on the subgrade allowed a wider vacuum distribution and less short circuiting by air." They concluded, "Vacuum assisted drainage does beneficially impact removal and redistribution of water (and hence air) in a soil profile."

GOLF GREEN IRRIGATION

Form follows function when it comes to irrigating golf greens, especially with automatic irrigation. It is nice to believe that all sprinkler heads throw precise patterns of water, and that their uniformity of distribution is such that all areas are irrigated the same. After all, enormous efforts have been made to get the green built to the highest levels of workmanship, the rootzone material is perfectly uniform and falls well within laboratory guidelines, and the design is the most aesthetic presentation of form follows function that could be imagined. So what would you think of an irrigation system that would give some portions of the green three to five times more water than other portions? Well, chances are this is exactly what is happening on 90 percent or more of the greens irrigated solely with automatic irrigation. The only sure method for uniform irrigation water distribution is hand watering, but certainly the severity of the problem caused by automatic irrigation can be reduced by understanding the causes of that problem.

The problem begins with the manufacturing standards of sprinkler heads, which give tolerances that can cause variability between heads even within the same batch of sprinklers. For instance, the sprinkler may have been designed to make four revolutions per minute, but the standard of manufacture is plus or minus one-half of the rotation speed. This difference is one-half of four, or two, so the acceptable rate of revolution is four plus or minus two, (4 ± 2), so the extremes can be anywhere between two and six turns per minute. Now, on long-run times, this doesn't make much difference, but on short-run times, on a green with an established mat layer of one-quarter to one-half inch, the slow turning head may deliver water faster than the mat layer will allow it to be absorbed, and the excess water becomes wasted or runoff. This excessive water runoff can cause the green surrounds to become wetter than the superintendent may want, so the dilemma is too little water on the green, or too much on the surrounds.

Then there are also differences in nozzle manufacturing, which again are practical but not precise for reasons of wanting to stay competitive in a very tough, price conscious industry. Nozzles are usually made of a nonferrous material and are either extruded or bored in large numbers. Say a nozzle was designed to deliver 20 gallons per minute (gpm) and the accepted manufacturing standard is plus or minus 10 percent. This means that as long as nozzles fall within the range of 20 plus or minus 2, or between 18 and 22 gpm, those nozzles are acceptable. Now just imagine the extreme situation where the largest acceptable nozzle was fortuitously installed on the slowest turning sprinkler head and the smallest nozzle on the fastest one. Consider how this would further compound problems of trying to deliver uniform irrigation. On top of that, as the sprinklers get warmer or colder they naturally expand and contract, which affects performance. Mechanical things like drive mechanisms and nozzles wear out and change performance. Heads get dirty and damaged just as a matter of course when installed in the golf environment. The point is that sprinkler heads are not precision mechanisms that all perform precisely identical to each other, and to expect that precision would double or triple the cost.

One small independent company does offer replacement nozzles for most popular golf course sprinklers, nozzles that greatly improve the sprinklers' overall performance and that save water in the process (see Figure 2-54). But they are also more expensive than factory replacement nozzles and some find it hard to justify the cost difference. This always amazes me, for these same superintendents will waste tens of thousands of dollars on some soil amendment that has no proven value.

Sprinklers are designed by very smart engineers who know these problems and are constantly trying to improve the quality of the product, but even if they perfected it, it wouldn't necessarily lessen the problem of different distribution of water on golf greens. To understand why requires understanding more about the process of sprinkler design and green design, as well as their nature and construction.

Sprinkler heads are designed and performance tested in buildings. Test heads are placed on perfectly level swing joints or risers set at the specified angle, the water pressure is perfectly controlled, water quality is usually very good, there is no wind, and the temperature is within an ideal range. The goal of this testing is to get a water distribution pattern that is very uniform and which, when graphed over the length of throw, forms an inverted wedge. Basically, for a sprinkler head rated at one-half inch per hour that throws 60 feet, the graph theoretically looks like Figure 2-55.

Figure 2-54: Full Coverage Irrigation Inc. produces replacement nozzles for sprinklers that can markedly improve the coefficients of uniformity and distribution. This is very important when greenkeepers depend heavily on automatic irrigation instead of hand watering of greens. (Courtesy of Full Coverage Irrigation, Inc.)

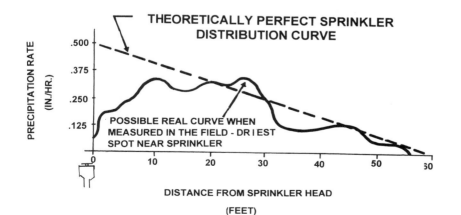

Figure 2-55: Ideally, a sprinkler head should have a precipitation pattern that looks like an inverted wedge, with the most water near the head and then decreasing with distance. Reality is that distribution is much more random.

Figure 2-56: Theoretically, when two perfect sprinkler distribution curves overlap, all areas between the sprinklers receive exactly the same amount of water. For example, at 30 feet from each head, the rate for each head is one-half that at the head, so that the spot receives the same amount of water from each head, and that amount is equal to what the grass right at each head receives from — and only from — that head.

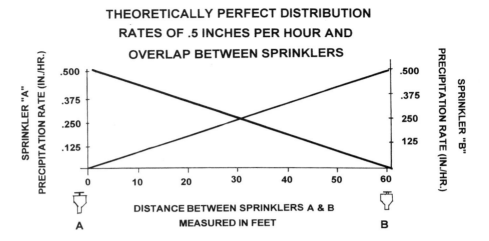

At the head, the precipitation rate is 0.50 inches per hour, and it decreases uniformly as the distance from the head increases, until 60 feet away the precipitation rate is zero. Thus, if two of these sprinklers were spaced 60 feet apart and one overlapped the precipitation curves, the graph would look like Figure 2-56. The area under the lines is where the combined precipitation rate is perfectly uniform and amounts to 0.50 inches per hour. At both sprinkler heads A and B the combined rate is 0.50 plus 0.0, and at the midpoint between the heads, or 30 feet, the rate 0.25 plus 0.25 inches per hour, and everywhere between the heads the combined rates deliver 0.50 inches per hour. However, the reality is that sprinkler nozzles rarely produce a perfect inverted wedge, and in many instances the least amount of water is at the head, so that dead grass doughnuts frequently appear around sprinkler heads. The serious student can learn more by contacting the Center of Irrigation Technology, California State University at Fresno (www.wateright.org).

So now you know that sprinklers turn at different speeds, that they have variations in nozzle delivery, that the uniformity of distribution can be poor, and that sprinkler components wear out and change performance characteristics. These problems are further compounded when sprinkler heads are not installed perfectly level, when they are not to the grade they are placed in but rather level to the earth, when swing joint angles are varied, when water pressures are not uniform, and when wind is a factor.

To really put this in perspective, realize that most greens are irrigated with between four to six sprinkler heads, which you now know can be very inconsistent, and that some places of the green will receive multiple applications of water from some or all of the sprinkler heads. Schematically this could look like Figure 2-57.

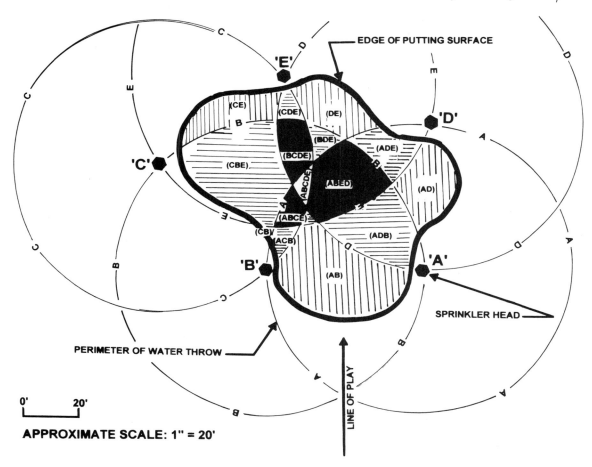

Figure 2-57: A golf green may typically have five sprinkler heads that theoretically throw water to the base of at least two neighboring sprinklers. When the distribution pattern for all five sprinklers is drawn together, it shows some parts of the green get water from five sprinklers, others only from four, three, or two. Consequently, middle parts of the green may receive two to three times more water than the outsides.

By tracing the theoretical arc of each sprinkler as it overlaps or touches each of its neighboring sprinklers, one should see that if five sprinklers are used around the green, all five converge at some point in the middle. In this area of convergence, the total water delivered would be two and a half times the amount applied on the outside of any area of convergence.

Chances are that, even with individual head control, the superintendent must decide on whether to overwater the middle, or underwater the edges, or both overwater and underwater parts of the green and hand water as necessary (see Figure 2-58). The rootzone mix in the middle of the green is no different than that on the edges, neither is the turfgrass, and neither is the mat layer, so it is reasonable to assume there is no water requirement differences between the middle and the edges, yet the middle gets multiple applications. It makes no sense to spend excessive amounts of money to get a perfect rootzone material, and then rely solely on irrigating it with equipment with so many inherent problems and potential opportunities for inconsistency. The point to remember is

Figure 2-58: Not only is it impossible to uniformly water a green in windless conditions, but also it is impossible if there is a wind. The only way to uniformly water a green is by hand.

that there is a tight linkage between agronomic theory and design concepts, and when individuals try to separate them, or favor one over the other, this is a recipe for failure. The real test for golf greens occurs not in the laboratory, or in test plots, or in any one given environment, but rather in each individual green site.

SUBIRRIGATION REVISITED

The search for a way to subirrigate greens inspired F. W. Taylor's research exactly 100 years ago, and many others have since tried to refine the concept as discussed earlier. It makes good sense to subirrigate for it would save water, reduce random dry areas, drain off excess water to maintain an optimum soil moisture, and could save money on irrigation installation and operation. To be able to subirrigate greens would eliminate one great environmental challenge and that is to save precious water.

Recently, a company called Evaporative Control Systems, Inc. (ECS), of Reno, NV, developed a system that it believes can save at least 50 percent of water consumption by greens. The patented system involves 4 foot by 4 foot plastic trays, or cells, that are buried about 12 to 15 inches deep, in series, and joined together by transfer pipes (see Figure 2-59). Inside the cell is placed a chamber system that looks like one-half of a 12-inch PVC double wall drain pipe, which can both add and carry excess water with its unique double chamber system (see Figure 2-60). The cells are then filled with two inches of small

ECS UNDERGROUND IRRIGATION AND DRAINAGE SYSTEM

Patent No. 5,921,711

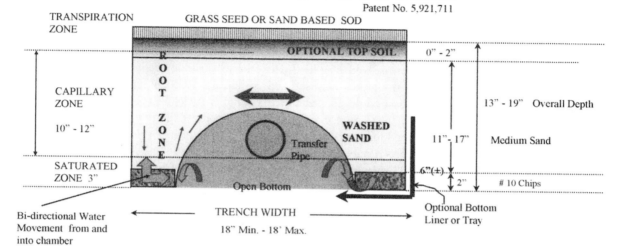

TRANSPIRATION ZONE

GRASS SEED OR SAND BASED SOD

OPTIONAL TOP SOIL

0" - 2"

CAPILLARY ZONE

10" - 12"

ROOT ZONE

WASHED SAND

Transfer Pipe

13" - 19" Overall Depth

11" - 17" Medium Sand

SATURATED ZONE 3"

Open Bottom

6"(±)

2" # 10 Chips

Bi-directional Water Movement from and into chamber

TRENCH WIDTH

18" Min. - 18' Max.

Optional Bottom Liner or Tray

Turf Construction
Structural cross section Details

Figure 2-59: Cross section of Evaporative Control Systems, Inc. (ECS) typical cell for subirrigation of turf-grass. (Courtesy of Evaporative Control Systems, Inc.)

Figure 2-60: Photo of a pan or tray that is the foundation of an ECS cell, and the double wall pipe that is placed in the pan to control water level in the cell. (Courtesy of Evaporative Control Systems, Inc.)

gravel. Next, 13 inches of washed sand is placed, compacted, and shaped. Finally, water flow from cell to cell and from cell to plant is checked. Water should wick to the surface for establishment and can be adjusted to lower depths as green matures and organic matter builds in the rootzone.

Working with the 4 foot by 4 foot chambers could potentially solve some of the failures of Taylor's and PURR-Wick greens. Because each cell could be filled with a sand of slightly different capillarity, like Taylor's lifting sand concept, a more uniform surface moisture may be possible than with PURR-Wick. Given the as yet unsolved problem of excessive sprinkler-delivered irrigation in the middle of the green, as discussed earlier, the ECS cells in areas of maximum accumulation could use sands with a higher hydraulic conductivity than those in areas of less intense irrigation. With some experimentation, and perhaps using embedded moisture sensors and some control valves, the system could become very efficient.

The ECS system seems best adapted to areas of low rainfall, but perhaps it might actually work best in areas of excessive rainfall, for the drainage capacity of these cells can be exceedingly high. The concept is very old, and now more than ever it makes great sense to investigate and develop subirrigation and drainage systems.

CHAPTER

3

Design Considerations for Golf Greens

FORM FOLLOWS FUNCTION

In 1859, Charles Darwin wrote a thesis on the natural selection of species, a thesis that hypothesized that slight genetic variations could result in some individuals with unique characteristics. We correctly know his theory as evolution, while some have simply and erroneously called it "the survival of the fittest." Paraphrasing Darwin's theory would be to say that under changing or life-threatening conditions, some members of a population have, through their genetic diversity, the capacity to adapt to those stresses and survive, while others of a different genetic makeup may not. This is somewhat true for golf course features, for those features that can cope with stresses will survive, and the others will get rebuilt (see Figure 3-1). Natural selection applies to living organisms, while for inanimate objects the "survival" theory is based on the ancient architectural axiom of "form follows function." This simply means that the most useful and common form of an object is based upon the function it has to serve.

For example, a room is normally defined as an enclosed space with a floor, ceiling, and walls. For a person to enter and exist in that space there is an architectural device called a door, and a typical door has the form of being about seven feet tall and three feet wide. This form of door follows the function of permitting most people to walk upright as they move in and out of the room. But suppose the door is turned sideways, so it is now three feet tall and seven feet wide. It is the same door but turned ninety degrees, but does the form follow the function? Well, without question, given the proper incentive, people

107

Figure 3-1: For golf features, especially greens, to survive harsh environments, they must respect the tenets of "form follows function."

Table 3-1 GOLF GREEN DESIGN CONSIDERATIONS—FORM FOLLOWS FUNCTION APPLIES TO GOLF GREENS AS TO OTHER EFFICIENT DESIGNS

Form	Function
Size	Reasonable target, adequate hole locations
Slope	Provide surface drainage and fair putting test
Shape	Visual interest, multiple drainage ways
Target	Defined easy and difficult strategic hole location
Hazards	Define shot value visual impact influence on maintenance
Irrigation	Quantity and quality of available water
Environmental	Reduce environmental stresses and impacts

could move in and out of the room, but not without more difficulty than when the door is properly oriented. Predictably, unless there is a strong and overriding reason to leave the door only three feet high, sooner or later it will be changed so that the form more properly follows the function.

On a golf green, there are many instances in which design decisions must be made about the form that should consider and be influenced by functional aspects of the green complex (see Table 3-1). Greens where form follows function will have a much higher survival rate then those that ignore that principle. Therefore, understanding forms and functions of a green make for a more stable and permanent final product.

The golf course architect sees the function of a golf green first as a target with defined shot values, measured by the difficulty of landing and leaving a golf ball at an intended spot, which is usually close to the hole; secondly as a test of putting skill; and lastly as a growing medium. As a result, if there are conflicts between being a great growing medium and environment and a sophisticated and strategic golf feature, chances are agronomy will be compromised (see Figure 3-2).

No one wants to see a golf green fail to produce a healthy turf cover, and liability lawsuits claming negligence in design or construction when greens do fail allegedly because they were improperly built, get everyone's attention. Therefore, no golf architect would completely ignore the functional aspects of agronomy, but he or she might just bend the concepts as necessary to achieve a design expression.

There is also a false notion among golf course architects that simply stating that the contractor shall build greens that conform to a standard design concept, such as USGA or California method, relieves the designer of liability for greens failure. That is simply not the case, for when problems with greens arise, everyone's role and action involved with those greens will be scrutinized for professional responsibility. There are no magic safety nets of phrases in specifications that can erase responsibility if a failure falls within a professional's scope of obligation. I say this not as a lawyer but rather as a person who has been an expert witness in almost 100 golf-related lawsuits, many of which involved disputes over design and construction.

Figure 3-2: Golf green design should consider agronomic and environmental factors like morning shade, which can make a green very difficult to maintain.

So although this chapter is about design, it also discusses the integration of the agronomic principles covered in Chapter 2. Form follows function in both physical design and agronomy.

SIZE OF GREEN

First among the design philosophies has to do with size or square footage of the putting surfaces. Greens can be as large as on the Old Course at St. Andrews, where double greens evolved to a half acre or more in size (see Figure 3-3), or as small as functionally necessary for a synthetic turf green that can measure only 800 square feet, or about the size of some of the old oiled sand greens. There are no rules or guidelines about the size of greens, so a golf course architect is free to make them whatever size best suits his or her design objective.

There are those who believe that strategically there should be large greens for long shots and small greens for short shots, but here is the first example of where such a design theory can be in conflict with agronomy. Suppose the golf course is very busy, playing 200 to 300 rounds per day, which results in a lot of foot traffic, which in turn produces a great deal of compaction and physical stress on the turf. Unless the playing surface is a synthetic turf, within two or three days, areas near the hole on a natural putting green turf would be so physically abused that it may require weeks of rest and nurturing to recover, if at all.

Figure 3-3: The double greens on the Old Course at St. Andrews, Scotland, measuring well over one-half acre in area, evolved to that size and shape through centuries of use and maintenance.

Figure 3-4: The key to any functional green design is adequately sized and sloped areas for hole locations, well-defined target areas, reasonably maintainable, and aesthetically pleasing.

The greenkeeper would like to move the hole to minimize this severe wear and allow the turf to rest and recover in a shorter period. Therefore, changing hole location on a green is usually done every day. Back in the days of steel golf spikes, unless there was a golf tournament taking place that required all competitors play to the same hole location, greenkeepers might have moved holes twice on stressful days. However, even with the advent of softer rubber spikes, the hole locations still get moved just about every day—*assuming* there is someplace to move it. So the issue of target size must now respect, or at least acknowledge, alternative hole locations for agronomic reasons, which means more than one target area (see Figure 3-4). The question then is how many hole locations are needed and what impact does that have on the total size of the putting green target area?

SIZE AND NUMBER OF HOLE LOCATIONS

We must first determine how much space is needed for one hole location. Generally the area of most damage around the hole location occurs within about an eight-foot radius. Then, applying the formula for the area of a circle, Area = πr^2 (where pi or π = 3.1459265 and radius or r = 8), the area for one hole location is approximately 200 square feet ($A = 3.14 \times 8^2 = 3.14 \times 64 = 200.96$). Now estimate the longest period of time needed for a badly damaged hole area to heal. If it takes 21 days to heal a hole location area, then there should be 21 separate hole locations on the green to allow for that length of a rotation for turf recovery. Then the total useable area available for hole locations should be 21 locations × 200 square feet for a total area of 4,200 square feet. Since the USGA recommends that holes be located at least three paces from the edge of the putting surface, and since there may be some steep areas on the green unsuitable for hole location, an extra 1,800 square feet of space may be needed. So, the form or size of a green that will functionally provide for 21 separate hole locations is 4,200 square feet, plus 1,800 square feet of perimeters and slopes, for a total size of 6,000 square feet. Form follows function.

Obviously, if the turf heals more quickly or more slowly than the 21 days in our example, or if the amount of play requires a different schedule than moving the hole every day, then a different functional area for the green is required and can be calculated. In any case, the *form* of the modern green is about 6,000 square feet because the *function* is to allow for 21 hole locations of 200 square feet each, plus an allowance for perimeters and steeper slopes.

SLOPE OF THE PUTTING SURFACE

So what is a steep slope? The answer is one on which, when the turf is kept at a normal daily mowing height, golf balls rolling down the slope will not lose speed. In other words, a steep slope is one on which the golfer cannot control the speed of the golf ball. At this point golf begins to lose the skill component of chipping and putting, replacing them with sheer luck. The steeper the slope, the less skill and the more luck required. It has been found that on North American golf greens maintained at mowing height of 0.10 inch or 2.5 mm, the maximum slope within 8 feet of the hole is approximately 1.5 percent, or to make that easier to visualize, it is one and one-half feet change in elevation over 100 feet of horizontal distance. Again the *form* of the green surface is a maximum 1.5 percent pitch or slope, and the *function* is to keep the skill factor in chipping and putting.

SPEED OF GREENS

Recently, one day of a professional golf tournament in Australia was canceled because the speed of greens increased so much as they dried out that they were no longer matched to the slope of the greens, making them unputtable, and thus making a golf game less than skillful competition. This is an extreme example of improperly matching form and function, or speed and slope, but it continues to happen with more frequency as the mania for fast greens grows among golfers and club officials. I have observed TifEagle Bermuda grass greens maintained at a daily cutting height of 0.085 inch or 2.1 mm, producing greens of extraordinary speed that were beyond the skill level of 90 percent or more of the members and guests at the course involved. The good news is that the greens were designed to have about 1.5 percent slope in pinable areas, so the greens were fast but fair. The problem is much more severe on older greens that were not designed to such soft slopes, but on which green committees still demand ultrafast green speeds. The choices are to either raise mowing heights to slow the greens down to allow golfers to control the ball, or rebuild the greens to softer slopes to fairly allow for putting on such very rapid greens. One test of whether a green's speed is properly matched to its slope is if a skillful golfer can leave a straight downhill putt short of the hole (see Figure 3-5).

This trend to superfast greens has caused some designers to overreact and build nearly flat or level putting surfaces so that green speeds are irrelevant. Although this sounds reasonable, this is another example of where design theory is in conflict with agronomy. Greens that are too flat will not surface drain excess water, resulting in overly saturated rootzones during periods of wet weather, or even after normal automatic irrigation. This problem is even worse in areas where ice can form in the rootzone, thus shutting off all normal infiltration and downward percolation of water, resulting in puddles that can freeze and predispose the grass to cold weather injuries or diseases. In short, it is agronomically imperative to build in some surface drainage on greens. Another reason is that slope is a mechanism to give putting surfaces an interesting character. To ignore surface drainage is to ignore function and to weaken survivability of the turf, as well as to miss a design opportunity.

If the maximum slope for a green is 1.5 percent in and around hole locations, what is the functional minimum? Oddly it, too, is about 1.5 percent, for anything less will not surface drain well enough, although many architects specify one percent as a minimum. So the pitch on a modern green in designated hole location areas is around 1.5 percent. Areas outside the defined hole

Figure 3-5: Green slopes around hole locations should be gentle enough that if a skillful golfer is above the hole, he or she can stop the putt around or above the hole.

location area can be as steep as the designer believes is necessary to carry his or her design intent, but typically it is between 4 and 7 percent. Form follows function.

SHAPE OF A GREEN

Another example of form that should respect function is the shape of the green. Greens can be very geometric in shape, ranging from circles and ovals to squares, triangles, and rectangles, as well as any other form the designer wishes, and still yield a functional number of hole locations with appropriate slopes. But geometric shapes with defined angles or shapes are unnatural looking, and all symmetrical shapes can be predictable and boring, so the preferred style of greens tends to be freeform in shape with flowing lines. Although one could design a course with 18 round or oval greens that would be exceedingly functional, the repetition of their appearance would be another missed opportunity to visually distinguish the green, and perhaps make a hole memorable (see Figure 3-6).

Figure 3-6: A green complex should be visually stimulating with lots of color, texture, and change of height.

The need for making strong visual statements with the green was best articulated by the famous golf course architect A. W. Tillinghast, who is credited with the statement that, from the neck down, all men look basically the same,

Figure 3-7: One of the most recognizable and beautiful golf holes in all of golf is the 15th green at Cypress Point.

but it is their heads and faces that give them memorable character. He used the same analogy for golf greens when he wrote: "Now, we are chatting on golf and faces, but there is a parallel. A putting green has features just like a human, or, at least, it should have to be worthy of the name." Later he writes, "No matter how excellent may be the distances, how cunningly placed the hazards, or how carefully considered has been the distribution of shot—if the greens themselves do not stand forth expressly the course itself can never be notable."

The logic of these statements is supported by thinking about how a golfer reads or senses a golf course landscape. Humans assess their environment through their five survival senses, but golfers do not smell a golf course, or taste it, or hear it, or touch it. They do, however, use their sense of sight extensively. It is that stream of visual inputs to the brain that conveys the messages to the golfer. The more varied and interesting a golf feature is to look at within given social norms, the more exciting and memorable the visual image and experience will be. Think for a minute about the island green at the 17th hole at TPC Sawgrass, the 15th or 16th holes at Cypress Point (see Figure 3-7), or the 12th at Augusta National. Even though you may never have played these holes, you can see pictures of them in your mind's eye. Therefore, golf course designers see one function of greens as being a means to communicate a design concept

Figure 3-8: The 17th green at TPC Sawgrass is an example of a golf green stripped down to its bare essentials, and the "message" from this Pete Dye creation is an equally blunt "do or die."

to golfers, and the form is the vehicle that carries the message. More precisely it is the collage of color, texture, and form that the golfer is reading in the green that carries the message and communicates the challenge set forth.

An excellent example is the 157-yard-long par 3 at TPC Sawgrass, for it is a golf hole stripped down to its naked essentials. It has tees, but no fairway, no rough, no fairway bunkers, no trees, no mounds, no length, no grassy hollows, just water and a green complex with one small bunker (see Figure 3-8). However, it is a terrifying golf hole for even the best players in the world because it has so many striking visual elements that communicate perhaps the harshest "do or die" concept in golf. (Perhaps the phrase here should be "do or Dye" in deference to the hole's designer, Pete Dye.) The green sits three to five feet above the water, supported by a wooden wall that is of an unusual brown/black color and hard linear texture not commonly found on most golf courses. The small bunker at the right front of the green is defined by its raised back face, the white color of the sand, and a color and texture of grass different from the putting surface. The green itself has a slow freeform shape that invites the golfer's mind to ask: How far is it? How big is it? How flat is it? The steeper slopes within the green are defined by patterns of light and subtle shades of green, and require the golfer to study the green and then be decisive about where he or she will aim. The only two outcomes for the tee shot are that it lands within the green complex or that it finishes in the water.

Any one of dozens of decisions about color, texture, and form could have been made differently and resulted in a different visual message and reaction from the golfer, but what Mr. Dye has chosen seems to be without flaw. However good this hole is, no one would enjoy a round of golf that had 18 holes of such extreme shot values. Again, it is the designer's ability to deliver variety and memorability (functions) by manipulating a proper balance of shapes, sizes, and slopes (forms) that communicate the safety, danger, and beauty that make for classic golf courses.

MULTIPLE DRAINAGE WAYS

Shapes of greens can serve not only as aesthetic functions, but also as agronomic ones because they permit designing multiple surface drainage ways (see Figure 3-9). Again, taking the simplest example of a perfectly round green with 1.5 percent back to front interior slopes, the designer should next question where the surface water of this green is going to drain to, and how will that water impact the golfer or golf course. If one assumes or knows that the soils outside the putting surface are finer textured than the rootzone mix, and hence will drain slowly, then one must consider how to get rid of that additional water by either using steeper slopes to nonplay areas or by installing underground drainage. A good functional solution is to direct the surface drainage

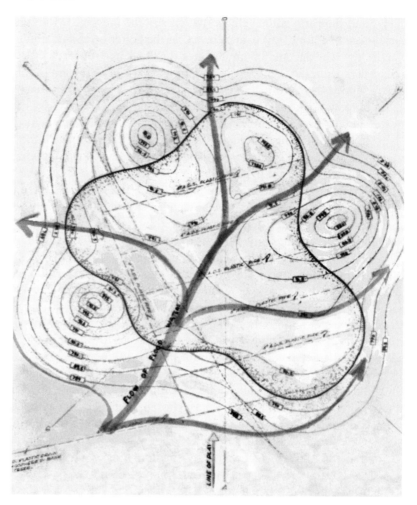

Figure 3-9: Even a simplified green drawing should indicate drainage patterns, and ideally the surface drainage should flow in three or four distinct directions, as in this example.

from the putting surface into three or four different directions, which reduces the magnitude of the problem for any one area. These functional multiple drainage ways are achieved by using form, in the context of slopes, between high and low places. Typically, it is easiest to drain surface water out the front of the green and to each side, for the back of the green is normally higher than the front. This typical form, where the back of the putting surface is higher than the front, probably goes back to the days when greens were set in hollows, and raised bunkers were the natural landform. Later, when greens were designed and built, raising the back of the green served the function of making the green more defined and easier to see, the upslope helped stop incoming shots, and it put a strategic premium on not playing too aggressively and thus having to face a down slope on the next shot; hence the adage: "Keep the ball below the hole."

CREATING DISTINCT TARGET AREAS

Another skill that the golf course designer should have is an ability to work the slopes and shapes of the green together, to create selected target areas within the putting surface (see Figure 3-10). We know the minimum-size target area within a green could be the area of one hole location, or 200 square feet, but even the most accurate player would have trouble consistently hitting that small an area from anything more than 40 or 50 yards. Consequently, target areas are larger than a 16-foot circle and are made up of multiple hole locations. To determine what would be a fair target size from any given length of approach shot, careful observation of lots of golfers of various skill levels from various distances is a help. Or one could guess what a fair target is or is not. Or consult the USGA *Course Rating Handbook* and simply use their table for 66 percent probability of accuracy for average and expert golfers (see Figure 3-11). This table suggests that, for any given distance, two out of three times golfers can hit an ellipse of a certain size from a certain distance. For instance, from 150 yards the expert or scratch golfer will land his or her shot within an area 15 yards wide by 16 yards deep 66 percent of the time, while a bogey golfer, from the same distance, needs an area 20 yards wide by 25 yards deep for the

Figure 3-10: A well-designed green like this one should have three or four well-defined target areas for hole locations, areas that have shot values ranging from easy, as in the right front, to very difficult where the hole is located in this photo.

Accuracy Table
(All Distances in Yards)

Dimensions of Expected Landing Area				
Length of Shot	SCRATCH GOLFER		BOGEY GOLFER	
	Width	Depth	Width	Depth
70	9	13	14	17
80	10	14	15	18
90	11	14	16	19
100	11	14	16	20
110	12	15	17	21
120	12	15	17	22
130	13	15	18	23
140	14	16	19	24
150	15	16	20	25
160	17	17	22	27
170	18	17	24	28
180	20	18	26	30
190	23	18	29	34
200	26	19	33	37
210	29	19	—	—
220	32	20	—	—
230	35	20	—	—
240	38	20	—	—
250	41	21	—	—

Figure 3-11: Although not intended for this purpose, this USGA table is an easy way for a designer to size target areas that are within the ability of various golfers to hit with a 66 percent probability, or two out of three times. (Courtesy of United States Golf Association)

same success percentage. Using this table and knowing the length of approach shots can help a designer intelligently determine fair target sizes. To separate and define these target areas, the designer will often use some variation in slope such as a ridgeline, valley, or terrace.

Mr. Tillinghast opined, "Nothing can supply a green with more character than bold undulations, and nothing can make a green more ridiculous looking than puny little kinks which some will insist are undulations." He continues, "But in introducing undulations the builder of courses must consider the shot which is to find the green."

True to the axiom of form follows function, the ratio of easy to difficult target areas within the green should be predicated upon the purpose of the golf course and the skill of the golfers who will use it. A golf course that is open for play and encourages beginning golfers to use it, with no intention of hosting a major competition, should have perhaps 90 percent of the hole locations easily reached by bogey golfers, while a course being designed strictly to test the best golfers may have only 30 or 40 percent of the hole locations easy to approach. A personal model used at Hurdzan/Fry for a resort or country club course calls for having perhaps 75 percent easy hole locations, with the other 25 percent being well-defined and well-defended to challenge the best players. The logical question is, of course, how does one apply the concept of form follows function to defining and defending hole locations?

GREENS AS THE FOCUS OF STRATEGIC DESIGN

We have already discussed sizes of target areas and the fact that interior slopes or undulations can separate and identify these areas. If a golfer is skillful enough to finish a shot near the hole, then his or her reward is a flatter putt than the one facing a golfer who misses the target area and must factor in putting over or through the undulation. Notice the operative phrase is "finish a shot," not land, or stick, or anything that implies that the hole location is always the target. In fact, a large part of strategic design is to reduce the "yard dart" style of attacking the flag and to emphasize intelligent shot making to a target and allow the ball to release to the hole. The drier and firmer the putting surface can be kept, the greater is the possibility of de-emphasizing trying to mindlessly knock pins down with approach shots. Every thinking golf course architect strives to design greens that reward strategic, thoughtful shot making over just sheer execution.

In fact, there is agreement among the most knowledgeable golf course architects that a properly designed strategic golf hole and golf green should force a skilled golfer to develop a strategy of attack, based upon the location of the hole that day. Different hole locations should reward different strategies for finishing a ball within a prescribed target area. This is an exceedingly difficult design goal to achieve, because it requires careful placing and balancing of each and every element of the golf hole, to give the golfer as many optional ways to play the hole as possible.

Truly strategic golf holes are rare, and rarer yet are golf courses made up of them, simply because it requires a remarkable design, based upon the conditions and the play of golf that will not change with time. For example, a design based upon dry, fast playing surfaces can lose its strategic intent when conditions turn soft and lush. A hole designed for wide fairways or landing zones changes its character if those zones become narrow and cloistered with trees or deep rough. Greens designed with dramatic slopes are well suited to slower putting so the strategy must change when green speeds are made lightning fast, as is currently fashionable.

The most timeless and exciting tests of golf are more commonly found in the old courses of the United Kingdom, Australia, and New Zealand, where the courses are maintained today much as they were when originally developed (see

Figure 3-12: Dry turf conditions such as found on the courses of Europe and Australia bring an exciting dimension to shot making not found on lushly maintained courses.

Figure 3-12). In America, I salute Newport Country Club and Fishers Island in Rhode Island, the great old courses on the eastern end of Long Island (National, Shinnecock, Maidstone), and a few others like Cypress Point and Prairie Dunes for resisting the urge of some members to modernize playing conditions and instead keeping these golf courses as designed. This doesn't mean that there can't be wonderful modern courses of strategic design, but to achieve that means giving the best golfers many optional ways to play a hole, based upon where the hole is located on the green, and then rewarding the best strategy to finish a ball close to it. The sophistication of design technique to achieve this is beyond this text and will be covered in greater detail in *Golf Course Architecture: Design, Construction and Restoration* (New York: Wiley, in press). However, a brief overview seems appropriate here, for it directly relates to designing greens and form following function.

The basic theory of strategic design is to reward good play without necessarily penalizing poor play. Penal design, on the other hand, seeks to penalize indifferent play and demands very clear and deliberate shot values. It really does not take much skill to ring a green with hazards, or provide target areas too small for most golfers, or demand that the golfer "work or shape" a particular shot in order to be successful, or be able to spin the ball or hit certain trajectory to hold a shot. It takes far greater design expertise to design a golf hole, or course, that allows a 20 to 30 handicapper to have one of the best rounds of his or her life, and yet challenges the best players in the game. There are limits to what can be achieved, of course, but that is the true test of greatness.

HAZARDS DEFINE SHOT VALUES

The controlling factors that define shot value are hazards such as water, sand, trees, rocks, vegetation, undulation, and length. Hazards involving turf can be types of grass, density, wetness, height of cut, grain, patchiness, and physical limits of the golf course. Each form of hazard requires a different skill level for recovery, and for some, like out of bounds, water, and very dense vegetation, there is no chance of recovery, while mild hazards, such as short rough, or gentle undulation, add little to the difficulty of the recovery shot for even beginning golfers. So there is a continuum of hazards exacting penalties ranging from slight to extreme that can define target areas. To properly prescribe a penalty that fairly fits the magnitude of the mishit shot, one must again turn to form follows function.

For example, a sand bunker is a common source of hazard, but it can be large or small, deep or shallow, soft or firm, sloped or flat, gathering or rejecting, and so on. A bunker can be made so gentle—that is, flat, with firm sand, no bunker edge or lip, and set at the same elevation as the green—that even a beginner can simply putt out and get up and down in two shots most of the time. This form of hazard is functionally worth about one-tenth of a shot penalty, which means that nine out of ten times the pro golfer can get up and down in two. The other extreme is a deep, sod-walled pot bunker with soft sand that produces "fried egg" lies and has such high edges that it is impossible to advance the ball toward the green. This bunker would be functionally worth one full shot penalty. Both examples are bunkers, but the form determines each one's functional value.

To an agronomist, the green is usually thought of as the putting surface alone. To a golf course architect, however, the concept of a green includes not only the putting surface but also all of the surrounding area of collar, fringe, apron, bunkers, mounds, hazards, and all elements that frame or influence play to the green such as trees, wind, fairway contour, and so on (see Figure 3-13). The golf course architect is trying to bring all of these together into a golf feature that fairly tests golf skills, all golf skills, and not just the high, soft shot right at the pin. This means that the architect will first determine the probable length of the approach shot, determine a fair target size, then properly mitigate the severity of the hazards around it. For instance, it is well known that average golfers are right-handed and that average to poorer players tend to finish

Figure 3-13: A golf green should be thought of as a complex, composed of the putting surface, hazards, and surrounds that complement each other.

their shots short and to the right of their target area. Consequently, one should avoid right front green hazards whose form dictates too harsh a penalty on the recovery shots. Likewise, better players tend to mishit the ball more often right to left, and long of the target area, thus opening up the opportunity to make the more difficult hole locations left and short. Of course, any green or hazard can be made more psychologically intimidating by raising the back edge of the feature or hazard so high that golfers can't see over it to the putting surface, or the front edge of the putting surface to "hide" their target area. Form especially follows function when trying to match swing errors to penalty.

READING AND INTERPRETING A GREEN DRAWING

There are no rules or guidelines for intelligently designing a golf green, but decisions must consider construction techniques, knowledge of the game and golfers, and agronomics. I hope that the reader thoroughly understands how these separate disciplines must harmoniously work together. To illustrate this point, it may be well to examine a green drawing by a master golf course architect, many of whose greens have passed the test of time by remaining unchanged because he understood that form follows function. The example chosen is from Donald Ross.

Donald Ross was one of the early designers to produce detailed plans for greens. Figure 3-14 is a Ross green plan drawn at a scale of each square is five yards. To analyze such a plan requires reading the information given for each design intent, beginning with size. Starting at the front of the green and measuring toward the back, you should measure that the green is about 100 feet long. Likewise, by counting the squares across the green at a midpoint, you can determine that the green is about 65 feet wide, more or less. Therefore, the total area of the green is roughly 100 feet × 65 feet = 6,500 square feet.

To evaluate slope, notice that the elevation at the front of the green is being called zero or "0," which means that all other elevations shown are in relationship to this point. At the very back of the green, the elevation is three and one-half, which means this point is three and one-half feet higher than the zero point. Since the green is 100 feet deep, the average slope is close to three and one-half percent; however, it is normal that many areas within the putting surface will be softer or flatter than that. Remember, back in the 1920s to 1980s, greens were mowed at perhaps one-quarter inch, so the speed of the green was perhaps six or seven feet off of a stimpmeter, or well within the skill level of most golfers. The point is that the function of the green was perfectly matched to its form as defined by size and slope.

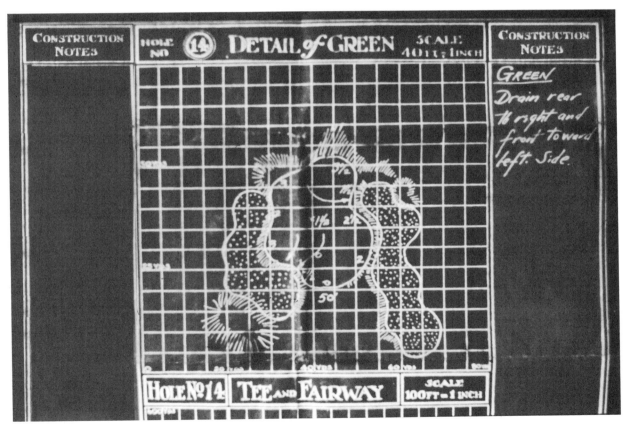

Figure 3-14: This Donald Ross green plan provides many insights into his design philosophy, as well as showing his concern for form follows function. Notice the size, drainage pattern, slopes, and target as defined by this plan.

Now consider the surface drainage and notice how Ross's written instructions in the upper right corner say, "Drain front of green to right, and rear to left side." This drainage pattern is shown graphically with arrows as well as by the elevations that make it happen. These drainage swales also define three or four distinct target areas: (1) the right, front half, (2) the right, back half, (3) the swale in the left middle, and (4) the flat at the left rear of the putting surface. These are all of different sizes, with the smallest and most difficult hole locations in the left swale and right rear plateau. Assuming a line of play from the bottom of the drawing, mentally draw a line parallel to the line of play, and notice that only the left 20 percent of the green requires a carry over a hazard such as a bunker. The other 80 percent of the hole locations can be reached with approach shots of any trajectory, spin, or shape. On the other hand, to miss the middle left hole locations would require putting down into the swale, while putts to the right rear target area must go up a slope. There is great variety in shots that could and would be played to this green.

Ross's use of sand bunkers on both sides of the putting surface, grassy hollows on steep slopes out the back of the green, and mounds in front and behind the left bunker give the green visual interest and character, as well as confound shot making without excessive penalty. The bunkers are below the putting surface and the sand appears to be flat. The interesting freeform shape of the green adds to the visual interest of the green, as well as complicating recovery shots from the bunker.

As previously stated, there are no hard and fast rules for designing green complexes, and if all golfers were playing a short approach shot to this Ross green, the front edge of the right bunker extending down the fairway might be justified. However, if they were playing a long approach, that bunker could be cut in half, keeping only the back one-half or one-third, and would still be an effective target delineator. The point is that, although this drawing conveys much information, it still requires a trained eye to make subtle field adjustments to better portray the design philosophy and intent.

FORM FOLLOWS FUNCTION FOR GREEN SURROUNDS

Since the surrounds of the green are so important to the golf course architect, they deserve a bit more evaluation as to form following function. Just outside of the actual putting surface, mowed slightly higher, is an area commonly called the collar, and outside of that area is an area of even higher mowed turf commonly called the fringe, and where the green transitions into the fairway is called the apron or approach. The relationship between the putting surface, collar, fringe, and the total outside edge of the green complex is also governed by

Figure 3-15: The maintenance of the entire green complex must be considered during the design process to maximize the benefits of form following function.

both the form and function of design philosophy, as well as the agronomics of maintaining the area (see Figure 3-15).

For example, how close hazards, such as bunkers, water, or steep slopes, are placed to putting surfaces should be evaluated with information about what maintenance equipment will be used on the putting surface, how much golfer traffic is expected, the drainage properties or textures of the outside soils, the aggressive or invasive nature of the grasses to be used, texture and color of the bunker sand, the normal rainfall distribution, Americans with Disabilities Act, and a few other things that may be specific to a given green site.

Not only is the theory of penalty of hazards, especially bunkers, governed by the concept that form follows function, so does their construction and maintenance. For example, if one expects to maintain any portion of the sand with a riding bunker rake, there has to be a place for the machine to get in and out of the bunker, it must be large enough to maneuver the machine, and the slope can't be too steep for it. In other words, there are certain forms that will be dictated by the maintenance procedure. If only hand raking of bunkers is expected, then a different style of bunker is possible. If bunker maintenance is to be by both mechanical and hand labor, then bunkers can have both large flat areas suitable for the bunker rake and steep flashed faces that will be hand raked.

Similarly, questions should be asked about what vegetation will be planted on the margins of bunkers or hazards, and how and how often these edges will be maintained, and is one form preferred over another to facilitate those functions (see Figure 3-16). Will these edges be mowed with fly mows, hand mowers, or riding mowers? Likewise, one should consider the influences on bunker maintenance of prevailing wind, sprinkler irrigation, subsoil material and rocks, certain sand or soil dwelling insects, maximum precipitation rates, and outside drainage. Each of these could be significant enough to cause one form of bunker to be preferred over another.

Another example is the shape and slope of the bunker edges with regard to surface drainage, playability, and aesthetics. Most golfers would agree that they prefer to see hazards, such as bunkers, for hidden hazards can often unfairly penalize a well-played shot. To define the locations of a bunker, it is a common practice to raise their edges above existing grade, which means that the bunker edge now has some kind of slope, which allows surface water and rolling golf balls to flow either toward or away from the bunker interior. Bunkers with gathering or inward slopes are often the most visually striking, and certainly become more intimidating than bunkers whose edges reject or direct rolling golf balls and water away from the sand interior. Again the question of which form to use can be logically answered by determining which function(s) to be served are given priority. If a major nuisance is having the sand wash off a steep

Figure 3-16: Although bunkers are important to the golf course, they can also be very costly to construct and maintain, and so these issues should be discussed during design phases.

bunker face with natural precipitation, then the margins of the bunker should be raised to cause water to drain away from the sand. If strong, prevailing winds, either in the summer or winter, cause the sand to blow off the faces and out of the bunker, then the bunker edge should be designed as a wind break, or the sandy interior should be oriented away from the wind, or only high grass faces should be used.

Don't consider bunker form only for aboveground functions, for it follows equally well where it can't be seen, below grade. The most obvious example is tile drainage, but there are others as well. For example, the use of a drainage matrix or grid, such as Bunker Aid®, SandTrapper®, or SandDam®, on a bunker face has been shown to be effective in reducing water erosion of sand off of very high and steep faces (see Figures 3-17, 3-18, 3-19, and 3-20 in color insert). It works by allowing the water to move vertically through the sand face and then move horizontally through the drainage matrix. It seems like a miracle to superintendents but it is really form follows function.

Similarly, there is the use of Bio-Barrier®, or a dense plastic buried between tree roots and sites where one does not want them surfacing, such as greens and bunkers. Placing an impervious plastic liner between the coarse-textured rootzone mix and the finer-textured surrounding soils can keep soil moisture from wicking away the green or from superheated sand faces of bunkers. These are all practices where form follows function.

PURPOSES OF BUNKERS

Bunkers can serve any one of five distinct purposes: (1) strategic—defines shot values; (2) retaining—keeps golf balls in play; (3) safety—separates or protects play areas; (4) directional—indicates line of play; or (5) aesthetic—they just look good. Each of these is a legitimate use for a bunker, but each bunker could have a very different form depending upon its function. For instance, a strategic bunker will tend to have its highest sand face oriented toward the putting surface, which not only makes the bunker more visible, but also complicates a recovery shot, which is the strategic bunker's primary function. If one agrees that the retaining bunker has the function of keeping golf balls from going out-of-bounds, down a hill, into water, and so on, then to be most effective and functional the high sand face should be on the outside and away from the putting surface. The point is that the designer must first determine the function of each bunker and then select a form that best suits that purpose. I am continually surprised by the number of ineffectual or poorly conceived bunkers I see, bunkers where the form doesn't fit the function. A good designer would deliberate the type of recovery shot required for any given bunker location, as well as the selection of sand used within its margins, and how the sand surface is maintained (see Figure 3-21).

Figure 3-21: How easy or difficult it is to recover from a bunker is dictated by the designer's philosophy and understanding of form follows function. (Courtesy of Doug Ball)

BUNKER SAND INFLUENCE ON SURROUNDS

Speaking of sand triggers thoughts about the impacts of bunker sand blasted out onto the surrounds. One commonly observed effect is that, if a lot of sand is blasted out and deposited on the fringe, then the sand can build up and effectively raise the bunker lip (see Figure 3-22). This may or may not change the design intent or shot value of the bunker, but it is something that should be watched and considered. [Recently, the Road Hole Bunker on the 17th on The Old Course at St. Andrews was made less deep and less penal because the R&A believed its shot value had become too harsh (see Figure 3-23).] It is not unusual to observe up to 18 inches of sand buildup above original grade on some heavily played, older golf courses. Such buildup areas tend to be droughty and require hand watering, usually don't hold a crisp edge, and they increase the difficulty of the recovery shot. Sand blasted out onto putting surfaces can complicate maintenance over time because of a textural discontinuity between the bunker sand and the rootzone material. Where possible, it is ideal to match the bunker sand and greens mix sand so such buildups are not a problem. Lastly, it has been observed that some dark color sands, when blasted out onto turf, can become so hot from sunshine that they weaken or kill the turf. This is especially true of the faddish black sand some designers have chosen to distinguish their projects.

Figure 3-22: After a long period of time, sand blasted out of bunkers by golfers can change the texture of the soil on the green complex, and often raise the bunker edge higher than originally designed. Whether this is good or bad is in the eye of the beholder.

Figure 3-23: Even historic bunkers, like the Road Hole bunker on the 17th green of the Old Course at St. Andrews, need occasionally to be rebuilt to maintain their image and character.

MOWERS' INFLUENCE ON SURROUNDS

If greens are to be mowed with walk-behind mowers, which can be turned within three or four feet, then bunkers can be as close as four to five feet from the putting surface. If most of the mowing is to be done with riding mowers, which require eight to ten feet of turning room, then obviously bunkers need to be moved back appropriately. The same logic applies to topdressing equipment, sprayers, aerifiers, and so on. Form must follow the function of accommodating maintenance equipment. To ignore this is to build in inefficiency and add to long-term maintenance costs.

Donald Ross's penchant for placing bunkers 20 feet or more away from greens has been credited by writers as a way to confuse a golfer's depth perception, and hence shot making. There is no question that placing bunkers that far away does produce some interesting impacts on golfers, but the reason that Ross gave for this technique was to allow for seven or nine unit gang mowers to be pulled between the bunkers and around the green to reduce maintenance cost associated with smaller mowers (see Figure 3-24). Donald Ross understood well that form follows function when trying to control maintenance costs.

RESOLVING CONFLICTS BETWEEN DESIGN AND MAINTENANCE

Throughout the chapter, the necessity of design theory respecting agronomic theory has been touched upon. A serious student of golf course design should be able to recognize such conflicts well in advance of the problem by understanding both sets of theories. It should be obvious that design theory should

Figure 3-24: Many golf course designers after The Depression, like Donald Ross, recognized the need to maintain golf courses with multi-gang mowers to keep labor costs low.

never compromise the total area required for hole locations, the slope or pitch within the green, surface and subsurface drainage parameters, depth and uniformity of rootzone, and the integration of surrounds into and with putting surfaces. If one were uncertain about possible conflicts, I would strongly urge erring on the side of good agronomy, drainage, and promoting good turf. Every golfer can recognize good playing conditions, but few to none recognize sophistication in design.

IMPROVING EXISTING PROBLEM GREENS

Up to this point, the discussion has dealt with new construction, but there are many instances in which greens must be rebuilt for a variety of reasons. One reason may be that the slopes are too steep for the current or projected mowing height. Other reasons might be ineffectual surface or subsurface drainage, substandard rootzone materials, poor initial design, a need to accommodate more golfers, buried layers of chemicals or soils that prevent a strong and healthy rooting, or a wide variety of other reasons that individually or collectively are contributing to the overstressing of turf.

There are several ways to renovate or improve older greens depending upon the major problem(s) that must be solved. To most accurately identify the problem green(s) and which course of corrective action to follow, James Francis Moore of the USGA Green Section Construction Education Committee has developed a method for grading or scoring existing greens. The complete method can be found online (www.USGA.com). Click on Green Section Construction, then "Helping your greens make the grade." Basically, scoring greens means working with a committee of golfers who have been familiar with the greens over at least five years. The step-by-step method allows the committee, led by the golf course superintendent, to grade each green for 12 factors that influence greens performance, and then average those grades to allow an understanding of why some greens perform well and others do not. The method also offers immediate ways to improve the grade for each green and perhaps the green itself, short of rebuilding. None of these suggestions are new or novel, but rather they reinforce the point that there is rarely just one factor that influences performance of a green. Rebuilding may be the only answer, and even that may not be sufficient to overcome critical influences such as dense shade, poor water quality, excessive traffic, and so on. The evaluation process does, however, identify, and somewhat quantify, the negative influences that rebuilding must overcome. This is an excellent exercise for any committee considering green reconstruction.

Short of rebuilding, there are a few techniques that can improve an old green, but not necessarily make it equal to a new one. The simplest involves doing a deep tine aerification, where holes are poked into the rootzone from 6

Figure 3-25: Older greens can be somewhat rejuvenated by deep aerification or deep aerification coupled to backfilling the hole with sand, called "drill and fill." Other machines use high-pressure water or air to inject inorganic amendments into the older rootzone. (Courtesy of DryJect)

to 18 inches deep. Some techniques refill these holes with sand or an inorganic amendment and hence are called "drill and fill," while others just leave the holes open for natural closure, and still others brush in sand or an inorganic amendment that has been topdressed onto the surface after the aerification (see Figure 3-25). Several deep tine aerifications or "drill and fill" operations will improve trouble greens to a point, but expect no miracles and keep in mind that it often takes three to five years of this operation to make a significant impact.

Recently, another method of improving older greens has been introduced by T. R. Wait, who also installs the green encroachment barriers that will be discussed in Chapter 5. Wait has developed a machine (see Figures 3-26 and 3-27) that looks like a mini-version of a subsoiler or mole plow and opens up a vertical channel in the green and fills it with sand. Then the green is rolled (see Figure 3-28) and washed down and syringed by hand to remove excess debris (see Figure 3-29). This method is called Water Wick™ and should improve poorly draining greens.

Figure 3-26: The Water Wick™ machine for cutting channels into existing green. (Courtesy of T. R. Wait)

Figure 3-27: Sand is immediately installed into channels to provide an open drainage way. (Courtesy of T. R. Wait)

Figure 3-28: Green is rolled to level out raised edges of channels. (Courtesy of T. R. Wait)

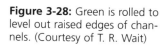

Figure 3-29: Excess sand and debris is washed off the green or into the mat layer. (Courtesy of T. R. Wait)

The next level of renovation is a bit more invasive in that it involves boring under or into greens and then installing a drainage tubing to keep the channel open, or force filling it with a small drainage tube bedded in sand (see Figure 3-30). The simplest of these operations is to remove a narrow strip of sod (three to four inches wide), cut in a narrow trench, install the drainage material and bedding, and then replace the sod. The trenches are cut on four- to ten-foot centers. This method has shown good success if the drainage material extends to or near the soil surface, and if the mat layer is routinely spiked or vertically mowed to keep openings to the drainage. Other systems have bored horizontally under a green and then inserted a perforated drainage pipe or tube. This system would work best if the pipe were sealed at one end and then attached to a vacuum pump to draw out excess soil water.

If all other negative influences have been addressed, and if laboratory evaluations confirm that the rootzone material is such poor quality that the green will not benefit from the methods described above, the next step might be to consider replacing or resurfacing only the top several inches of the putting surface. This means stripping off the old sod and either disposing of it, or setting it aside for reuse to sod the new green surface if the textural quality of the old rootzone surface is physically compatible to the new one. Once the sod is gone, either a portion of the existing rootzone can be dug out and removed, or drainage can be installed in the old surface, which is now used as a base. Then fresh rootzone is placed either into the excavated and tiled cavity or on top of the new subgrade. Rarely does it work to simply add sand or rootzone mix and then attempt to incorporate it to some depth in an effort to dilute the negative

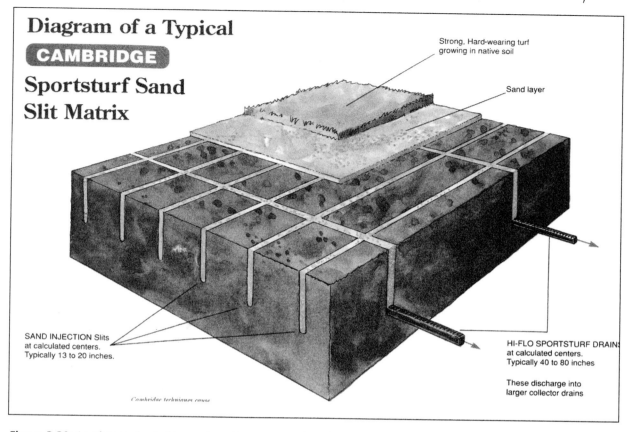

Diagram of a Typical

CAMBRIDGE

Sportsturf Sand Slit Matrix

Strong, Hard-wearing turf growing in native soil

Sand layer

SAND INJECTION Slits at calculated centers. Typically 13 to 20 inches.

HI-FLO SPORTSTURF DRAIN at calculated centers. Typically 40 to 80 inches

These discharge into larger collector drains

Cambridge techniques cause

Figure 3-30: Another method of improving older rootzones is with sand-filled channels, often called the "Cambridge System." (Courtesy of Cambridge Systems, Ltd.)

aspects of the old rootzone. This has the same problems as trying amended soil, as discussed in Chapter 2. The only reason to attempt this resurfacing procedure would be if funds to replace the entire rootzone are not available and if laboratory testing has suggested that the old rootzone would not be a chemical or physical conflict with the new rootzone material.

If the problem on the old green were isolated to the top inch or two of the old rootzone, one could consider simply removing the sod, as outlined, excavating and hauling away the problem soils, and then relying on the remaining profile to provide the growing medium that is needed. Again, in each and every scenario, rely on an accredited soil-testing lab to advise on the quality of the rootzone. The USGA has several great publications on the correct method for taking samples for lab testing. These procedures are available by contacting the USGA or one of its field agronomists. Also check the website under Green Section and Construction Education.

REBUILDING OLD GREENS

If and when it is determined that nothing short of total rebuilding will serve to correct the problems of a green, then a more elaborate and methodical process and detailed considerations should be expected (see Figure 3-31). Rebuilding an old green is much more difficult than building a new one from scratch for several reasons.

One reason is that the rebuilding is being done to solve a problem that may have nothing to do with the physical, chemical, or biological influence within the green site, for the source of the problem may be strictly environmental. As mentioned before, these influences include dense shade, morning shade, poor or excessive air circulation, poor water quality, unstable soils, excessive moisture or humidity, normal ambient temperatures in the growing season, and so on. Standard construction techniques may not work if the problem is not well defined and addressed to relieve stress on the putting surface turf. It is not uncommon for uninformed committees to rebuild a problem green only to have it fail again because the primary problem(s) was (were) not addressed by the design or construction technique of the new green.

However, assuming the problems have been thoroughly investigated, the usual and recommended process is to develop a scaled plan, which shows the existing green complex and the proposed new green (see Figure 3-32). It should contain sufficient detail to allow a knowledgeable and interested person to fully

Figure 3-31: Rebuilding greens is often the only way to improve them, but it should be a last resort.

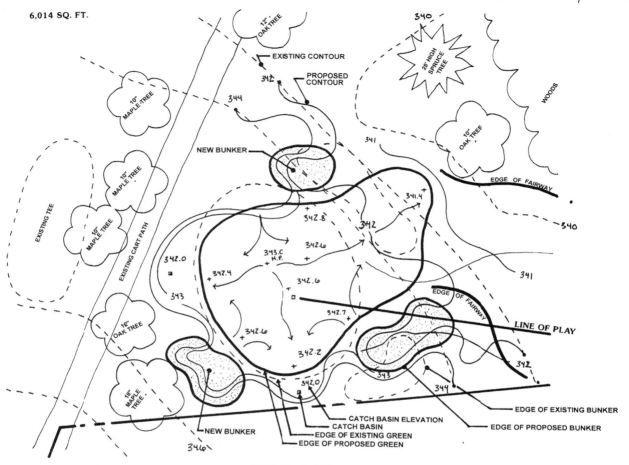

HOLE # 17

NOTES:

1) ARROWS DENOTE SURFACE DRAINAGE OF APPROXIMATELY 1.5%.
2) TILE DRAINAGE ESTIMATED AT 800 LINEAR FEET, PATTERN TO BE LAYED OUT AND APPROVED IN FIELD.
3) CATCH BASINS DO NOT CONNECT TO GREEN DRAINAGE.
4) IRRIGATION TO BE DONE BY GOLF COURSE STAFF.
5) ALL AREAS TO BE SODDED EXCEPT GREEN AND COLLAR - SEE SPECIFICATIONS.

understand the scope and specifics of the proposed rebuild. This does not mean fancy, rather this means complete. Typically, a golf course architect will be called upon to prepare this plan, but before that person is retained, it is a good idea for the owner to investigate previous projects the architect may have done, especially those with the same project requirements. It is an uncontested fact that 50 percent of all golf course architects graduated in the bottom half of their class, so make certain you get one who understands all of the nuances of greens and not just design theory. End of sermon.

Figure 3-32: When rebuilding greens, it is best to have a scaled plan that shows the existing green and the proposed new one. This plan should be approved before construction begins.

Minimally, the plan should give existing and proposed size shapes and elevations of the putting surface and surrounding features. Spot elevations are acceptable, but contour lines convey more information such as tie-in points, transitions in grades, and drainage patterns. The plan or plans should show proposed drainage, both subsurface and surface, catch basins, and tie-in or exit points for the drain lines. The location of sprinkler heads can be shown on this plan and/or on a separate plan that details the existing and proposed locations and sizes of pipe lines, electric wires, valves, valve boxes, sprinklers, quick couplers, drain valves, and so on. These two plans should also be accompanied by a very comprehensive set of specifications that cover all aspects of the project, to include permit information, licensing, general conditions, contracts, and detailed specifications of the *entire* scope of work. Under the watchful eye of the designer and superintendent, this is all that an experienced contractor needs to bid and subsequently rebuild a green. The actual construction and grow-in process are detailed in Chapter 5 of this book.

The summary statement is that there are many design considerations that must be identified and addressed by form following function, if a green is to survive the stresses placed on it.

Making Intelligent Compromises in Green Construction

In an ideal world, all golf greens would only be built on sites that had perfect and predictable growing conditions. There would be lots of sunshine, with very little or no influence of trees, fabulous air movement, low relative humidity, favorable temperatures, and long growing seasons (see Figure 4-1). The air would be fresh and clean, natural precipitation would be light and frequent, and pests would be few and nonthreatening. The irrigation water would be pure and plentiful, the golfer traffic light and light footed, and the grass perfectly matched to the environment. The building material for these mythical greens would fall right in the middle of the laboratory selection and performance criteria, they would be consistent and uniform, inexpensive, and well matched to the best available topdressing and bunker sands. The greens amendments would be similarly perfect. There would be no legal or environmental restrictions on maintenance materials or techniques, construction and maintenance budgets would be limitless, and greenkeepers would love their work and be highly paid. Yes, this seems like the perfect world as seen through the eyes of folks who do research on test plot golf greens, or speak at turf conferences, or opine on a single aspect of the entire topic of greens.

Figure 4-1: A favorable, if not perfect, green setting with no environmental stresses.

A METHOD FOR DECISION MAKING

Unfortunately, the reality is much different than the ideal, so intelligent compromises must be made to find the best balance among influencing factors. There are no stock answers that work, and no standard methods that can guarantee results. Rather, one must be prepared to be open-minded to all credible information, consider the physical, chemical, biological, and environmental characteristics of the green site(s), and then follow a methodical but flexible process of selection for what is available, affordable, and predictable. Proper green construction can be a complex effort of problem solving, and what follows is my personal method of analyzing and deciding.

CHECK AVAILABILITY OF MATERIALS

The process must begin with a realistic look at budgets of time and money. A push-up, native soil green can cost as little as fifty cents ($0.50) per square foot, a California style green at least two dollars ($2) per square foot, while a USGA green can cost as much as six dollars ($6) or more per square foot. Clearly, each has very different performance characteristics and long-term costs as well, which must also be considered, and that consideration follows a cost-to-benefit analysis as discussed in Chapter 2. Factors that influence setting a realistic budget include the amount of anticipated play, the golf market demands, the microclimate of the green site(s), the quality of the sand and soils available, and the skill and resources of the maintenance staff. One would hope this analysis would support the conclusion to build a green with some sort of a high sand base in order to realize the benefits afforded by the resistance to compaction, better soil water to air balance, and more forgiving rootzone matrix.

Intuitively, growing putting green turf on a proper sand base is much easier than not. But oftentimes proper construction materials are not locally available and cost to import them makes it impractical. The most extreme example I have heard of was for the nearest available and approved rootzone mix to cost $25 for the mix per ton and another $110 to truck it to the site. This made the total estimated cost for the golf course greens mix almost $1 million—uninstalled. When no local materials will meet laboratory selection criteria, alternatives must be considered if golf course construction costs are to remain reasonable. So realistic construction and operational budgets should be established before making too many decisions about green construction methods.

CHECK QUALITY AND QUANTITY OF IRRIGATION SOURCE

Another equally important decision factor is the quality of the irrigation water (see Figure 4-2). In the ideal world it was pure, but increasingly water for irrigation is becoming higher in salts, heavy metals or silicates, suspended bioma-

Dealing with water problems

A water test reveals whether a particular source of water is suitable for turf irrigation. Here are guidelines for various water problems in irrigation water (1,3), compiled and adapted by M. Ali Harivandi, Ph.D.

Water problem	How measured	Units	Irrigation management		
			No irrigation restriction if:	Slight to moderate restriction if:	Severe irrigation restriction if:
Salinity	Electrical conductivity (EC)	Decisiemens per meter (dS m⁻¹)	less than 0.7	0.7 to 3	Greater than 3
	Total dissolved solids (TDS)	Milligrams per liter (mg L⁻¹)	less than 450	450 to 2,000	Greater than 2,000
Soil water infiltration	Electrical conductivity (EC) and sodium adsorption ratio (SAR)	SAR = 0 to 3 and dS m⁻¹= SAR = 3 to 6 and dS m⁻¹= SAR = 6 to 12 and dS m⁻¹= SAR = 12 to 20 and dS m⁻¹= SAR = 20 to 40 and dS m⁻¹=	greater than 0.7 greater than 1.2 greater than 1.9 greater than 2.9 greater than 5	0.7 to 0.2 1.2 to 0.3 1.9 to 0.5 2.9 to 1.3 5 to 2.9	less than 0.2 less than 0.3 less than 0.5 less than 1.3 less than 2.9
Sodium ion (Na) toxicity in roots	SAR		less than 3	3 to 9	greater than 9
Sodium toxicity in leaves	milliequivalents per liter (meq L⁻¹)		less than 3	greater than 3	
	milligrams per liter (mg L⁻¹)		less than 70	greater than 70	
Chloride ion (Cl) toxicity in roots	meq L⁻¹		less than 2	2 to 10	greater than 10
	mg L⁻¹		less than 70	70 to 355	greater than 355
Chloride toxicity in leaves	meq L⁻¹		less than 3	greater than 3	
	mg L⁻¹		less than 100	greater than 100	
Boron ion (B) toxicity	mg L⁻¹		less than 1	1 to 2	greater than 2
Bicarbonate	meq L⁻¹		less than 1.5	1.5 to 8.5	greater than 8.5
	mg L⁻¹		less than 90	90 to 500	greater than 500
Residual chlorine	mg L⁻¹		less than 1	1 to 5	greater than 5

Figure 4-2: The quality and quantity of available irrigation water should be a determining factor in turfgrass cultivar selection and construction method for golf greens. In general, good water quality favors USGA construction while poor water quality works best in a California green. (Harivandi, M. A. 1999. Interpreting Turfgrass Irrigation Water Test Results, *California Turfgrass Culture.* Vol. 49, Nos. 1–4, pp. 1–6)

terials, and other "stuff" that can negatively affect turf growth. In addition, depending upon the source, the quality of the water can change over the growing season. The first key to successfully using low quality water is to select turfgrasses that have the highest tolerances for the identified impurity, yet that will deliver a marketable putting surface. The second key—also important—is to select methods to keep the irrigation water moving through the rootzone profile. When low quality water is allowed to evaporate, the result will be a deposition of its impurities, which can subsequently result in an accumulation, with negative impacts on plant growth. The easy solution to this problem is to flush out the rootzone with larger quantities of water, but often this is not possible or practical. The best approach is to never let the bad stuff accumulate. Avoiding accumulation means understanding and predicting the nature of the problem in advance, and building in as many safeguards as possible.

For example, if the effluent water that will be used for irrigation can reasonably be expected to be high in salts and heavy metals, one would encourage downward movement of these materials by considering a rootzone with a low cation exchange capacity (CEC), a high hydraulic conductivity (Ksat) or percolation rate, over a gravel drainage blanket, perhaps supplemented by vacuum-assisted drainage capability. This means avoiding any rootzone amendment that would add CEC or retard complete and thorough drainage. Likewise, thought should be given to increasing the depth of the rootzone mix, and to topdressing with only inert materials.

A CASE STUDY: BULLY PULPIT, MEDORA, NORTH DAKOTA

A good case study mentioned earlier is a golf course called Bully Pulpit in Medora, North Dakota (see Figure 4-3). Medora is a town of about only 80 full-time residents, but in the summer, it becomes North Dakota's largest tourist attraction by hosting about 250,000 guests. They come to Medora because it is the gateway to the Little Missouri National Grasslands and the Theodore Roosevelt National Park (he had a ranch nearby), as well as being the beginning of the Badlands. The restored western character of Medora is a further draw. It is a wonderfully historic and beautiful place, complete with an outdoor musical production, but tourists generally stay only a short while. Therefore, the Theodore Roosevelt Medora Foundation decided to build a golf course to expand the region's points of interest. However, as is usually the case in western North Dakota, the course had to be affordable, which meant low-cost construction and maintenance.

The area is very dry, getting only about 11 inches of precipitation per year, mostly in the winter. In addition, it is subject to wide temperature swings. The only available irrigation source is the Little Missouri River, which flows by the site, but to use that water the golf course can only draw water out during high runoff peri-

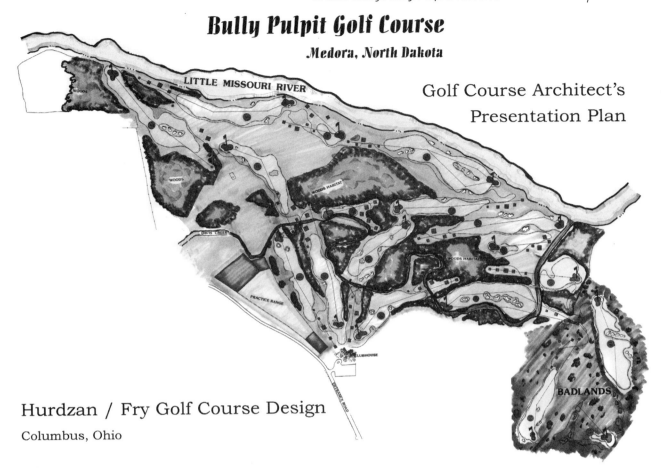

Figure 4-3: Bully Pulpit Golf Course, Medora, ND, is a good case study in making compromises in green construction in response to water quality, budget, and environmental conditions.

ods, typically in the spring. A review of 20 years of river water quality tests showed the water to be high in salts, except during spring snow melt when the river was high. The prudent decision was to plan for large storage ponds with greater than a year's supply of water (100 acre feet), assume the water to be salty, and plan accordingly. This would include investigating water treatment techniques such an acid injection system or a sulfur burner (see Figure 4-4).

Next began a search for suitable turfgrasses that could tolerate potential winter temperatures of −35°F and summer extremes of 108°F, *and* handle salty water. It was decided that, for greens, Seaside II would be best and that all other maintained areas would be seeded to a blend of Seabreeze and Dawson Fine fescues with a small percentage either a colonial bentgrass, alkali grass, or bluegrass, all of which would have superior salt tolerance.

Figure 4-4: In the summer, river water becomes increasingly high in salts and bicarbonates. Storage ponds are filled during peak flows in spring and water is then treated by a sulfur burner to produce a reasonable quality irrigation source. (Courtesy of David Solga)

Figure 4-5: For the past 10,000 years or more, the Little Missouri River has flooded the golf course site, depositing various layers of sand and soil, which were suitable for modified green construction. (Courtesy of David Solga)

The Little Missouri River had over the aeons of time carved a mile-wide valley, and then slowly filled it with sediments from Badland erosions during flood times (see Figure 4-5). The soils of the golf course site were sent to an accredited rootzone mix testing lab, which determined them to be a fairly consistent source of sandy loam material. As was expected, there was some variability in the soil between locations and depths of the sediment, which meant there might be the same degree of variability in the rootzone performance. Although some materials were coarser or finer than others, all fell into a reasonable range of acceptability, *if* adjustment in depth of profile were done. Coarse sands could be 12 to 14 inches deep, while finer sands would have to be closer to 16 to 18 inches deep. Soil samples were submitted periodically during construction to verify that the rootzone materials were still within an acceptable range. Since the budget for the entire golf course, excluding the irrigation system, was less than $650,000 in 2002 dollars, the only place where tile drainage was to be installed under greens was where there was no sandy textured subsoil.

The process was to core out the green 16 inches deep from existing contours and, if the soil below was sandy, then selected native sand was used to fill the cavity. If the soils in the bottom of the core drained slowly, then a limited amount of tile was added.

Since the goal was a reasonably fast draining profile to keep the salty water moving downward, that meant the top inch or two could be a bit droughty. To compensate for this dryness, particularly during germination and early establishment, about 12 percent inorganic amendment was incorporated into this two- to three-inch deep top zone (see Figure 4-6). The site is somewhat windy so over the course of the summer a thin coating of dust, mostly silt and clay, developed on the surface of the greens' rootzones. So the top half-inch or so was scooped off or incorporated in by using a walk-behind Knolte sand screener. Fertility amendments were added and greens seeded and mulched by late fall.

Bully Pulpit is indeed a worthy textbook example of having to make intelligent compromises, simply because there was no budget to do otherwise. The lockstep process was to let the potential golf market establish budget limits, study the irrigation water quality, select grasses well adjusted to the climate and the irrigation water, test for available rootzone material within the context of

Figure 4-6: The top two inches of the native sand was amended with 12 percent inorganic amendment to reduce surface drying. (Courtesy of David Solga)

budget, select the most prudent rootzone material and adjust as practical, amend with appropriate rootzone amendment, and manage the turf for stress avoidance. This evaluation process begins before the golf course is designed and then continues through construction, grow-in, and long-term maintenance.

ANOTHER CASE STUDY THAT WAS NEVER BUILT

Sometimes this process can tip the scales against a project, but in the end such a decision might well save hundreds of thousands of dollars. For example, a project in southern California was moving through the preliminary phases when a study of the only potential irrigation source revealed a high level of suspended silicates. Further research showed that, when this water was pumped out onto turf and soil and allowed to evaporate, the silicates remained and formed a very impervious soil colloid. Checking with a nearby golf course using a similar water source, the researchers confirmed that it took about three or four years for the problem to become chronic, but once it did, the only solution was aerification once or twice a month and topdressing to fill the holes. Since there was no practical way to remove the silicate, the golf course was condemned to slowly worsening conditions, which would result in higher and higher costs.

This information, in combination with a few other factors, was enough to force a decision against the proposed new golf course. It would have been a fabulous golf course on a great site, but the prudent choice was to abandon the project.

DESIGNING FOR STRESSFUL ENVIRONMENTS

Other important factors that may force compromise or creative thinking also need evaluation. One often cited factor is shade (see Figure 4-7). Full sunlight is commonly accepted as the best for turfgrass growth. Shade is loosely defined as sunlight that has been altered by reflectance, selective absorption, transference, and reradiation. Compared to sunlight, shade generally has a different proportion of wavelengths with reduced intensities. Consequently, light-driven physiological processes of plants will be different from sun to shade environments just on the basis of light alone. In addition, compared to full sun, shade environments tend to be cooler, more humid, with less air movement, any or all of which can influence plant life processes. Although some plants prefer shaded environments to sunny ones, most turfgrasses do best in full sun. Conversely, many plant pests prefer the cool, damp, and even reduced-light regimes of shade. Taken together, shade generally disadvantages turfgrasses and advantages the pest. While building greens in full sun is preferred, the reality is that this is often not possible because of restrictions or current attitudes about saving trees.

Figure 4-7: Greens built in full sun perform best, especially if there is good air movement around them.

Figure 4-8: Early morning shade, and shade in general, on putting greens is a source of severe environmental stress.

The recommended development process is to try to avoid shaded green sites, especially ones that receive morning shade (see Figure 4-8). Morning shade seems particularly bad because the afffected area is generally the slowest to warm up, especially if there is any frost or snow cover. The shaded plant cannot reach full photosynthetic capacity during the cooler and more optimum morning hours. Moisture remains longer on leaves, increasing the predisposition for diseases. Shaded soils tend to be wetter, making them more prone to compaction, as well as excessive organic accumulation. Hence turfgrasses face increased competition from mosses and algae in shaded areas. Some plants like *Poa annua* can more easily invade turfgrass swards, and once there can become dominant. Shade areas of trees are also areas most likely to have tree roots, especially surface roots, which can invade the green rootzone and outcompete the turf for limiting supplies of moisture and fertility. Consequently, for a multitude of reasons, green sites with morning shade should be avoided or made sunny by tree removal and pruning.

If shade avoidance or removal is not possible, then measures to advantage the selected putting green turf should be studied.

COMPROMISES FOR GREENS IN SHADE

The first step, obviously, is to see if there are suitable cultivars of putting green turf that do better in the shade than others. This may even require establishing a test plot or visiting and evaluating new courses in the region with shaded greens. In acute cases, one might turn to alternative grasses, such as marketed *Poa annua* types or *Poa trivialis*. If the situation is that some greens will be in the sun and some in the shade, strong consideration should be given to using two different turf types best suited for each location. Nothing says that all greens *must* be planted to the same grass. It is critical that the quality of irrigation water be examined as previously discussed, for to use low-quality water on turfgrasses not tolerant of it will only compound the problems of shaded greens.

Two other considerations are to use root washed sod cut from greens already established in shade, or to blend in a significant percentage of a companion grass, such as a fine fescue, that is shade adaptable. If the shade prohibits the principal turf from flourishing, then the companion turf may proliferate. The companion turf may not be ideal for lots of reasons, but it may provide a more acceptable overall playing surface than possible with more traditional turf types.

The use of lights and mirrors to supplement the light requirement is simply not practical, and does little good, except perhaps to warm the air, reduce relative humidity, or alter dark periods that benefit some pests. It would take an enormous amount of artificial light to mimic the effects of even weak sunlight.

Prewiring the site for fans, however, may make good sense, for although electric fans cannot help overcome light problems, they can dry the turf surface more quickly and allow for better gas exchange in the turf canopy.

Another approach to dealing with shade is to think in terms of installing a root barrier of sufficient depth to stop the encroachment of tree roots that compete with the turf for moisture and nutrients (see Figure 4-9). Geotextiles with root-limiting herbicide materials attached or embedded are designed for that very purpose and last a long time (see Figure 4-10). A more open or rapidly draining rootzone architecture should be favored in shaded areas to permit

Figure 4-9: Having a tree to separate two greens is novel, but it does add some maintenance problems.

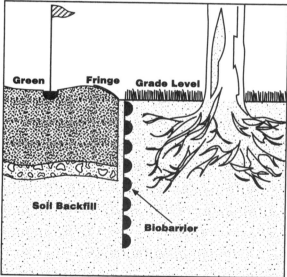

Figure 4-10: Biobarrier™ is a very popular brand of root encroachment barrier that consists of a geotextile with embedded nodules of trifluralin to control root growth. (Courtesy of Biobarrier)

more thorough drainage from surface layers, hence combating compaction somewhat, as well as discouraging excessive organic matter accumulation and wet soil pests. Also, it is easier to warm up air-filled soil than it is one filled with water. Consideration should also be given to accommodating vacuum-assisted drainage, by separating the drainage field of the most heavily shaded areas from that of lesser-shaded areas. This would permit removing excess moisture from

Figure 4-11: Shaded green sites are dramatic but may require special construction techniques to lessen the environmental stress. They should be evaluated during the design process.

the most shaded areas only. A final suggestion would be to adjust the sprinkler placement and capacity to apply less water in more shaded areas, and install a quick coupler in those areas so they can be hand watered as best management practices would determine (see Figure 4-11).

Again, the teaching point is that one cannot simply treat all green sites, all of which might have different microclimates, in the same way and still expect optimum performance from each one of them. Understanding the confounding influences of long-term maintenance and building in stress relievers is a more intelligent approach.

COMPROMISES FOR PESTICIDE RESTRICTIONS

There continues to be growing public pressure to maintain greens using no chemical fertilizers or pesticides (see Figure 4-12). Many golfers, on the other hand, do not really care how greens are maintained as long as the results are firm, fast, true putting surfaces. Maintaining older greens without the benefit of all of the modern products and tools available is a challenge that I do not think can be met at present. However, if greens are designed and built with the idea of low or reduced inputs of water, fertilizer, and pesticides, *and* if golfers do not expect unblemished putting surfaces, it may be possible to get closer to zero impacts on the environment. However, it will require some very unique circumstances to even approach the environmental standards being required by overzealous regulators, who falsely believe golf green management damages the environment.

To begin with, all greens should be built in full sunlight, for any shade will disadvantage the putting green turf and complicate maintenance. The irrigation water should be pure, with a neutral pH, with no use restrictions. The rootzone blend should be selected to be the most biologically active possible, again with a neutral pH and great aeration. Any organic matter amendment should be a proven substrate for active microbiobal activity, in particular mycorrhizae or tricoderma species, and inorganic amendments should be considered in the top six inches of the rootzone to keep the aeration porosity high. A gravel drainage layer and hook ups for a vacuum-assisted drainage would be required. The selected turf or turf blend should be well adapted to low fertility inputs and have exceptional disease resistance for diseases associated with low nitrogen levels. Ideally, planting with a mature sod that included a healthy quarter-inch mat layer would complete the process.

The long-term maintenance program should permit the use of foliar feeding with transcuticular materials that can be absorbed through the pore spaces in the cuticle, as well as a wide array of biological pest controls. The maintenance budget must be generous in allowing for more hand labor than for conventional greens. A system for brewing and delivering protective and antagonistic organisms on a daily basis should also be included.

Figure 4-12: Golf and environment are integrally linked, so green maintenance is prime public concern. (Courtesy Golf & the Environment Conference, 1995—Center for Resource Management)

THE IMPORTANCE OF THE GOLF COURSE SUPERINTENDENT

However, the single most important ingredient should be a golf course superintendent trained in and dedicated to the zero impact philosophy (see Figure 4-13). This person must ignore conventional greenkeeping techniques and concentrate on developing a maintenance program for each green. Granted there will be large areas of overlap among greens, but not to identify the nuances of individual greens would hinder success. This would include training the greenkeeping staff in the intricacies of pest and problem identification. Embracing emerging technology such as tissue testing, enhanced spectral reflectivity analysis, conventional and soil pest testing, and detailed monitoring and record keeping of microclimatic factors will be necessary. Microclimate measurements should include light quality, quantity, and duration, air and soil temperatures at two or three different levels, relative humidity, periodic water and precipitation quality and quantity analysis, and air quality and movement (see Figure 4-14).

Figure 4-13: The golf course superintendent is the most important ingredient in a program to have great greens with minimum environmental impact.

Figure 4-14: Several supply houses offer a wide variety of scientific instrumentation to monitor microclimates on a golf course. (Courtesy of Spectrum, Inc.)

A program of routine mapping of incidence of turf problem areas, using global positioning systems/geographic information systems (GPS/GIS), will allow historic analysis of trouble spots, which can then allow for adjustments or problem solving, reducing the incidence. Growing an indicator nursery of many different varieties of turf may provide an early warning system that will warn the superintendent when treatment is indicated. Detailed record keeping of turf treatments, both biological and cultural, with a postapplication analysis of the efficacy of the treatment, should prove valuable over the long term. Naturally,

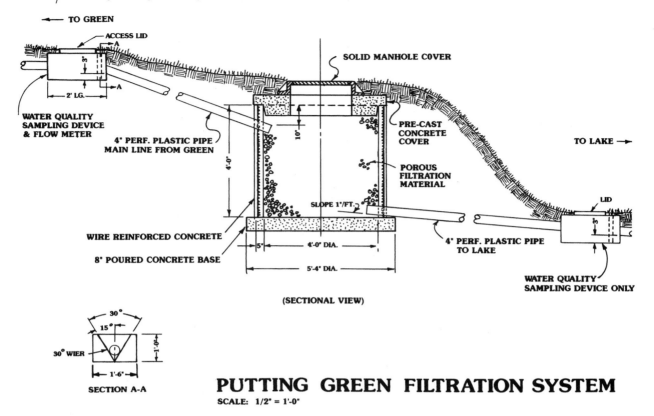

← TO GREEN

ACCESS LID

SOLID MANHOLE COVER

2' LG.

WATER QUALITY
SAMPLING DEVICE
& FLOW METER

4" PERF. PLASTIC PIPE
MAIN LINE FROM GREEN

PRE-CAST
CONCRETE
COVER

TO LAKE →

POROUS
FILTRATION
MATERIAL

10"

4'-0"

SLOPE 1"/FT.

LID

WIRE REINFORCED CONCRETE

8" POURED CONCRETE BASE

5"

4'-0" DIA.

5'-4" DIA.

4" PERF. PLASTIC PIPE
TO LAKE

WATER QUALITY
SAMPLING DEVICE ONLY

(SECTIONAL VIEW)

30°

15°

30° WIER

1'-0"

1'-6"

SECTION A-A

PUTTING GREEN FILTRATION SYSTEM
SCALE: 1/2" = 1'-0"

Figure 4-15: A system for sampling leachate from greens, putting it through a charcoal or filtration resin, and resampling the treated leachate before release.

an ongoing program of soil and water monitoring would prove the impact, or lack thereof, on the environment (see Figure 4-15). The cost of such maintenance is difficult to estimate; however, it would not be surprising if it were 50 to 100 percent greater than maintaining turf with currently approved and conventional methods and products. To deny the golf course superintendent any of those tools listed above, or not to provide the general physical conditions as described will jeopardize the success of the program. Even then, it may take a blend of science, art, skill, common sense, and luck to achieve zero impact. However, if that goal is never set, it will never be reached.

MICROBIAL ACTIVITY OF GREENS

Fortuitously, some things take care of themselves in golf green construction and maintenance. One prime example is the soil microbiology. Although it would seem logical to "seed" some beneficial microbes into a new green rootzone, they seem to establish quickly enough without any assistance. Intuitively, if some organisms are good, some must be bad or deleterious to turf growth, and when

Figure 4-16: When droughty and nutritionally impoverished test plots are treated with certain beneficial organisms, there often can be seen positive results. However, under conditions of adequate water and fertilization, the effect is not as noticeable.

the good and bad are mutually antagonistic, and when the amount of good organisms is sufficient to counteract any negative effects of the others, they are said to be "in balance." Attempts to identify specific good and bad organisms have been complicated by the sheer number of microbes found in an active rootzone, as well as by the fact they have also been found in different proportions or populations (see Figure 4-16).

One broad family of microbes that have been known and used for over 100 years in forestry and horticulture are called mycorrhizae. The one of greatest interest is a fungus that lives in association with plant roots. The mycorrhizae are naturally occurring and can exist by forming a sheath around plant roots, by actually penetrating the surface layers of young roots, or by both penetrating and forming a sheath around roots.

For greater detail, please reference an article published by Chris Martin, Professor of Urban Horticulture at Arizona State University, in *Grounds Maintenance* in October 1994. Professor Martin nicely summarized information that showed that even a decade ago, over 150 species of mycorrhizae were identified from six genera. The fungi demand up to 15 or 20 percent of the simple sugars produced by a plant during photosynthesis, and in turn serve as extensions of the plant's rootzone, helping to absorb water and inorganic nutrients, especially phosphorous. This mutually beneficial association is credited with the ability some plants demonstrate to survive harsh environments. Supplementing planting beds with mycorrhizae is a routine part of horticulture and forestry planting methods. So if other plant industries know what they are, how they work, and the benefits they provide, why isn't the turf industry more knowledgeable about mycorrhizae?

Some USGA-funded research, done at the University of Rhode Island and published in the *USGA Green Section Record* of November/December 1995, showed some remarkable benefits of mycorrhizae on putting green turf. Doctors R. Koske, J. N. Genna, and N. Jackson first sampled existing bentgrass and *Poa annua* greens and sand dunes to isolate 29 species of mycorrhizae from 200 rootzone samples. These were subsequently screened down to seven isolates, and grown in a greenhouse in a pot culture. Various treatments of water and fertility were given and positive interactions were observed and evaluated. The greatest promise seemed to come from the mycorrhizae isolated from the sand dunes. The researchers found establishment of young turf was enhanced by inoculating the rootzone, and differences were apparent within three weeks of seeding. Older mycorrhizae-treated turfs had up to 60 percent more chlorophyll than untreated turf, and 39 percent less water stress after five days of drought and 60 percent less after eight days. Mycorrhizae-treated turf recovered more quickly from the drought and, where phosphorous was limiting, treated turf had much greater growth.

Mycorrhizae are, however, sensitive to some pesticides and at normal to higher levels of soil moisture and fertility, their benefit may be marginal. Furthermore, they seem susceptible to "take all" organisms. The researchers further concluded that mycorrhizae would naturally colonize new greens without being added as inoculums, but inoculation doesn't hurt. Similar, positive effects of inoculation of new greens with *Trichoderma* species were observed in Southern Australia. The turf was observed to grow in more quickly and vigorously, and had better drought tolerance and disease resistance. The USGA sponsored research on two Trichodermas, *T. arzianum* and *T. (Gliocladium) virens,* research conducted by Dr. Gary Harman of Cornell University, which showed these organisms quickly colonizing root surfaces even when the roots were a meter or more away in the soil. The Trichodermas hold great promise as biocontrols for several diseases as well as offer enhanced root development and function. They show innate resistance to most agricultural chemicals and fungicides, but resistance varies among strains. Harman's research showed colonized corn plants needed 40 percent less nitrogen and showed improved drought resistance.

The point of discussing these organisms is to point out that the rootzone and/or rhizosphere of turfgrass plants is dynamic and can contribute to the health of the plant. Although these colonizations appear to occur naturally, additional research may suggest that inoculation of certain organisms will improve the performance of putting green turf. For now, however, there is too little solid information to suggest a best management practice. A useful tool for learning more about such soil organism is the Internet.

COMPOSTS

Another topic of concern to environmentally concerned golf course superintendents has to do with the use of composts and compost teas for biological control of pests as an alternative to chemical pesticides (see Figure 4-17). Some tremendous successes have been observed, but no approaches are foolproof. For example, one very interesting trial showed that topdressing with one particular compost was highly effective against snow mold, and, in the spring, the superintendent was impressed. The problem was, however, that this same plot became very susceptible to such summer diseases as Brown Patch. Other composts in the same trial did fair in disease control during both winter and summer. The differences arise from the variable nature of the compost.

Compost in the broadest terms simply refers to an organic source material that has gone through a thermophillic process of decomposition, often followed by a mesophillic stabilization phase. There are no minimum standards for calling something compost, and so the materials vary widely. The most common expectation of compost is that, since it was produced by microbial decomposition, it has the potential to be biologically active and thus can convey the benefits of organism-to-pest-organism antagonism, as well as offer by-products

Figure 4-17: Greens amended with compost as an organic source seem to show better disease resistance and more vigorous growth with lower inputs of water and fertilizer. However, these results are highly variable with the source of compost, the microclimate of the green, and the type of turf grown.

produced during the decomposition that will stimulate plant growth. But not all compost offers these benefits and, in fact, depending upon the source material and organisms to compost it, compost can be high in salt, silt, carbon-to-nitrogen ratio, heavy metals, or even phytoxins. Again, it is another case of "buyer beware," and it is important to do a cost-to-benefit ratio analysis to see if compost is really a good value or not. Some unscrupulous compost companies have even been found to "fortify" their compost with chemical fertilizers. On the other hand, there are some excellent materials on the market that provide benefits that can only be achieved with composts. More details of this topic are discussed in Chapter 6 on Rootzone Sampling, Testing, and Evaluation.

One last natural product that is being touted as a great biological management tool is worm castings. Ads read, "...[R]ichest natural fertilizer known to man," of course without any data to back up the claim. Clearly, earthworms are a vital part of any biosphere, and healthy ecosystems seem to be those with lots of earthworms. The problem is that there are probably thousands of species of earthworms, and their excrement can only be reflective of their food source, minus what the earthworm needed personally. Therefore, the same warning of "buyer beware" applies to this group of products. However, it becomes a bit more disconcerting, because nowhere in the many discussion sources on the Internet is there any indication of the amount of silt found in these excreta. Without question, such materials show great promise and should be investigated. However, their benefits may not be applicable to golf greens, per se.

Making intelligent compromises in green construction for special situations requires understanding of the full spectrum of factors that influence plant growth, along with some speculation and observational trials, and a solid strategy for stress management based on science, not miraculous amendments.

Green Construction Techniques

METHODICAL PROCESS

There is a statement from the Bible, specifically Ecclesiastics 3:1–8, that begins: "[T]here is a time for everything, and a season for every activity." To me this indicates that angels build greens in heaven, for that phrase is directly applicable to green construction. There are many different ways to design and detail a proposed green construction, but there are few variations in how to get it built. Granted, some greens are less complicated and complex than others, and so some steps or operations may be omitted, but the same progression of steps must occur if maximum efficiency and quality are to be realized.

The full process, starting from the beginning, is as follows:

Step 1: Survey or designate the center of the green.

Step 2: Remove all vegetation in all areas of proposed grade change.

Step 3: Remove shade-producing vegetation or microclimatic concerns or factors that would affect putting green performance.

Step 4: Strip and save topsoil, if suitable.

Step 5: Lay out or stake out the limits of the putting surface and surrounding features that are to be constructed.

Step 6: Mark out areas and elevations within the green and surrounds that are to be cut or filled.

Step 7: Cut or fill green and surrounds to bring to design subgrade elevations.

Step 8: Insure design subgrade base is stable and reflects finished grade elevations, to include surface drainage patterns.

Step 9: Lay out and install drainage tile and drop inlets for surface flows.

Step 10: Remove spoil, reestablish subgrade.

Step 11: Place vapor barrier between rootzone cavity and outside soils (optional).

Step 12: Install gravel layer (optional).

Step 13: Install intermediate layer (optional).

Step 14: Select, blend, and install rootzone mix.

Step 15: Fumigate if required (optional).

Step 16: Place topsoil on the surrounds.

Step 17: Install irrigation and compact or flood settle trenches.

Step 18: Test irrigation system function, patterns, and tightness.

Step 19: Fine-grade green and surrounds.

Step 20: Create a punch list of deficiencies and make appropriate repairs.

Step 21: Apply preplant materials and work in.

Step 22: Finalize finish grade.

Step 23: Plant (seed–sod–stolons).

Step 24: Mulch or cover (optional).

Step 25: Add sod ring collar or sod surrounds (both are optional).

Step 26: Begin light frequent wetting of top one to two inches of rootzone.

Step 27: Keep top of rootzone continually moist.

Step 28: Avoid, if possible, traffic, pesticides, topdressing, fertilization, and so on.

Step 29: Monitor for physical, chemical, biological, or environmental damage—treat or repair as required.

Step 30: Allow young grass to grow to two to three inches long before removing mulch or covers.

Step 31: Begin mowing at one-inch height of cut—gradually lower to one-half inch by six to eight weeks of growing weather after planting.

Step 32: Install encroachment barrier (optional).

Step 33: No topdressing or hollow tine aerification, but continue to water and fertilize as necessary—ideally, use pesticides only as curative until turf is at least ten weeks old.

Step 34: Gradually lower cutting height to sustainable levels over next four weeks.

Step 35: Edge bunkers, clean and shape bottoms, check drainage, and purchase and place bunker sand.

Step 36: Encourage and develop a mat layer of at least one-quarter inch before topdressing of hollow tine aerification.

Step 37: Begin topdressing and aerification as needed to maintain mat layer at one-quarter to three-eighths of an inch.

Figure 5-1: Deciding who should construct a golf course—and how—requires intelligent decision making based on many considerations. (Courtesy of P. J. Barton)

Those are the steps, but before the explanation of why, how, and how much leeway for variation there is in each step, one must decide on who will build the green(s). The choices can be: (1) build with in-house staff and equipment, (2) subcontract out portions of the work, (3) hire full-service contractor, or (4) some combination thereof (see Figure 5-1). Each choice carries with it different liabilities and obligations, as well as requirements for documentation.

CONSTRUCTION RESPONSIBILITIES

Intuitively, the greatest liability for the golf course owner occurs when the work is done in-house for, as they say, "You have no one to blame but yourself." Of course, the owner can blame the construction crew, but they work for him or her and are legally the owner's representatives, as long as they are acting legally, morally, ethically, and within the limits of authority granted to them. This includes their work in securing any permits or approvals, selecting construction materials, and meeting the requirements of the Occupational Safety and Health Administration (OSHA) and the Environmental Protection Agency (EPA), employee training and performance, construction impacts or accidents, and finally, the quality of the workmanship and finished product are other areas of liability concern. In-house work does not need as much documentation in the form of plans or specifications, because there is no formal bid process involved and there is no need for extraneous information as required for contracted work. There is a reward for taking all of the risk through in-house construction, and that amounts to about 15 percent lower cost, which is just about what a contractor hopes to average in profit on a project.

The second alternative is to subcontract out the work that in-house crews cannot do because they do not have proper equipment, training, or time. Typically, this amounts to contracting out the earthwork, tile installation, and rootzone purchase and placement. The in-house staff can usually prepare a site to receive the subcontractor, and then once the rootzone is in, can install and test the irrigation, do final grade, plant, and grow-in. Alternatively, an owner may just have in-house staff prepare the site, plant, and do the grow-in, while letting a subcontractor install the irrigation. There are lots of options, but each time work is subcontracted there is a shift in liabilities and responsibilities. Therefore, this approach requires more documentation in the form of plans and/or specifications. Good plans and specs should detail exactly where the subcontractor's work starts and stops and what he or she is responsible for in between. Naturally, the profit for each task that is contracted out now flows to the subcontractor. The owner may save a little money, but he or she is also assuming a great deal of risk to grow the green in, particularly from risk erosion or turf pests.

The third alternative is to hire a full-service contractor who can do all phases of the work, with no assistance from in-house staff (see Figure 5-2). Obviously, this option needs lots of plans and specifications and documentation, but the risk is mostly assumed by the contractor. Contractors usually do not mind taking on manageable risks, but things like weather-related damage during grow-in scare the heck out of them—and well should they be scared. A heavy storm on newly planted areas can cause lots of expensive damage. Therefore, full-service contracts are usually written so the contractor's responsibility can end at any one of several options: (1) seed, sprigs, or sod on the ground, (2) planting plus x number of days, (3) "establishment" in the opinion of a designated consultant, or (4) "complete and ready for play." In the seed, sprigs, or sod on the ground option, the moment the green is properly planted, the contractor's work is done, and the green becomes the owner's responsibility. Contractors like this option because there is a clear-cut point where their work is complete. Equally if not more imporant, they don't usually have the equipment, staff, or know-how to grow in the green, not compared to a golf course superintendent. So each time a contractor's obligation is extended beyond planting, that contractor must charge or overcharge for the potential work to be done. For a complete new golf course, the grow-in charge is between $50,000 and $100,000 per month.

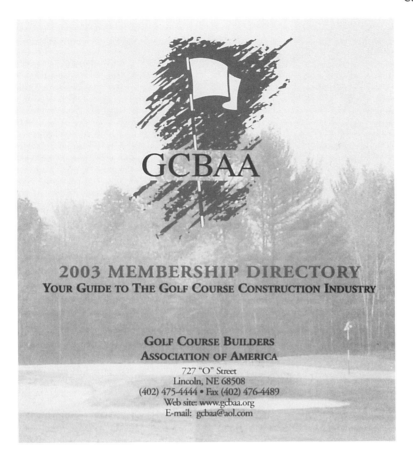

Figure 5-2: The Golf Course Builder's Association of America is the best source of information on contracting and construction of golf courses (www.gcbaa.org). (Courtesy of Golf Course Builders Association of America)

CONSTRUCTION DOCUMENTS

Trying to determine the exact point where the contractor's work is done and where the responsibility shifts to the owner can become very subjective; to continue the biblical references, it can require the wisdom of Solomon. The designer or agronomic consultant is usually named in the contract or construction documents as the final authority of when that point is reached. The owner wants the contractor to do as much as possible, the contractor would like to do the least possible, and the consultant is the referee. Even making the contractor produce a "complete and ready to play" facility still requires making some tough choices.

What constitutes a suitable set of construction documents (CDs) is also subjective (see Figure 5-3). They can range from a simple sketch on a cocktail napkin to elaborate scaled drawings and three-dimensional models. Specifications can be a few pages or hundreds of pages. Regardless of their sophistication, the CDs should clearly and precisely quantify the work, how it is to be done, and

Figure 5-3: Construction documents (CDs) can be complex or simple, as long as they tell the contractor exactly where the work is to start and stop, and what to do in between.

how to resolve disputes or differences of opinions. So, although there are lots of ways to express design intent and quality, the more detail that the CDs have, the less room there is for disputes and disagreements.

PERSONAL EXPERIENCE

Back in the 1960s, through the 1980s, our firm used to draw greens at a scale of one inch equals 10 feet (1" = 10'), with six-inch contour lines, and lots of spot elevations on top of that. In addition, each green was cross-sectioned in four to six different directions. It took a full day at the drawing board to design, refine, draw, cross-section, label, and shade one green drawing done that way, but they were chock-full of detail—perhaps needless detail.

Today, we rarely draw greens, because our one to fifty (1" = 50') scale drawings are computer generated and are so accurate we can work directly from them. In addition, greens are so flat that we might only have one or two contour lines going through a green, and most cross sections look like parallel lines. When we do make green drawings, they are usually at a scale of one to twenty (1" = 20') with no cross sections but lots of spot elevations and arrows to show surface flow (see Figure 5-4). Typically, our firm simply gives the contractor a square footage of putting green area, based upon the computer calculations of our one to fifty (1" = 50') drawings, and that is what he bids on, and that becomes our allowance of useable space. This method gives the designer in the field the ultimate flexibility to fit a green to its site, but it does require the principal designer to visit the site just about every week during active construction times to approve the work and to lay out more greens.

We evolved from our earlier superdetailed format, taught to us by engineers, to the freewheeling, do-it-in-the-field approach, *not* because we are lazy, but rather because we could produce a more attractive golf course. The reason was that no matter how accurate the site maps we generate, they were usually off by about one-half of a contour interval, that is, a two-foot contour map might be off one foot plus or minus, *and* they often failed to show features near the green that made it interesting, like specimen trees, rocks, off-site views, shade

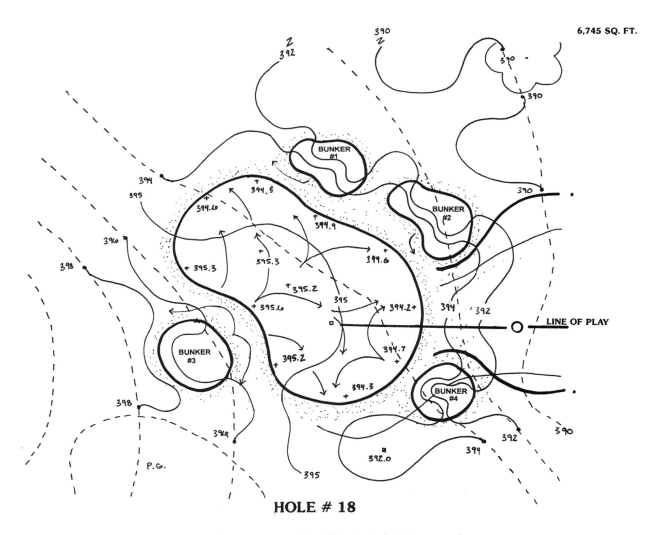

HOLE # 18

Figure 5-4: Green drawing at a scale of one to twenty (1 " = 20'): simple, but it may require a great deal of field interpretation.

patterns, sight lines, and a host of other things we care more about today. Granted, contractors must have enormous trust in the designer to bid work without detailed drawings, and there is no easy way to settle disputes like going to the drawings, but it does produce greens that fit the site better. Even though one of our designers is on site every week or so, that is sometimes not enough to answer questions or solve problems, so the answer has been to use e-mail. The contractor takes a picture(s) of the problem area, e-mails them to the designer or our office, and then has a phone conversation about how to resolve the issue. There are some risks of misinterpretation of information, but the system does work well, especially with skillful and experienced contractors who already know how to solve most problems. The key element providing protection for our client, making sure he or she gets what was paid for, is not detailed drawings but rather an extremely detailed set of specifications that is usually in excess of 100 printed pages. Whatever the question is, the answer can be found in the specs.

STAKING OUT THE GREEN

However the design is communicated and the green is to be built, it needs to be laid out on the ground. Generally on new construction, the owner's surveyors put a stake in the middle of the green from coordinates or measurements taken from the architect's staking plan (see Figure 5-5). Once the center of the green is located, generally the designer will review the site and golf course routing plan to see the length and kind of approach shot that might be played to the green. Then, based upon that, the designer will designate the area for vegetation removal using ribbons, flags, stakes, paint, or whatever. Generally, a 6,000-square-foot green may need about 20,000 square feet or more of space to allow for the green surrounds, as well as permit reasonable light and air movement to reach the green.

If the green is part of a remodeling project, I advise getting approval of that committee of bosses that we all work for, and explaining the concept of the green at this stage as well as what vegetation is going to be removed. This can be critical if large trees are involved, for there can be a great deal of resistance to removing trees, even though everyone knows they need to go (see Figure 5-6). The other reason is that very few people can visualize what a green will look like based on a drawing, but if the green is laid out in the ground using stakes, flags, ribbons, paint or whatever, then they better visualize and approve the design. On remodeling work, I would advise bringing the committee back again to approve the green in the subgrade phase before tiling for one last approval. On new work, such committee involvement is more of a courtesy than in remodeling, where committee members and golfers feel more possessive about the old golf course.

Figure 5-5: Center of green is located on the ground from the plan and marked with a pole.

Figure 5-6: Once green is located, surrounding vegetation must be removed. This often includes removing trees that have been marked by the architect and approved by the owner's representative.

As the green is being staked or laid out, the designer should look for micro-climatic problems to correct or plan for, as well as decide on how to strategically integrate the green and surrounds. Sometimes greens are out in the middle of open, flat fields so it doesn't matter, but other times greens are placed in the middle of dense woods, on a steep slope, or surrounded by a swamp or some other confounding feature. Only after the site is cleared of vegetation can the best strategic design for the green and golf hole be determined and staked out.

TOPSOIL AND SURROUNDS

If the green site is blessed with topsoil, it should be stripped and saved for replanting the green surrounds after the subgrade is approved (see Figure 5-7). Sometimes the topsoil is stripped before the green is staked out; other times the green must be laid out first, the topsoil stripped using bulldozers or scrapers, and then the green restaked along with green surrounds.

"Surrounds" is a term that generally applies to all constructed earthwork features outside of the actual putting surface. This includes the green's collars, fringe, apron, approach, bunker(s), support mounds, grassy hollows, chipping areas, or backdrops. These are, of course, integrated as artistically as possible into the existing natural features of the green site, and when done properly make the entire green area seem to be one composition, or green complex.

DESIGN SUBGRADE

The actual physical building of the green and surrounds generally involves either removing or adding material (cutting or filling, respectively) to achieve the design subgrade of the green (see Figure 5-8). Design subgrade is a term used to designate the green and surrounds as constructed to the general size, shape, elevations, and outslopes of the final product, but before any tile drainage, irrigation, rootzone mix, or topsoil is added (see Figure 5-9). Design subgrade looks like what the green will look like except there is a cavity where the green mix will go, and the finish grade of the surrounds will be raised by the addition of topsoil and rootzone material. It is the equivalent of the green with no clothes on, but should clearly communicate exactly what the final constructed green will look like when fully dressed out.

A professional and competent designer will generally inspect this subgrade phase and make his or her final adjustments to the design, for at this stage of construction making changes or alterations is easy, fast, and cheap (see Figure 5-10). At any subsequent step in construction beyond design subgrade, making changes is going to be complicated and expensive, as well as jeopardizing the form and function of the green and rootzone. The world of greenkeeping is

Figure 5-7: Topsoil is stripped from green site for later replacement on the surrounds.

Figure 5-8: Often the grade at a green site must be raised or lowered by "filling" or "cutting," respectively, the subsoil layers.

Figure 5-9: "Design subgrade" is the term used to describe the green and surrounds after it has been graded with subsoil, prior to topsoiling or adding drainage or rootzone.

Figure 5-10: Final adjustments are made to the subgrade prior to installing drainage in the green cavity.

filled with horror stories of designers making changes in the final grades of the green, only to screw up the depth and function of the rootzone. Anyone who lacks the vision or commitment to inspect and approve design subgrades, and then not mess with them, is a rank amateur dabbling in golf green design; such a designer doesn't know what he or she is doing, and doesn't have a clue about the big picture.

With final adjustments made to the design subgrade, the next step is to refine the drainage system. Some surface drainage is already built in and is reflected in the subgrade elevations of the green cavity. The goal is to be close to 1.5 percent slope in useable cupset areas, with greater slopes used to separate and hence define target areas. If the greens are to be built to the USGA concept, although their recommendations say the limit of tolerance for the subgrade is plus or minus one-half inch, it really isn't as critical as for a California green. The reason, of course, is that the USGA green will have a gravel drainage blanket that can vary between two and four inches, or more, in depth, so as long as its surface of gravel is within plus or minus one-half inch of design finish grade, it is acceptable. The important thing is the uniform depth of the rootzone layer, not the gravel layer, but it is good workmanship to keep all layers of a parallel depth. The California green, however, requires that the design subgrade to be "spot on," as should any modified version of construction that does not use a gravel blanket. The subgrade should be stable and compact and relatively smooth.

TILING THE GREEN

Now comes the step that most folks just cannot seem to get correct—laying out the tile drainage pattern *perpendicular* to the flow of water across the slope. For emphasis, I am going to repeat that concept—lay out the tile drainage pattern *perpendicular* to the flow of water across the slope. (There, I've told you twice.) The main reason for the all-too-common mistake of not doing this is that most people are more concerned with "pretty" than with "function." In nearly every textbook, specification, recommendation, or published picture, tile drainage patterns are shown as a perfect herringbone or grid pattern, when in real life the green surface is not a perfectly flat sheet or surface. The design subgrade of a well-designed green will twist and turn, and so should the tile drainage pattern (see Figure 5-11). This is not as important with a USGA green, but for any green that does not have a gravel drainage blanket, getting the tile perpendicular to the slope is important, especially California greens. Forget how it looks—make it drain efficiently. They award points for "pretty" in figure skating, but not in tile installation, so forget "pretty."

An easy way to determine if tile drainage patterns are perpendicular to the slope is to observe the subgrade after a rain and look for the small erosions or water rivulets (see Figure 5-12). The other way is to do the best possible, using a level or laser to determine the slope, paint arrows on the subgrade indicating the drainage direction, install the drainage based upon those observations and

Figure 5-11: Install tile drainage perpendicular to slope of green subgrade. Some architects specify installing a tracer wire with the tile. (Courtesy of Karl Olson)

Figure 5-12: Drainage lines must be installed perpendicular to the surface flow or slope of the green. Notice how surface erosions show water is flowing between the tile lines, not into them. Drainage water should travel no more than 18 feet, especially on California greens. (Courtesy of Ed Walsh)

readings, and then after the irrigation is installed but prior to rootzone placement, run the irrigation to check the direction of water flow. Be prepared to add short runs of additional drainage if needed.

The idea is to minimize how far the water flows along the subgrade before reaching a tile line, with the optimal distance determined by laboratory test results of the rootzone, the quality of the irrigation water, and common sense and experience. If the rootzone has a high saturated hydraulic conductivity rate (Ksat) (sometimes called "perc rate") and the water quality is good, a wider (15 to 20 foot) spacing of tile makes sense. If the perc rate of the rootzone is low and/or the water quality is poor, then a closer spacing (5 to 10 feet) may be needed. Again, if there is any question about tile spacing, it should be discussed with the rootzone-testing lab or with a specialist in green construction.

Conventional or round tile for green drainage is generally of four-inch diameter, although in some locations only two- or three-inch diameter tile is available. Granted, there is not enough water going though a mature rootzone to even half fill a two-inch tile, but even so the preferred material is the four-inch because it is readily available and is more forgiving of construction errors than is a smaller tile.

If vacuum-assisted drainage is planned for the green, then the main line should be a six-inch tile, or the drainage area should be separated into two sections, each served by a four-inch main line. Some designers and contractors are partial to rigid pipe instead of flexible, but with four-inch pipe, laid on at least

Figure 2-41: A 1992 test to evaluate using flat pipe for green construction. The flat pipe was installed with and without the geotextile, and blended with various aggregate materials. Initial testing indicated that no geotextile was best, but now the recommendation calls for a coarse-weave "sock" — not traditional close-weave filter cloth.

Figure 2-42: Tile pattern is laid out on green subgrade. Notice catch basins around the green protected by straw bales.

Figure 2-43: Tile is overlapped, marked, and cut to fit together.

Figure 2-44: The tile is nailed into soil using 60-penny nails or long spikes.

Figure 2-45: Tape across joints keeps tile clean.

Figure 2-46: Rootzone mix is dumped directly over tile.

Figure 2-47: Small dozer spreads rootzone to grade stakes.

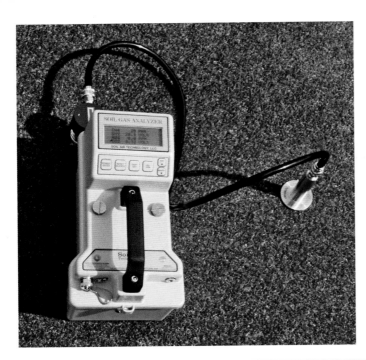

Figure 2-51: A portable gas analyzer can quickly measure rootzones for levels of oxygen, carbon dioxide, hydrogen sulfide, and methane. This permits the greenkeeper now to intelligently manage rootzone air.

Figure 3-17: Once the subgrade for bunkers is complete, the drainage matrix is rolled out on the steep slopes, the bunker edge painted on, and the matrix terminated into a drain line. (Courtesy of Bert McFadden)

Figure 3-18: A hard edge of plywood, plastic, or Masonite™ is established around the bunker perimeter and held in place by stakes until the bunker edges are grown in and stable. Once shape is determined, then topsoil can be installed on outside edge for planting or sodding. (Courtesy of Bert McFadden)

Figure 3-19: After the outside is topsoiled, lightly compacted, and finish graded, the outside of the bunker can be planted; in this case, it will be sodded. (Courtesy of Bert McFadden)

Figure 3-20: A nearly finished green side bunker on the 18th hole at Georgian Bay Club. Once turf is well established, sand will be installed and hard-edge material removed. (Courtesy of Bert McFadden)

Figure 6-1: Soil-testing laboratories specializing in, and accredited for, rootzone testing are the best estimator of potential performance; however, numerical test values should not be overemphasized. (Courtesy of Hummel & Co., Inc.)

Figure 6-10: To determine particle size distribution, a set of standard screen and shaker are used to separate the various textural fractions. (Courtesy of Hummel & Co., Inc.)

Figure 6-17: A tension table has a saturated base pad that is connected to a tube to create a fixed "suction," or tension, equal to a 40-cm column of water. This simulates bringing a sample to field capacity in a rootzone profile. (Courtesy of Hummel & Co., Inc.)

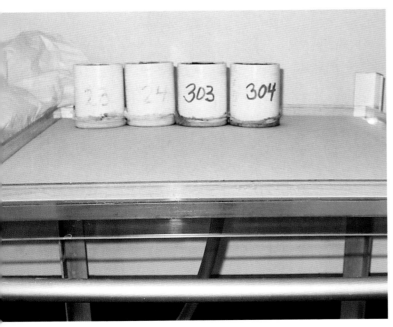

Figure 6-18: The sample core is compacted by dropping a standard weight 15 times from a height of one foot. (Courtesy of Hummel & Co., Inc.)

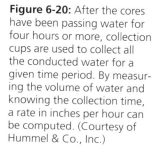

Figure 6-19: The permeameter is used to thoroughly saturate the core by keeping a constant head of water on the sample for at least four hours; the water is allowed to freely pass through the core. (Courtesy of Hummel & Co., Inc.)

Figure 6-20: After the cores have been passing water for four hours or more, collection cups are used to collect all the conducted water for a given time period. By measuring the volume of water and knowing the collection time, a rate in inches per hour can be computed. (Courtesy of Hummel & Co., Inc.)

Figure 6-21: After samples have been again brought to field capacity on the tension table, the samples are weighed, oven dried, and reweighed to determine water retention. (Courtesy of Hummel & Co., Inc.)

Figure 6-22: Particle density requires an apparatus called a pycnometer. Using all of the measured values, the technician can complete the performance analysis. (Courtesy of Hummel & Co., Inc.)

Figure 6-27: Ash content can be measured by weighing a sample, burning off the organic matter in a high-temperature muffle oven, and weighing the residual. (Courtesy of Hummel & Co., Inc.)

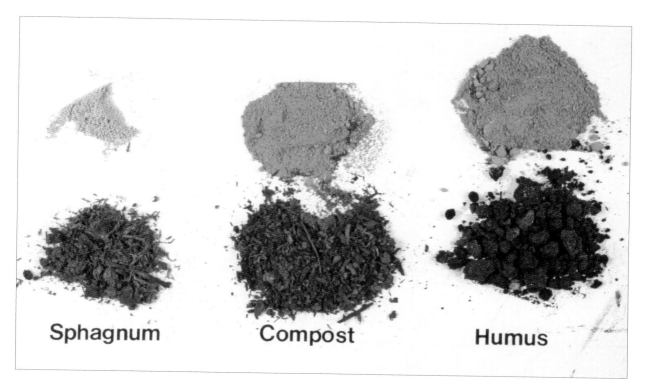

Sphagnum

Compost

Humus

Figure 6-28: Three samples of organic matter that look similar but contain very different amounts of ash. Low ash is preferred. (Courtesy of Hummel & Co., Inc.)

Figure 6-34: A penetrometer is currently the best measure of how well a bunker sand will resist displacement to avoid the dreaded "fried egg" lie. The test golf ball is pushed into the sample up to its equator, and the amount of force required is measured. (Courtesy of Hummel & Co., Inc.)

Figure 7-20: An artificial turf green built in the mid-1990s at Hurdzan/Fry Golf Course Design offices.

Figure 8-6: Some green sites, such as the par 3, 12th at Westwood Plateau, first had to have tree clearing done to reveal steep rock slope.

Figure 8-7: Rock was drilled and blasted into large chunks, to be hauled away and replaced by soil.

Figure 8-8: Soil subgrade is hauled in, compacted, shaped, and tiled at 12th green site of Westwood Plateau.

Figure 8-9: Green is tiled and ready for rootzone material. Notice topsoil and irrigation are also installed. The contractor is responsible for protecting the area against erosion and vandalism.

Figure 8-10: Procuring and protecting rootzone material until the area is planted is also the contractor's responsibility, unless otherwise specified in the contract documents.

Figure 8-12: Once the contactor has completed his or her work, the owner assumes the responsibility for the green, unless there is failure in the material or workmanship provided by the contractor. In addition, the owner is responsible for any employee, paying and nonpaying guests, as well as trespassers who visit that green.

Figure 9-1: Jack Kidwell, my late mentor, and me at Pinehurst. Jack's grass-roots approach to golf and golf courses shaped my thinking to try to do more with less.

one half of a percent (0.5 percent) grade, there is no functional difference between them. There is also no significant difference in the crush strength of either rigid or flexible, so they should be considered equal.

There are some designers who prefer to use perforated pipe inside the green cavity, and solid or nonperforated pipe outside it. I really do not understand why, unless the soil outside the green is so open that there is concern about it entering the tile, or unless vacuum-assisted drainage is to be used and there is a need to keep the system sealed. Otherwise, it makes good sense to use properly bedded, perforated pipe, both inside and outside the green cavity. There is some advantage in using smooth wall pipe for drainage in that, since it has no corrugations, it flows water better. In fact, it flows water 20 percent better and on flatter slopes. The minimum fall for a corrugated pipe is about one-half of a percent (0.5 percent), while for a smooth wall pipe it is one-tenth of a percent (0.1 percent). On flat sites, this is an important difference.

The usual method of tile installation is to dig a trench that allows for at least one inch on either side of the tile, that is, a four-inch tile needs at least a six-inch-wide trench (see Figure 2-3). The depth of trench should allow for at least two inches of gravel or coarse sand bedding on the bottom and the top of the tile. Therefore, the minimum trench size for a four-inch tile is six inches wide and eight inches deep (two inches of bedding, four inches of tile, two inches of covering, plus one inch of bedding on either side). These are minimum dimensions, but unless there is an overriding reason to expand them, such as keeping at least one-half percent fall or slope in the line when passing over high places, that is all that is needed. Even this minimum trench size will create enough excavated spoil to mess up the subgrade, so there is no reason to do any more than necessary.

Some contractors use trenchers that directly load the spoil into a truck or trailer for disposal; others simply dig the trench, then remove the spoil and regrade the subgrade, and yet others will try to "lose" the spoil between the trenches by slight mounding directed to the trenches. Most designers and agronomists would like to see the spoil taken away so there is no chance the spoil would block the overall surface drainage of the subgrade. This is even more critical when building greens without gravel drainage blankets.

One other tip is to mound the gravel above tile lines and French drain trenches, about one inch above the outside edges of the trench (see Figure 2-3). This mounded gravel acts like a "beehive" grate used to keep trash from covering over flat surfaces of drop inlets. If the grate or gravel were flat, it would be easy for a thin layer of silt to filter cake over the area and shut off the drainage. That is why during construction, contractors usually extend the pipe of drop inlets up in the air a couple of feet above grade, until the turf is well established around them and no erosion can take place, before cutting them off at grade and adding protective grates.

FLAT TILE

The other method of tiling is called by many names such as trenchless tile, flat pipe, flat tile, waffle drain, panel drain, and a few others. Basically, it consists of a tile material that is about 2 inches thick and either 12 or 18 inches wide, laid flat on the subgrade—perpendicular to the flow line. Since there is no trenching, no gravel or sand bedding, and no spoil to clean up, flat tile is about 25 to 50 percent less expensive to install than trenched tile, and works as well or better. However, it is also more critical that the subgrade surface be properly prepared and that the tile be laid out correctly. The flat pipe is generally nailed into the subgrade with 60-penny nails (barn nails, gutter spikes, or staples). This is meant only to hold the tile in place until the rootzone is placed over it. Flat pipe was also discussed in Chapter 2 (see Figures 2-42 through 2-47).

No round or flat tile should ever be used with a tight weave geotextile, which can filter cake and clog. Avoid using geotextiles anywhere in drainage systems. The *only* time a geotextile is acceptable is when it is an extremely open weave, like a burlap bag, and when the material in which it is being bedded is extremely fine. Otherwise, all geotextiles are subject to filter caking and are destined to fail. Below is a quote taken directly from the drainage manual of a very large drainage pipe manufacturer:

> A drain envelope has two major functions, one, to restrain soil from entering the drain, except for the very fine particles suspended in the drainage water, and two, to allow unrestricted entry of water. A drain envelope is not successful unless both of these functions are satisfied.
>
> The role of the envelope "to stabilize the soil" cannot be over emphasized. Drain envelopes are often considered to be "filters." A drain envelope that operates as a filter as commonly defined is doomed to failure. The filter may perform well in preventing sediment from entering the drain, but because soil particles accumulate on the filter or within its voids, flow is drastically reduced. Continued filtration results in progressive reduction of flow. Thus a filter prevents sediment entry, but in so doing causes the drain to fail as a drain. (Courtesy of *A.D.S. Drainage Handbook,* Appendix D)

If at all possible, substitute fine gravel bedding for any and all geotextiles. Only when there is no other alternative should geotextile around drain tiles be considered, and then only with a written guarantee from the manufacturer to take full responsibility if the material doesn't function properly as an envelope for the life of the tile. Geotextiles clog up; that is why they are used for silt fence. In fact, take a piece of silt fence and hold it up to the light and observe the openings, and then hold to the light a piece of the geotextile you are considering using, and decide which one has more openings for drainage. If it is the silt fence, which is designed to stop silt, then keep looking for another geotextile—or for a source of fine gravel.

SMILE DRAIN

The single most important piece of tile in any green is the smile drain, or the tile that is placed as close to the interface of the rootzone cavity and the collar of the green as possible, at places where surface drainage is expected to leave the green. The name comes from the fact that the tile looks like a facial smile (see Figure 5-13). Without the smile drain, free water could move horizontally through the rootzone and accumulate where it meets the edge of the green cavity and finer textured soils. This is particularly true where a plastic liner or moisture barrier is used around a USGA green. This excess water could weaken the turf, allow the area to become more compacted or subject to displacement by traffic, or allow water to seep into the soils beneath the collar and cause problems there. Smile drains usually follow the shape of the green and ignore the rest of the overall tile drainage pattern. In fact, some designers like to ring the entire outside perimeter with a smile, now called "circle," drain, especially if the green is an area with lots of natural precipitation or poor water quality. In any case, round tile works better than flat tile for smile drains because it bends more easily when going around corners. There is no problem

Figure 5-13: The "smile" drain is the single most important part of the drainage system, for it catches the water in the lowest or outfall sections of the green cavity. In this picture, the tile line on the far right was installed to catch runoff onto the green from the surrounds. (Courtesy of Ed Walsh)

using round tile for smile or circle drains and flat tile for the rest of the drainage field. The key is to lay out the tile (now think, yes, that's right) *perpendicular* to the flow of the water on the subgrade.

There are some designers who separate green drainage from any other drainage of the surrounds, such as bunkers. The theory is that bunkers are a source of contamination to the drainage pipe, but that is only true if the pipe is not properly installed or bedded. Otherwise, tying green and surround drainage together is not a problem. The only time that green and surround drainage must be separated is if a vacuum-assisted drainage system is going to be used. Since the vacuum will cause the air to follow the path of least resistance, it is more likely most of the vacuum will be lost through the bunkers and not the green. Of course, if it is a championship course in an area that gets big rain during tournament week, then having a drainage system dedicated to greens and a separate one for bunkers or play areas might make sense—at a course like Augusta National, for example.

As stated earlier, if a vacuum-assisted drainage system is expected to get a lot of use, then using 18-inch-wide flat tile, with a 2-inch gravel layer between the tile lines, and connected to a 6-inch round tile as the main line, will give best efficiency (see Figure 5-14). In extreme cases, it may be advisable to have two main lines of 6 inches, with each main draining about half of the green surface. The halves can be front and back, left and right, sun and shade, upper and lower, or whatever makes the best sense to have the vacuum system make green maintenance easier.

Figure 5-14: Green at Tucson Country Club that shows correct method to install 6-inch round tile and 12-inch flat pipe with gravel backfill to maximize efficiency of vacuum-assisted drainage. (Courtesy of Karl Olson)

DROP INLETS AND CLEAN OUTS

Any discussion of tile drainage should include drop inlets and "clean outs" (see Figures 5-15 and 5-16). Drop inlets are simply ways for surface water to drop directly into drainage lines and not filter through sand, gravel, or soil. Drop inlets are usually nothing more than a "tee" in the drain line that comes to the surface and is covered by a grate or strainer of some kind. As a rule of thumb, it is a good idea not to allow surface drainage to run more than 150 feet across a play area before it goes into a drop inlet. This means that just outside the green cavity but into the surrounds, there should be as many drop inlets as required to handle the anticipated flow. Our office actually uses a combination of drop inlets and French drains tile in gravel-filled trenches capped by soil and turf in the surrounds, with gravel placed around the drop inlets to keep that area as dry as possible.

Where the notion of "clean outs" came from I have no idea, but they began to be used in the late 1970s, perhaps when someone had too much time on his or her hands, for I think they are a waste of money and actually pose more potential problems than they can solve. The idea is that at the extreme upstream end of the main line, or of the laterals if you are really anal, the end of the tile will be turned up and capped at the surface. Then, in the event that the tile line gets clogged, you simply remove the cap, insert a water hose into the end, and "Away go troubles down the drain," to quote an old ad jingle. Now this seems commonsensical enough if you do not give it too much thought.

Figure 5-15: "Clean outs" or "flush outs" installed as part of the green drainage are of questionable value, in the author's opinion. (Courtesy of Shaun Henry)

Figure 5-16: Drop inlets may also be installed as part of green drainage or separately, but they allow the designer to drain hollows in the green surrounds.

My questions are: Where did this blockage, large enough to fill a four-inch tile, come from? Where are you going to flush it, assuming you could flush it? Why won't the flush water simply run out the perforation in the tile above the blockage, run around the blockage in the bedding, and get back in the tile on the other side of the blockage? How did you know you had a blockage to begin with and that it was in the main line and not in a lateral? Why won't the water build up in the tile behind the blockage and flow out into the laterals, tile bedding, and rootzone? And a bunch of other equally valid questions can be asked. I have never seen a blockage in a properly installed tile, except for an occasional animal that might crawl into the discharge pipe, get stuck, die, bloat, stink, and then decay. The answer here is to simply put a grate or a flapper valve on the discharge end of the pipe to keep animals out. Clean outs are a waste of time and money and they simply become a place for debris (grass clippings, leaves, dirt, etc.) to enter an otherwise sealed and protected tile system.

The only—repeat only—time such a "clean out" has merit is when nowhere along the entire length of the tile system does the tile "daylight" or come to "atmosphere." These are descriptive terms, for they indicate that the tile is directly open to the atmosphere so there can be no vacuum or pressure buildup in the tile. The only way such buildup can occur is if the tile drainage from the green has no drop inlets in the outflow or discharge pipe, and the discharge pipe is terminated below water level in a water body. Then the tile will not function properly, and a relief opening like a drop inlet, just one, is all that is needed, somewhere along the length of the system.

ANIMAL GUARDS

Speaking of discharge pipe, it is a good idea for the last ten feet of the pipe to be of a sturdier material than the rest of the tile. Typically, this can be corrugated metal or aluminized pipe, schedule 160 or 200 irrigation pipe, or some other material that critters will not eat. Animals will chew holes in polyethylene or thin PVC pipe, UV light breaks it down, and mowers can grind it up. The best idea is to terminate the discharge line with a sturdy pipe, bedded in concrete to hold and protect it, and put some stiff wire or a couple of bolts over the opening to keep out God's little creatures.

MOISTURE OR WICKING BARRIER

Once the drainage system is installed and the subgrade is reestablished where disrupted, the next step is to place the plastic liner, or moisture, or wicking barrier around the outside perimeter of the green cavity (see Figures 5-17 and 5-18).

Figure 5-17: Wicking or moisture barrier placed around perimeter of green to prevent soil of surrounds from "sucking" moisture out of green's rootzone. Note how tile exists below barrier. (Courtesy of Cole McInnis)

Figure 5-18: Note how tile drainage goes under or through the wicking barrier placed around the green cavity. (Courtesy of Cole McInnis)

This is an optional step and is based upon the likelihood that the soils outside the green cavity will wick water by capillarity out of the rootzone mix that has been selected. The finer textured these outside soils and the coarser textured the rootzone mix is, the greater the chance there will be moisture retention problems along the outside perimeter of the green. If there is any doubt this moisture barrier is needed, first check out an accredited soil-testing lab that does rootzone testing, or just put the plastic liner in. There have been some problems with water building up on the inside of the moisture barrier, especially if there are not enough smile drains installed on the green. In this instance, removing the wicking barrier once the green has matured solves the problem.

The usual way to install a moisture barrier is to cut a roll of 10- to 20-mil plastic into 24- to 30-inch wide rolls. Then unroll the plastic around the edge of the green perimeter and sod staple one edge to the bottom of the green cavity. Lay the plastic up along the vertical edge of the green cavity and either sod staple it in place at the top or tuck it in under some loose soil of the subgrade material. Some contractors prefer to install a row of sturdy stakes around the perimeter of the green and then staple or glue the liner to the stakes. After the rootzone material is in place, and the surrounds are topsoiled, then the remaining plastic above grade will be cut off about one-half inch below finish grade. If the wood stake method is used, the stakes should be removed before final grading is done.

ROOT BARRIER

Similar to the moisture barrier, tree root barriers are either thick plastic liner or geotextiles made with root-stopping chemical materials that are placed vertically in a trench just outside the putting surface (see Figure 5-19). Depending upon the species of the tree, these barriers may extend downward four feet or more, and digging a trench that size yields a lot of dirt, and hence mess. It is best to place this root barrier outside the collar of the green, and this can be done either before or after the tiling operation. If it is done before tiling, the root barrier material will be cut by the exit lines from the tile and the entrance lines for the irrigation, so appropriate repairs should be made to the barrier. If it goes in after tiling, then the root barrier will cut the exit lines of the tile, and of course repairs will be made there, too. Irrigation entrance lines will cut it regardless, so those repairs should be expected, but by placing the root barrier material far enough out in the collar, multiple disruptions of the barrier can be avoided as the irrigation loops system goes in around the green. Obviously, the root barrier material needs to come right to the top of the finish grade if it is to stop "surface roots."

Figure 5-19: Detail of geo-textile designed to control root encroachment. (Courtesy of Biobarrier)

REESTABLISH GRADES

Regardless of the concept of green construction to be used, the next operation is to reshape the subgrade of the green well, reestablish its edges or walls, and then grade stake the cavity of the green to receive the rootzone material. The regrading of the subgrade is to assure that there are no pockets in the subgrade where water could puddle and cause soft spots that may settle or displace. Every place within the green cavity should slope toward a drain line, at a minimum of 1.5 percent.

If USGA greens are to be built, then cavity walls need to be vertical, and if the concept is California, the walls are laid back at a 4:1 or 6:1 slope. But in all cases, grade stakes should be placed every 10 to 20 feet, and the finish elevations of layers to go into the cavity are marked on the grade stakes (see Figure 5-14). It is wise to place the grade stakes along and immediately adjacent to the tile lines. This permits the builder to know where these lines are and to protect them from crushing by subsequent construction equipment.

Grade stakes for USGA greens should reflect the depth of the gravel layer specified, the depth of intermediate layer if used, and then the rootzone material. These grade stakes should be maintained through each and every operation of adding material to the green well or cavity. This permits a quick inspection of the depth and grade of the layer, as well as assures that tile lines are identified and protected from heavy traffic. It is also a good idea to check depth of layers by probing as they are spread (see Figure 5-20).

Figure 5-20: Checking depth of gravel layer with a probe as layer is smoothed out to receive rootzone material. (Courtesy of Steve Miles)

Figure 5-21: This method of filling the green uses both a conveyor truck and a small bulldozer. Simply dumping rootzone at the edge of the green and spreading works well too. Notice rootzone being watered down as it is installed so it will compact better. (Courtesy of Karl Olson)

FILLING THE GREEN CAVITY

The best way to install material inside the cavity is to dump it along the edge, and then push it out with a small dozer or other high flotation machine, or with a conveyor truck (see Figure 5-21). By working on the filled material, there is less chance of contamination from the subgrade and better protection for the tile drainage system. Of course, spreading the material by hand with landscape rakes and shovels is permissible too, as is using trucks with built-in conveyor belts and shoots. If the subgrade is especially firm, then backing in loaded, small trailers or trucks between the tile lines works, but equipment should never be allowed to run directly over the drainage lines, only between them. Any tracks left by such equipment must be filled and smoothed out or they will become water filled and remain soft long after construction. Although there are lots of ways to fill the green cavity, dumping on the inside edge and working to the middle is the most popular.

Just about every kind of green cavity fill, except pea gravel, will settle appreciably. This is why maintaining the grade stakes is so important. Typically, rootzone material will settle 2 to 3 inches, so contractors will usually place 14 to 15 inches of it in the green, knowing it is going to settle to around 12 inches. Even then, more rootzone material may be required, for the tolerance of workmanship is usually plus or minus one-half inch. If grade stakes are pulled out before the material has settled, determining whether the depths of layers are correct becomes a guessing game. Sure, one can take a probe and probe and measure every five feet or so across the putting surface, but leaving the grade stakes in place is easier, faster, and more accurate.

COMPACTING THE ROOTZONE

Settling fill material can be done several ways. One of the most common is to wheel track or compact the finished surface with a light farm or turf tractor by simply running back and forth until the material doesn't compact any more (see Figure 5-22). The material should be moist, not wet or dry, but with enough moisture so it compresses. The best way to compact rootzone materials is to use lots of water and time, but adding a roller or wheel tracking works when time is short. If the irrigation system goes in before final compaction is needed, then running the irrigation frequently and heavily will often work. Putting a vibrating roller on the rootzone helps settle materials whose particles are rounded, but even then proper moisture is important to get best results. If in doubt, compact or settle the rootzone some more, for it is essential that the rootzone not sink once it is planted. When that does happen, the edges of the putting surface will usually be lower than the collar, which blocks surface drainage. These areas will tend to scalp with mowing, they deflect balls unfairly, and they look horri-

Figure 5-22: Compacting the rootzone material requires a combination of watering to moisten the sand and then using a machine to compress it. Notice water hose in the foreground to add additional moisture needed to get good compaction. (Courtesy of Matt Wolf)

ble. I would liken an uneven interface between putting surface and collar to hammer marks on woodwork and corners on a cabinet that do not butt up evenly.

There is some argument among academicians and theoretical agronomists about the wisdom of working the rootzone so heavily once it is placed on the green, their concern being that the mechanical operations of hauling, dumping, spreading, and compacting rootzone material create more fine particles. I personally never subscribed to that notion, but recently we have had test results that showed that the fines do increase with hauling by as much as 8 percent. Samples were taken at the sand source and tested. Then once the material was in the green and compacted, samples were again taken, sent to the same lab, and the results indicated increased fines. It would be easy to dismiss these results by saying the problem was contamination during movement and placement, but not 8 percent worth. This area needs further study.

PROTECTING THE ROOTZONE

If the rootzone is going to be on the green for several weeks or more, then efforts should be made to protect it from contamination. Typical sources of rootzone surface contamination are blowing dust and water erosion. It is not uncommon to have the top one-half inch or more of rootzone accumulate enough contamination to cause it to crust or even make it impervious to rain or irrigation water (see Figure 5-23). The first line of defense is to put up a fence;

Figure 5-23: Wind and water-driven contamination of the rootzone, once placed in the green cavity, can make the top one-half inch crusty and, in some cases, dramatically change the infiltration rate. Irrigating with muddy or murky water can do the same thing.

either ring the green in three-foot high silt fence material or, in extreme cases, use five-foot snow fencing and then add the silt fence over that (see Figure 5-24). If water erosion is the problem, straw bales may be needed to redirect the flow. Of course the other alternative is to simply scoop off the accumulated foreign material prior to final grading, but this takes a delicate touch so as not to mix the contamination into the upper profile of the rootzone itself. If there is any doubt, carefully skim the rootzone surface to get a sample of material, then send it to the lab for testing, along with a sample taken four to six inches down for comparison.

Another problem that can occur in a rootzone mix between blending, placement, and planting is the decomposition in organic matter if any was blended in. By its very nature, organic matter is some state of decomposition, between its original source and its final end products of mineralization. Some materials are very stable, while others with low cellulose and lignin, and high carbon-to-nitrogen content are very unstable. The unstable ones can nearly be totally lost in six months or less, plus one must be concerned about the by-products of that decomposition. Typically, these by-products will be humic and fulvic acid derivatives, which are known to coat sand particles and make them hydrophobic. Remember, this rootzone blend has been tested and retested, but just sitting in a pile or in a green well can change properties enough for the blend to become unacceptable by test criteria. It doesn't happen often, and at first I was surprised by this event, but as time goes on, I find it happens much more frequently than any of us would like to believe, although usually not too dramatically.

In an established green, the problem manifests itself as localized dry spot (LDS), particularly in the top few inches, or as the old timers would call it, "dry mulch." Once the sand gets this coating, there is little that can be done but keep the rootzone well aerated and use wetting agents or surfactants. If this hydrophobic situation happens in the stockpile before placement, one approach is to try to rewet the material and keep it moist, or blend the material with fresh sand to dilute the problem. None of these solutions is easy or cheap, but the problem is real. To lessen the problem, use only lab-approved organic matter sources, try to avoid long stockpile periods, and if there is any question, retest the material before placement.

A final word on this phenomenon of the rootzone material changing performance characteristics after blending: some theorize that the addition of fertilizer during blending, especially nitrogen-containing fertilizers, will exacerbate the potential problem. This is especially true if the carbon-to-nitrogen ratio of the organic matter is greater than 40:1, and hence potentially somewhat unstable, so ideally one would like to see that ratio closer to 20:1 or lower. Also it is possible that if the stockpile is subjected to very much moisture, active composting can occur within the stockpile. This has led some contractors to cover the rootzone stockpile with huge plastic sheets, or to keep it under some sort of roof. This may be worrying too much about an infrequent problem, but like snakebite, once you've had this trouble, you don't soon forget it.

FUMIGATION

Fumigation of the rootzone material only needs to be done when it has been conclusively determined it is required to control some endemic pest, such as nematodes or weed seeds (see Figure 5-25). This is a reasonably expensive operation, especially because the chemicals used are so dangerous, and hence tightly regulated by government agencies. The fumigants can be solids, liquids, or gases, and usually are short-term with no residual effects, which means the possibility of reinfestation, especially by nematodes.

The most common fumigant for large-scale areas has been methyl bromide, and it is usually applied after the rootzone mix is in place, but before compaction. This more open state of the rootzone allows the gas to penetrate more deeply and kill more pests. A commercial applicator will inject the material into the soil profile and then immediately cover the area with a plastic sheet for a few hours. Methyl bromide has been suspected as a casual agent in the depletion of the ozone, and is being phased out of use as stocks are used up; however, there is hope that the ban will be reduced to just heavy restrictions for professional use only.

Alternatives to methyl bromide are being used, such as compounds using dichloroproshone and chloropicrin, metham sodium, methyl isothiocyanate,

Figure 5-25: Fumigation of rootzone once it is in place is the most common way to kill weed seeds and nematodes, which may complicate establishment and future maintenance of putting surfaces.

and a few other research compounds. None of this material is quite as good as methyl bromide, but there is hope for fumigation if it is required. Fumigation is generally most common in hot humid climates, which tend to favor nematode population. It is rare to fumigate greens above the transition zone, and is not recommended unless critical, for fumigation is nondiscriminatory and kills beneficial organisms as well as harmful ones. After the covers are removed, the greens need to breathe for a day or two, and then be compacted. Care should be taken to not recontaminate the greens during the compaction, finish grade, and seeding operations that follow. Cleaning wheels and tracks of equipment, staying on the putting surface with equipment as opposed to tracking on and off the surrounds as much as possible, and using general common sense is about all that can be done.

RETOPSOILING

Placing or replacing topsoil can either precede or follow placing the rootzone mix (see Figure 5-26). The advantage of placing it before the rootzone is that the green well is well defined and is nearer to finish grade to hold the vapor barrier in place. The disadvantage is that the topsoil gets compacted where equipment must run during rootzone placement, and unless fluffed up, will be difficult to grade out and grow turf on later. Waiting to place the topsoil after the rootzone placement obviously avoids the differential compaction described above, there is less contamination of topsoil with the rootzone material, and no

Figure 5-26: Replacing top-soil around the green can take place either before or after rootzone installation, and there are advantages and disadvantages to either time.

topsoil is lost or wasted through the traffic of rootzone placement equipment. The disadvantage is that greater care must be taken in placing the topsoil at interface of rootzone to collar. Some designers solve this problem by carrying the rootzone material out into the collar, but this is an expensive solution. Others place thin Masonite® sheets, cut 18 to 24 inches wide, as a temporary barrier to protect the rootzone material during topsoiling. Slow and easy with emphasis on good workmanship is the best way to reduce unwanted mixing of the rootzone and topsoil used on collars. Grade stakes are often used to ensure a uniform layer of topsoil on the surrounds, and as a rule the sandier and deeper the topsoil, the better it is for growing turf. The most difficult place to establish acceptable golf course turf is within three or four feet on either side of the interface between collar and putting surface. I believe much of the reason is compaction caused by construction and maintenance equipment. Recently, I have observed superintendents requiring their crews to place four-foot by eight-foot sheets of plywood down along the collar of new greens, on which to turn their mowers, to reduce the physical injury to turf on the collar, as well as to minimize soil compaction.

IRRIGATION INSTALLATION

Before the topsoil is finish graded, the irrigation must be installed, and here again the question is whether this should be done before or after topsoiling (see Figure 5-27). Trenching for irrigation lines is going to yield a fair amount of spoil that must be cleaned up either off the topsoil or before the topsoil is

Figure 5-27: Irrigation installation can either precede or follow topsoiling of surrounds, based upon various site conditions. When there is lots of rock, it is better to install irrigation first, then topsoil. (Courtesy of Ed Walsh)

placed. Most contractors would prefer to work on the subgrade for as long as possible before putting down the topsoil, especially if very much rock is going to be found during trenching. If the rock is small, it can be dug out. If it is large, it may require jackhammering, rock saws, or even drilling and blasting, all of which can cause a huge mess. There are also the advantages of being able to settle the trench by flooding and/or compaction without contaminating surrounding topsoil, as well as setting the irrigation heads close to grade. Trenches that settle after planting are a huge problem for everyone, so good contractors work hard at getting all trenches compacted (see Figure 5-28).

The disadvantage of topsoiling after irrigation installation is that irrigation heads must be set high above proposed finish grade, so workmen readily see their location, and there is a high likelihood of damaging heads during the topsoiling operation. From the designer's point of view, it really does not matter whether topsoiling or irrigation installation comes first. If topsoil is at all limiting or a precious commodity on a particular project, I would opt for topsoiling as late as possible, for the earlier it goes down, the greater is the probability of loss, contamination, and compaction.

Once the irrigation is installed, it should be flushed clean of any debris or dirt in the line, brought up to pressure, and each head cycled using the control system, then brought to maximum line pressure and isolated to check for a 24-hour leak down. A pressure gauge installed on a quick coupler key can give quick readings. If no pressure drop is detected, then the next step in construction can begin.

Figure 5-28: Compacting trenches to avoid settling after seeding is a prime concern for the best contractors. To a golf course contractor, a settled trench after grow-in is like a hammer mark on wood trim to a finish carpenter.

CONTROLLING WEEDS DURING CONSTRUCTION

Early topsoiling can also produce a serious crop of weeds from seeds that are in the soil or that get scattered from adjacent areas. The greatest nuisance is, of course, a grass weed such as common Bermuda grass in southern regions, and panicum in northern ones. Foxtail, crabgrass, *Poa annua* spp., and a few other grass weeds seem to be common everywhere. The problem is that, if left to grow to any size, these weeds produce their crop of weed seeds, they are very difficult to kill, and trying to finish grade the topsoil is next to impossible unless all of the plants' crown and root system are loosened, raked up, and removed, or hand picked. The grass weeds can be controlled with materials like Round-up®, Fusilade®, Finale®, or MSMA (monosodium methylarsonate), but the older the plants become, the more difficult they are to kill, frequently requiring multiple treatments, with seven- to ten-day waiting periods in between. On top of that, it is doubtful that the contractor has anyone on the crew who is a licensed pesticide applicator, or has proper spray equipment, and pesticide storage can be an issue. Even though contracting out the spraying solves some of the problems, weed control still adds time and money to the construction project. Although leaving the topsoil stockpiled as long as possible tends to allow a healthy weed crop on its exterior, inside the pile lots of weed seeds are being destroyed by soil organisms. Covering topsoil piles with plastic not only tends to kill the seeds that germinate on the surface but also, through heat buildup, can reduce the viability of remaining seeds.

FINISH GRADE ON SURROUNDS

Final or finish grading of the green and surrounds requires a higher degree of skillful workmanship in grading than anywhere else on the golf course. The reason is that, since this area will be mowed so closely, every little bump or dip will ultimately show up as a scalped area or an area of longer grass. Typically, the soils of the surrounds, both subsoil and topsoil, will usually settle at a different rate and depth than the rootzone material, so trying to produce a seamless edge between putting surface and surrounds takes some extra planning and time (see Figure 5-29). It would be nice if all soils and rootzone blends would be firmly compacted before final grade out, and if they would both settle uniformly over time. Rarely does that happen, so some designers and agronomists suggest building the collars and fringes of the green out of the rootzone material, especially with the USGA type green that has a vertical edge to the cavity. This is an excellent idea but can be very expensive, almost doubling the rootzone material cost. Since the recommended method for building a California type green is to lay the edges of the green cavity back into

Figure 5-29: Creating a seamless edge between putting surface, collar, and surrounds requires lots of skill, patience, and determination. The finish grade process is much easier if rootzone material is spread out onto the collar area.

Figure 5-30: Soil in the surrounds should be loosened before final grade.

194

the collar at a soft angle (4:1 to 6:1), this isn't as big a problem. In fact, in my opinion, tapering the edges of USGA greens back this way would not at all affect their function, and would reduce the problem of differential settling at the interface.

Some contractors like to have crews hand rake the green and surrounds, but this often produces a worse result than if machine graded, and at a higher cost. The reason is that, although a hand-raked green and surround may look nice, this operation hides the hard or compacted spots, or fills in low areas with fluffy soils that blow, settle, or wash out later, leaving the low spot. Hand raking is hard work, usually done under miserable working conditions, and is exceedingly boring, so workmen are usually low paid, poorly trained, and just going through the motions, so their level of workmanship is often also low.

It would be far better if the contractor used a machine like a disc, rock hound, or rotovator to loosen the topsoil down three or four inches. I have seen one contractor use a quadratine aerifier to loosen tee tops and green collars, prior to final grading. If a plow down or corrective fertilizer application is required based upon soil tests, it can be applied just before or just after the loosening operation. Most agronomists would like to see it applied before rather than after this loosening operation. Then use a light grading tool like a Harrogator, Gill, Viking or some other small hydraulically controlled grading tool to lightly recompact and grade the green surrounds (see Figure 5-30). The key is for the operator to be able to raise and lower the cutting or grading edge to cut or fill areas as necessary. It takes a highly skilled and caring craftsman, taking his or her time, to do this well. It is virtually impossible for this final grade person(s) to work alone, for there should be an equally skillful and caring person on the ground with a rake and shovel, working in tandem with the machine. The ground person checks grades, picks up rocks or debris, identifies areas to be cut or filled, protects sprinkler heads, and rakes and shovels small areas that the machine misses. The ground person should also identify areas of soil that are too compact and need loosening, as well as areas that are too loose and need compacting.

FINISH GRADE ON PUTTING SURFACE

Once the outside of the green is pretty close to grade, wash or clean the machine, then go to the inside green or onto the putting surface and grade it (see Figure 5-31). Before this happens, the ground control worker, using a soil probe and measuring device, needs to probe the depth of the rootzone and mark any areas that are too deep or too shallow, and put in a grade stake (see Figure 5-32). Many of the original grade stakes may, or should, still be in place, which will help speed up this process, for one can usually see where adjust-

Figure 5-31: Once the outside of the green is close to grade, then the machine goes onto the putting surface to begin to grade it. (Courtesy of Ed Connor)

Figure 5-32: "Rubbing down" or "floating out" a green means smoothing and compacting the surface as well as checking all grades to make sure that percentages of slope are correct.

ments in rootzone depth must be made. The goal is a rootzone depth that is within a half inch, plus or minus, of the depth specified by the laboratory testing and the specifications. Once the rootzone depth is pretty uniform over the entire putting surface, the grade stakes can be pulled out. Now the machine should work inside the putting surface in large, open circles to "rub down" the green into smooth grades that transition one into another as per the designer's instructions (see Figure 5-32). This shouldn't take very long, 20 to 30 minutes, after which time the machine should be stopped and the machine operator and ground controller should set up a laser level and verify all slopes within the putting surface. This means maintaining adequate surface drainage to drain the green, but yet keeping the designated cupset or hole location areas gentle enough (characteristically 1.5 percent) to allow for skillful putting when the greens are firm and fast. Using different color wire flags (also called pin flags) and a felt tip marker, mark out areas that need to be raised or lowered. Again, the amount of material moved should be less than an inch if all of the previous operations were properly done.

The last step before preparation for planting is normally called final grading, and it means just that. Very little effort should be required for this step, and it primarily focuses on the blending of the interface between collar and putting surface. Now the machine and ground controller will start in the middle of the green and slowly work the grades from that point across the putting surface, out onto the collar and fringe and to the outside of the surrounds. Then the machine lifts the grading tool and goes back to the center of the green and again grades or drags a very small amount of material from the middle of the green to the outside. This operation is repeated until the grades of the putting surface and the collar are harmonious. The final pass with the machine may be around the perimeter of the putting surface, with half the cutting edge on the putting surface and the other half on the collar.

PREPLANT SOIL AMENDMENTS

By now there is no clear defined edge between putting surface and collar, so the next step is to probe the area to find where the rootzone is at full depth and mark it with wire flags every 15–20 feet, or as necessary, to define the shape of the putting surface. This is a good time to run a second test of the irrigation system and controllers. Now is the time to bring in the hand rakers if needed, to pick up rocks and debris, cut out any remaining weeds, clean around and level sprinkler heads, and make slight adjustments to the grades. Some contractors prefer to spread the preplant fertilizer and amendments (remember, the plow down or corrective fertilizer went down at soil loosening—this is the preplant) before raking or final grading, while others believe that this can often result in windrowing or uneven displacement of the fertilizer, especially if any small

Figure 5-33: Preplant soil amendments should be applied immediately prior to seeding but after final grade has been approved by the golf course designer.

adjustments to grade are required (see Figure 5-33). Therefore, they prefer to apply preplant fertilizer after all approvals are given to proceed with planting. Some designers specify that preplant materials can only be applied within 72 hours of planting to avoid losses by natural causes such as wind, water, or other displacement. This may seem to be a trivial precaution until one observes the difference it makes in the speed and uniformity of seed germination or stolon or sod rooting. In fact, our firm not only endorses the 72-hour rule but also further requires that all broadcast or topically applied materials must be lightly raked into the top inch or so of the planting area, in a straight-line manner. In other words, it is unacceptable to use a sand trap rake and/or a drag and drive around in circles on the planting bed to work in the preplant application (see Figure 5-34). When someone violates that straight-line raking procedure, it is very obvious from the time that the turf starts to grow and lasts many months.

Some preplant specifications may require individual applications of materials that do not share spreading or distribution characteristics. For example, a light, fluffy organic material like seaweed powder or a micronutrient package may be physically incompatible with a poly-coated, slow-release, large prill-sized fertilizer. One may go down better with a drop spreader while others may be best broadcast. Some may require mixing with a carrier such as dry sand, a fine-grain organic fertilizer, or some inert material like ground-up corncobs. There is a trend to use a total preplant package that is uniformly blended and can be applied in one operation with a drop spreader. The fewer times a piece of equipment must go across the planting bed, the fewer footprints and wheel marks there will be to contend with later. One last test of the irrigation at this point may help settle the dust and firm up the planting areas. However, be careful not to make the surrounds too wet and soft for the operations that follow.

Figure 5-34: Once preplant amendments are applied, they should be incorporated into the top inch or so in a straight-line pattern. Driving in circles windrows the amendments and often results in uneven germination and establishment. (Courtesy of Matt Wolf)

PREPLANT PUNCH LIST

A "punch list" is jargon for a list of deficiencies or errors in construction that contractors must fix before their contractual obligations are complete. Typically, the punch list is put together by having representatives from the owner, contractor, and designer review the contractor's completed work together and agree on a list of remaining items of work that are the contractor's responsibility. It is almost like a contract within a contract, for unless otherwise specified, most contract laws would support the notion that once the punch list items are satisfactorily completed, the contractor is done with his or her work, except for guaranteed items. Consequently, punch lists are usually one of the last items of business, and for other building trades, this makes good sense, but not necessarily for a golf course project that is a living complex that must now be nurtured into maturation. This nurturing normally involves frequent, light irrigation, restriction of traffic, protecting soft soils, and so on, all of which can enormously complicate making construction repairs after planting. A better procedure for green construction is to do a punch list prior to preplant and/or planting, for at that point it is easy to make any needed corrections. Doing punch list work later, after the turf is well enough established to support whatever construction equipment is needed, often means doing patchwork repairs that never blend in and hence detract from the finished product.

There is no set procedure for writing a punch list, so techniques range from wandering around the work until a deficiency strikes someone to a more methodical approach of using a checklist. Since this is a textbook, it will advocate the checklist approach. Being that there are no standard checklists, the owner, his or her representative, and the designer have full freedom to add or delete items from this suggested list as best suits their needs, and as reflective of the contract obligations and limitations. As a starting point I have included a sample checklist below:

SAMPLE GREEN CONSTRUCTION CHECKLIST

I. Rootzone Material

A. Spot-check depths with probe.
B. Make small composite sample, air dry, label, and save in water-proof container for future testing if required.
C. Insure rootzone is well compacted and stable.
D. Check rootzone blending with collar.
E. Check that grades are smooth and harmonious.
F. Verify slopes within putting surface.
G. Insure removal of all weeds, debris, and contamination.
H. Observe that moisture barrier is not exposed at surface.
I. Check that encroachment barrier is in place and continuous (optional).

II. Irrigation

A. Check that heads are at proper spacing.
B. Check that heads are level (whether set to grade or not).
C. Flush quick coupler and all lines and heads.
D. Cycle all heads with controllers.
E. Look for:

1. Sunken lines or trenches
2. Uncompacted backfill
3. Broken or damaged heads or equipment
4. Wet spots indicating leaks or tile cuts

F. Inspect valve boxes and grade around them
G. Verify isolation valves work
H. Conduct 24-hour pressure test

III. Drainage System

A. Check drop inlets for cleanliness
B. Verify grades around drop inlets
C. Check function of vacuum-assisted drainage valves (if used)
D. Inspect discharge pipe if close by:

1. Animal guard in place
2. Durable final section (metal, PVC, concrete, etc.)
3. End section or riprap in place (if used)
4. Solidly anchored, cut off flush to grade

IV. Surrounds

A. Verify depth of topsoil
B. Check that topsoil is not overly compacted
C. Make sure surrounds are cleaned of rocks, stones, vegetation, and debris, as per specifications.
D. Verify slopes of drainage swales—all the way to drop inlet or discharge point.
E. Check other key grades and slopes.
F. Grades should be smooth and harmonious.

V. Bunkers

A. Check drainage system.
B. Check that bottoms are compact and clean.
C. Check that gravel bedding for drainage is clean.
D. Check that geogrids are properly installed (if used).
E. If bunker sand is in bunker, ensure it is well protected from loss or contamination.

VI. Miscellaneous

A. Check that tree root barrier is in place.
B. Check that cart path is correct.
C. Make sure proper clearing and thinning for air and light have been done.
D. Check that encroachment barrier is correctly installed.

This is far from a comprehensive checklist, but if just the items listed are to everyone's satisfaction, chances are the final checklist for the project will be quite small. While everyone is together making the preplant punch list, it is a good time to review those portions of the specifications or contract that spell out where the contractor's responsibility ends and the owner's begins. Likewise, it is helpful to have a discussion of who is responsible for watering, mowing, erosion, repair, replanting, irrigation and drainage maintenance, to reduce disagreements later.

PLANTING AND SODDING

Once the preplant punch list is complete, planting is the next step. There are so many ways to plant that there can be confusion about which method to use, when, where, and how. The important thing is the result, and regardless of how planting is done, there are a few common basics. Whether it is seed, sod, or stolons being used for revegetation, soil contact is critical. Plant roots will rarely grow into or through a void, unless it is within a certain range of size for that particular plant part. Generally, this means that the better the seed-soil, sod-soil, or sprig-soil contact, the better the rooting process. This, then, favors the use of those pieces of equipment that can provide the best distribution of revegetation material and ensure its best contact with the soil or rootzone material. This means a golf green that is seeded with a drop spreader (see Figure 5-35), followed by a cultipacker-type roller, is going to have faster and more uniform establishment than a green hydroseeded with seed, fertilizer, and mulch combined, but not compacted. In fact, even stolons benefit from a cultipacker-type rolling. An acceptable substitute is to use a light leaf rake to straight-line rake in the seed, then roll the planted area with a sand trap rake with knobby tires (see Figures 5-36 and 5-37). Such rolling or compaction must be done in a straight line so as to avoid the displacement of materials that results from driving in circles. Straight-line compaction is best.

Another generality about seeding is to avoid the temptation to "up the rate." When seed is planted too heavily, the resulting population of seedling is so dense that the plants take too long to begin to vegetatively propagate themselves. This effect of too heavy a seed rate can be seen for years after seeding. Vegetative spreading or tillering allows the plant to regenerate tissue damaged by physical injury, disease, traffic, and so on. Sod growers who want to get a crop tight enough to be cut as sod as quickly as possible use about one-half to one-third the amount of seed specified for golf courses, for they have learned

Figure 5-35: A drop seeder is the best way to plant the very small seeds of bentgrass; it should go at half rate in two perpendicular directions, such as front to back and then left to right. (Courtesy of Matt Wolf)

Figure 5-36: After seeding, a very light raking with a leaf rake will slightly cover the seed before rolling or compacting. (Courtesy of Matt Wolf)

Figure 5-37: A bunker rake with knobby tires works well to ensure good seed/soil contact. Only drive in straight-line direction and make all turns off the putting surface.

this gives the best results. On the other hand, greens planted with stolons can greatly benefit from high rates of stolons, because the material is already at a mature state of vegetative regeneration. In fact, one technique that is often used is to "up the rate" of stolons, more and more when planting will occur later into the final stages of the growing season. One might start out planting 450 to 600 bushels of stolons or sprigs per acre (10 to 15 bushels per thousand square feet) but then increase that rate by about 20 percent per week as the prime growing season gets shorter.

Figure 5-38: Sodding green surrounds and erodable steep slopes within sprinkler pattern, immediately before or after seeding, allows areas to be irrigated and grown in simultaneously.

Sod can be laid just about anytime it can be cut and immediately irrigated after installation (see Figure 5-38). Sod can even be laid on frozen ground (soil, not ice or snow) and will "peg down" or take root when soil temperatures rise to favorable levels. Therefore, greens constructed in northern latitudes should not be seeded when soil temperatures fall below 50° to 52°F, while sodding can be successful as long as the sod can be cut.

A sodding technique that seems periodically to fall in and out of favor is root washing. This essentially means using water under pressure to remove nearly all of the soil from field-grown sod before laying it. The idea is to avoid creating a textural discontinuity between the soil type that the sod was grown on and the rootzone it will be laid on. For example, bentgrass sod grown on a mineral soil that texturally is a clay loam, silt, or any combination thereof other than sand, and then planted on a high-sand rootzone, would take on the infiltration characteristic of the mineral soil, not the sand rootzone that is desired. Root washing makes sense, but costs extra money; the newly laid sod is a little more difficult to get smooth, and frankly, for unknown reasons, the procedure is not always successful. Generally, the sod roots will simply not grow into the rootzone, or if they do, they are very shallow, but it's not clear what causes this.

Most experienced agronomists favor seeding greens over sodding them, if possible. Without question, sodding greens gets them green and into play more quickly, perhaps by four to six weeks, but the best quality putting surfaces seem to come from seed. Perhaps the reason is that sod requires so much topdressing, aerification, and rolling to get smooth that the plants are being physically damaged, and it takes a while to overcome such chronic injury. Stolons are midway between seed and sod in the speed of establishment and final quality of putting surface. With some cultivars of putting green grasses, the only choice is to plant stolons, sprigs, or sod, but the advantages and disadvantages remain.

One common technique for sodding greens is to grow the sod on the same basic high sand material as the rootzone it will ultimately be planted on. This takes a great deal of lead time and money to select the sod bed and rootzone materials, grow the sod, build the green, and then sod it. To reduce the number of seams that must be topdressed and grown-in, the sod is often cut in big rolls 50 feet or more long and four feet wide, instead of the more usual four- to six-foot long, 12- to 18-inch wide stuff (see Figure 5-39). Big roll sod must be lifted and moved by tractors or forklifts, working off of three-quarter-inch plywood sheets of four-foot by eight-foot size to avoid wheel tracking or rutting the work area.

Recently, an experimental technique of growing putting green sod on a thin layer of compost, tied together with a thin mesh net, on concrete slabs has proved successful. However, one must be sure the organic layer the sod is grown on will decompose quickly and not form a textural layer that will be different from the rootzone below.

Regardless of the source of sod, or on what it is grown, the usual method of sodding greens is to prepare the sod bed exactly as one would a seedbed. The difference, of course, is what gets planted. Sodding greens usually means working off the plywood sheets described earlier, and making sure there is good contact with the soil, as also discussed earlier. One way to do that, once the sod is

Figure 5-39: Big roll sod reduces seam matching problems but requires specialized care such as working off heavy plywood sheets.

laid with edges butted up as tight as possible, is to put the plywood sheets on top of the sod, and then roll the sod through the plywood. This allows using a heavier roller, even a small blacktop roller, to firmly press the sod into the root-zone. A word of caution is that the roller will not have very good traction on the low frictional surface of the plywood, so the operator will need to be careful about sliding. It is called common sense.

The surrounds within the sprinkler pattern of the putting surface should be planted immediately before or after the putting surface itself (see Figure 5-40). If it is planted before, then the normal activities of planting the green will wreak havoc on the surrounds, and if one waits until the sprinklers are turned on to establish the putting surface, the surrounds become an unmanageable muddy mess. Between the time the surrounds and green are planted, hand watering or roller base sprinklers are the only way to keep sprigs, stolons, or sod alive. Seed will remain dormant in the seedbed until it receives sufficient and prolonged moisture to start the germination process, and then watering must begin or there will be a high mortality among the seedlings.

Planting of the surrounds seems to work best if there is at least a ring of sod laid at the edge of the putting surface and bunkers to stabilize and separate their edges. The sod ring keeps the stuff with which the green was planted separate from the stuff used on the surrounds. The sod around the bunkers permits a faster establishment of the bunker edge, which must be stable before edging can take place. If construction budgets are small, then everything can be seeded appropriately, but if budgets allow for more sod, it should be used as close to greens in the surrounds as possible. For an 18-hole golf course, a minimum sod budget would be 25,000 square yards; a typical one, 100,000 square yards; and the ultra-high-end is to sod everything.

Figure 5-40: Green surrounds within sprinkler pattern should be planted at the same time as the green. Notice how approach is already seeded and mulched prior to seeding green.

MULCH

The values of mulch, covers, and hydromulch are widely debated, except by people who do a lot of seed planting, and they all favor using them (see Figure 5-41). They, however, are often divided about which is best, and having personally tried almost every such product out there, I, too, have an opinion. For the money, it is difficult to beat straw mulch (see Figure 5-42). Before I justify why I favor straw, there should be some basic understanding of the form and function of mulches and covers. The purpose of mulches and covers is to:

Figure 5-41: Straw blower or hydromulcher can apply a uniform application of material to speed establishment of planted greens. (Courtesy of Ed Walsh)

Figure 5-42: The benefits of mulch are often not readily apparent until you move away some of the mulch.

1. Reduce the erosive actions of water and wind
2. Reduce evaporation from the seedbed surface
3. Allow frequent light applications of water
4. Permit some sunlight to reach seedlings
5. Reduce excessive peak soil temperatures
6. Retain heat in the seedbed after sunset
7. Permit seedling growth and development
8. Protect seedling from injury by early maintenance
9. Alert humans that area is seeded
10. Protect crown of plant from freeze drying in winter
11. Provide carbon source for soil microbes (if needed)

Anything that accomplishes these goals will definitely assist in the germination, emergence, establishment, and maturation of plants from seed. There are many kinds of materials that can be applied to a seedbed that would provide many of those functions; however, sorting out which is best for a particular application requires a bit more study of their limitations.

Covers or green blankets work well to reduce evaporation from the soil surface, but some are so tightly woven it is difficult to get water to the soil surface to keep it moist. Covers tend to filter or severely reduce the quality and quantity of needed sunlight that will reach the developing seedlings. There can also be excessive heat buildup under covers, but they do an excellent job in retaining heat after sunset. Covers can be pricey, require a good bit of manpower and time to install, staple or weight down, then remove and replace as needed. On the other hand, they are reusable and provide excellent winter protection against freeze drying (desiccation) by winter winds. In fact, perhaps their greatest benefit comes from their application as winter protectants.

Hydromulches are generally a slurry of water and ground-up paper and/or wood fibers, mixed with a tackifying or binding agent, that are sprayed out onto the soil surface. The machines and materials were designed to seed and mulch roadsides, restoration areas, or sites too difficult to seed and mulch by conventional methods. These areas tend to be very steep or soft, often rough graded compared to a golf course, and the technique was simply to get such areas revegetated, not to get them planted to fine turfgrasses. Although hydroseeding and hydromulching are very fast, there is no way to calibrate precisely what is being applied; the procedure doesn't result in good soil–seed contact, and the machine is very heavy and tends to overcompact the soil in the wheel tracks. The mulch itself is a great use of recycled materials but it, too, is fairly pricey in that it costs two to three times more than straw mulching.

Straw mulch is generally taken to be a weed-free grain straw such as wheat, oat, barley, or rye. Hay is not an acceptable substitute because it contains so many weeds and weed seeds, although in coastal areas a product called "salt hay" is available that is clean of noxious weed and seeds. The straw is often

Figure 5-43: A straw crimper works well on the stiffer soils usually found on green surrounds but is too damaging to sandy rootzone mixes for use on putting surfaces. (Courtesy of Ian McQueen)

baled and is applied by putting it through a straw blower that chops and separates the bale, and then feeds it into a high-speed air stream, which blows the straw out much like the hydroseeder blows seed. Straw mulch can be mixed with a tackifier or binder by spraying the straw as it leaves the blower tube. Another technique, preferred by some, is to blow the straw on and then use a straw crimper to push the straw into the soil, assuring a good contact between straw and soil and locking the straw down to resist erosion or disruption of the mulch by wind or water. A straw crimper is like a straight-blade notched disc, and although not suitable for use on greens, except surrounds, it is a mechanical way to hold the straw in place (see Figure 5-43). When straw is used for mulching the putting surface, it is usually blown on, with or without a tackifier, or immediately wetted down with the irrigation to make the straw heavy, which helps it resist wind movement. In addition, some rootzone material is splashed up on the straw to slightly bury it. Some contractors prefer to mulch putting surfaces by "hand shaking" the straw, which is an acceptable practice but one that takes lots of time and careful workmanship.

A perfectly mulched area can be judged by looking straight down at it and seeing 50 percent seedbed surface and 50 percent mulch. This balance allows adequate water and sunlight penetration, yet resists the erosive forces of wind and water, while providing good shade protection and evening heat retention. If the mulch is too heavy or too clumpy, it will only work ideally at the edges of the clump or blanket, for too much light and water will be blocked. If the mulch is too light, then there is not the maximum benefit of shading some sunlight and retaining soil warmth into the night. It takes no skill, but lots of patience, to apply mulch that is the perfect 50–50 rate. If one must err on the side of caution, it would be better to apply too little as opposed to too much.

If wind, water, vandals, or other forces displace the mulch, it must be repaired back to the ideal, or the mulch will not provide its full benefit. If the surrounds are properly mulched with either straw or hydromulch, there is no need to remove the mulch as the turf seedlings begin to emerge.

EARLY IRRIGATION PRACTICES

If the mulch is too thick to allow adequate sunlight, however, then it must be respread or removed. It always surprises me when a greenkeeper fails to keep a seedbed moist once the seed starts to germinate (see Figure 5-44). It is imperative to never, ever let the top inch or two of the rootzone dry out. Often this requires running the irrigation or hand watering 10 to 12 times per day or more. This is why proper mulch is so important. Granted, if one is going to rely on using automatic sprinklers that may throw a full 360° circle, the surrounds with tighter soils may only need one or two wettings per day or they will become mush, but there is no excuse for allowing germinated seed to dry out and wither. Commonly, irrigation designers will place two or three sets of irrigation heads around the green—one 360° head, one 180° or part circle head, perhaps a low gallon mist head, and at least one or two quick couplers. If the 180° or part circle head is installed, it is initially adjusted to throw on putting surface only to keep the seed on the rootzone moist; then, once the green has matured, that head will be readjusted or aimed to only water the surrounds or areas that dry out faster than the putting surface. The use of roller base sprinklers and hoses connected to quick couplers may be the greenkeeper's only way to fight a windy situation during germination.

Figure 5-44: Once irrigation begins, the planted areas should never be allowed to dry out on the surface until the turf is established. (Courtesy of Bert McFadden)

FERTILIZERS, PESTICIDES, AND TOPDRESSING

During the period between germination and about six to eight weeks into the growth cycle of the plant, it is best to limit traffic, pesticides, topdressing, and heavy applications of fertilizers. This is young turf that needs to be nurtured. This means plenty of water, mowing every couple of days at a high height of cut (initially at one to one and one-half inches or more), and no pesticides unless absolutely necessary. The intent is to vigorously grow the plant with light, frequent water and fertilizer applications, and nothing more, if possible, while protecting the green from physical, chemical, pathological, or environmental stresses that could retard growth. The mulch that is left will decompose by the action of microbes, leaving a desirable form of organic matter, which will be the foundation for the mat layer that the greenkeeper should be trying to cultivate. Since the carbon-to-nitrogen ratio of the mulch is so high (perhaps 150:1 or more), the microbes will tie up most of the available nitrogen, so an additional application of quick-release nitrogen may be necessary to provide enough to green up the seedlings. This additional nitrogen will be released and available to the turfgrass as the carbon-to-nitrogen ratio is reduced during decomposition. Generally, one to two *extra* pounds of nitrogen per thousand square feet are sufficient to satisfy the requirements of both microbes and seedlings. The mulch is usually totally broken down within a growing season or less.

MULCH REMOVAL

On the putting surfaces proper, even a perfectly mulched area has a bit too much to allow for getting a clean playable surface within 10 to 12 weeks of good weather, so about half of the mulch is removed when the seedlings are two to three inches tall. Some greenkeepers use a low set rotary mower to mow the turf for the first time or two, which chops the mulch and speeds up decomposition (see Figure 5-45). Others use a reel-type mower set at two to three inches and catch the clippings for removal. However, I believe the preferred way should be to use a leaf or broom rake, and lightly rake up about

Figure 5-45: A rotary mower set as low as possible works well to chop mulch and trim young turf seedlings.

Figure 5-46: On putting surfaces, about one-half of the mulch can be removed after the turf is about two inches tall, by *lightly* using a leaf rake.

Figure 5-47: Before mowing with a green mower, putting surface should be rolled every day with a drum-type greens mower but without engaging the reels. (Courtesy of Matt Wolf)

one-half of the straw, while not uprooting seedlings (see Figure 5-46). This raked-up straw is removed, and then the green rolled with either a greens mower with the reels not engaged, or a light lawn roller before mowing to level up the rootzone surface (see Figure 5-47).

EARLY MOWING

Turfgrass plants are wonderfully balanced organisms with almost half of the plant living in the soil environment and the other half living in the atmosphere. (There is also a small portion of it that lives in the mat or thatch layer, which is important to the health, durability, and playability of the green, and that is discussed later.) The aboveground part of the plant supports the belowground portions and functions, and vice versa. So the shorter the green leafy part is mowed, the less photosynthetic area is available to produce the energy sources for a robust root system; at the same time the aboveground plant, because it is kept small, does not need an extensive root system. The amount of top growth is directly and physiologically linked to the bottom growth. Because this seems so self-evident, one wonders why greenkeepers are so bent on dropping the cutting height of new greens. They are not forcing the plant to tiller, for that is internally regulated in the plant, they are not training the turf to grow short; and they are not making the stand more dense. All they are doing is stressing a young plant, limiting the full growth potential of the roots, and risking exposing the turf crown and soft tissue to injury or damage.

My recommendation is to maintain the turf no shorter than one inch for the first six weeks or so of active growth, then gradually lower the mowing height to one-half inch by the eighth week of active growth, then winter at this height or continue to lower the mowing height to a reasonable green speed level.

ENCROACHMENT BARRIERS

With some grass varieties, there is a long-term maintenance concern about encroachment of surrounding grasses into the putting greens. Bermuda grass is especially troublesome because of its aggressive stoloniferous growth habit, which lets it spread several feet in one growing season. One technique to control this is to plant the collar of the green to a nonaggressive or slow-growing turf like zoysia grass or 328 Bermuda, thus placing an obstacle between the aggressive Bermuda grass aprons and fairways and the putting surface. This does help reduce the problem for a few years, and longer if the greenkeepers actively fight the Bermuda encroachment by physically cutting the runners, or by using chemicals to regulate growth or burn back the Bermuda once the zoysia goes dormant. But, with aggressive turf types, this is such a labor-consuming task that it is usually easier to just strip out the contaminated collar and resod it to clean material. Of course, the other problem is that mixing Bermuda grass culture with zoysia grass maintenance can complicate maintenance as well as change the playing characteristics of the green surrounds.

Another method is available, however: install an encroachment barrier or track around the green and then use a special edger to trim back the stolon (see

Figure 5-48: One method for controlling encroachment of non–putting green grasses onto green uses an underground track system to guide special vertical mower to trim invading stolons. This machine pulls in the barrier after establishment. (Courtesy of T. R. Wait)

Figure 5-49: The track that is pulled in is less than two inches wide, and not readily visible. (Courtesy of T. R. Wait)

Figure 5-50: The key to controlling encroachment is to periodically cut and remove invasive runners from grasses on the collar. (Courtesy of T. R. Wait)

Figures 5-48, 5-49, and 5-50). The system costs about $2,500 per green and has been well accepted by superintendents in the southern United States. If such a track system or a root encroachment barrier is to be installed, it should be after the green's edge has finally established and somewhat grown in. The encroachment barrier track is then pulled in about four to six inches from final edge, which places it into the rootzone. There is little chance of disrupting or damaging the already installed drainage, irrigation, or wicking barrier. When properly installed, the encroachment track is barely discernible. However, if the thatch layers of the surrounds are not kept to one-half inch or less, the track system will be buried and lost in this organic layer and thus lose its functional value.

DEVELOPING A MAT LAYER

There should be *no* topdressing of the putting surface, unless there has been some extensive damage to the seedling turf, for the goal of grow-in is to produce a mat layer of one-quarter inch, and topdressing retards mat formation (see Figure 5-51). If the putting surface is bumpy, roll it smooth, but forget the topdressing until there is a well-established mat layer. This can take as little a one year with intensive effort, or as much as three to five years if one tries to treat a new green like an old green.

The key is to get the turf to spread vegetatively by tillers and not remain a single plant. Tillering will begin once the plant reaches a level of functional maturity, so that it can sustain the original plant tissue, and has excess energy reserves for new. Seeding at too high a rate can retard the tillering mode and maturity because the plants are growing so densely there isn't room for tillers, and the competition for vital growth resources (water, nutrition, light) does not

Figure 5-51: Developing a mat layer that is about one-quarter-inch thick is key to the playing performance and wearability of putting green turf. Allowing clippings to fall every third or fourth mowing helps develop the mat layer. (Courtesy of Matt Wolf)

allow the plant to create excess energy reserves. This doesn't apply to stolons because they are by definition already in a stage of vegetation repropagation, so the greenkeeper must work on stimulating the existing physiological system, as opposed to maturing the plant to that state, as must be done when it is started from seed. Obviously sodded greens are both mature and vegetatively active, so the grow-in task there is to encourage rooting and seam healing—which sounds easier but often is not. There is a shift in attitudes about topdressing and aerification as well about the assumption that the sod comes with a fairly well-developed mat layer.

Some believe that topdressing sprigs or stolons speeds up their establishment. If the sprigs and stolons were properly planted *into* the soil, rather than just spread on the surface, then the same philosophy that topdressing retards mat formation applies. If the sprigs and stolons were only surface spread, then one heavy topdressing to lightly bury the material may be necessary.

There is some truth to the idea that topdressing will reduce leaf blade width and produce a finer textured turf, but this is at the expense of mat layer development. A more practical method to get a finer textured turf is to reduce excessive fertilization and watering, and make the turf lean.

If the greenkeeper believes that aerification is necessary before the mat layer is developed, then it should be done with solid tines or air or water injection (see Figure 5-52). Hollow tine aerification should only begin once the mat layer is well established. Spiking or verticutting are often needed during mat formation to control grain on the putting surface, or to facilitate good air and water exchange into and out of the rootzone. If possible, apply no pesticides until the plant has reached the vegetative growth state, and the chances of phytoxicity are markedly reduced. This can be difficult if a young turf is hit with Pythium or Rhizoctonia, for the cure may do as much damage as the disease.

Figure 5-52: Solid tine or water injection are the preferred methods of aerification until the mat layer is established.

MAINTAINING ROOTZONE FERTILITY

During these early states of growth, with large volumes of water being applied and a young, sparse root system growing on a well-drained rootzone, leaching of nutrients can occur more rapidly than once the green matures. In particular, I have repeatedly observed nutrient deficiencies, especially with phosphorus and the micronutrient package in general, and particularly with magnesium, manganese, and iron. This depletion of needed nutrients in the upper part of the rootzone can happen in weeks, if not days. The only answer is to be vigilant, know how these deficiencies manifest themselves in young plants, and do comparison soil and tissue tests. Over the years, I have come to believe that the proper grow-in fertilizer ratio is 1–1–1 (N–P–K), with an application of the micronutrient package every other week. Some products used for grow-in (like Grow-In®) are formulated to address these deletions, and take a lot of guesswork out of maintaining a good fertility balance. Recently, I have worked with a fertilizer formulator to develop a total package of all essential nutrients, organic sources, biostimulants, and other amendments shown to stimulate seedling growth and development. For more information, contact Ocean Organic Corporation at 207-832-4305 and inquire about "Architect's Blend."

BUNKERS

Once the putting surfaces and surrounds are fairly well established, the next step is to address the process of finishing the bunkers. Contractors would prefer to deliver a pile of sand to the bunkers and dump it on plastic, or better yet, spread it as early in the construction process as possible, and certainly before planting bed preparation (see Figure 5-53). Their reasons are that, before planting and grow-in, the soils are firm and thus they can haul in large vehicles. In addition, when bunkers are completed early, the contractor doesn't have to wait for the establishment of turf to complete all contractual obligations, which limits his or her exposure to possible problems with erosion, damage, and bad weather. The designers and greenkeepers would prefer to wait as long into the construction process as possible, until the turf is fully established, before any bunker finishing is done for a number of reasons that make long-term maintenance easier.

During grow-in there are usually excessive amounts of water being applied, which inevitably causes soil erosion, which in turn means some soil displacement into the drainage system. Cleaning the drainage inlets to keep them functioning can be an almost daily occurrence, and if a monster rainstorm hits, there can be several feet of sediment deposited in or near the drainage network. This means not only mucking out drainage basins but also cleaning the upper layer of surface-graveled drain lines and placing clean gravel. This is time consuming, costly, and difficult to include in a bid or to estimate the cost before it

Figure 5-53: Finishing bunkers needs to be coordinated with establishing the turf on the greens and surrounds.

happens. However, someone must take this responsibility, and that is why contractors like "seed or sprig in the ground" completion clauses. On the other hand, very few greenkeepers and maintenance staffs have the manpower and equipment to handle the job, and grow in the turf, too.

So while turf is being established, bunkers are generally eroding, and if sand is placed early, the effect is either to contaminate the sand with soil from the bunker edges and/or the outside, to erode the sand, or both (see Figure 5-54). Although some repairs and sand replacement can help address long-term maintenance issues of contamination and drainage, bunkers are never as good as when done the ideal way of finishing them only after turf establishment.

Once the turf on the bunker edge is grown in and anchored, the designer will normally designate the exact bunker shape he or she wants by painting, flagging, or staking the bunker outline and elevations. Then workmen can edge vertically down from that outline to form the bunker cavity. My experiences have led me to believe that the best method is to establish a six-inch vertical edge that flows harmoniously into a bowl-shaped bunker bottom, with tile drainage placed in the lowest areas (see Figure 3-19). Since the turf is mature, it will hold this edge with little soil contamination occurring. Some superintendents prefer to place a six- to eight-inch edging material on the vertical face, such as masonite or thin plywood cut into long strips, for added insurance against edge erosion. Once the sand has settled in and the turf grown for another season, they then remove the edging strip.

If a bunker liner, either sprayed or placed on the inside of the bunker cavity, is to be used, then it should go in after edging and bottom shaping. Although some claim good success with spray-on bunker liners, there is almost universal

Figure 5-54: If sand is placed in the bunker before the perimeter turf is well established, there is a high probability the sand will become contaminated by erosion of perimeter soils.

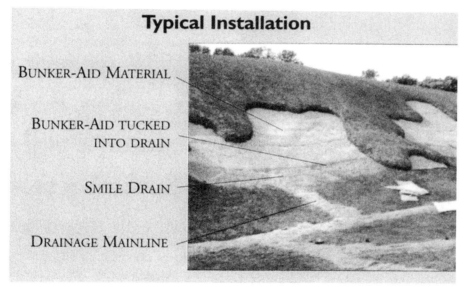

Typical Installation

BUNKER-AID MATERIAL

BUNKER-AID TUCKED INTO DRAIN

SMILE DRAIN

DRAINAGE MAINLINE

Figure 5-55: Bunker liners should terminate into a tile drainage for greatest effectiveness. (Courtesy of Bunker Net)

agreement that it is better to use three-dimensional blankets on the surface, for they are almost miraculous in curbing sand face washouts. There are a number of products, but all generally look like a furnace filter type material, ranging in thickness from three-eighths of an inch up to three-quarters of an inch, and coming in large rolls (see Figures 3-18, 3-19, and 3-20). These blankets can be made of natural materials, such as coconut coir, or of a synthetic fiber. Although the coconut coir is mostly lignin and cellulose and should decompose very slowly, without question the synthetic fiber should last longer. Rarely are natural materials used now.

The key to successful use of a bunker liner is to start it at the bottom of the vertical edge, and terminate the liner into a drainage line (see Figure 5-55).

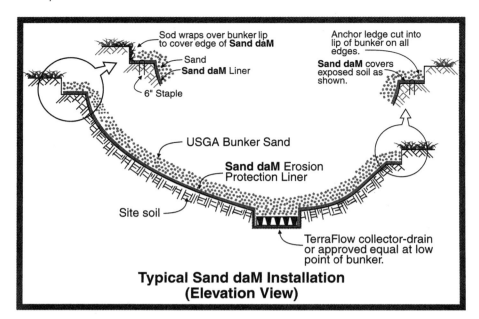

Sod wraps over bunker lip to cover edge of **Sand daM**

Anchor ledge cut into lip of bunker on all edges.

Sand
Sand daM Liner

Sand daM covers exposed soil as shown.

6" Staple

USGA Bunker Sand

Sand daM Erosion Protection Liner

Site soil

TerraFlow collector-drain or approved equal at low point of bunker.

Typical Sand daM Installation (Elevation View)

Figure 5-56: A well-shaped bunker bottom should be smooth, compacted, and bowl shaped with a six- to eight-inch vertical edge. (Courtesy of Sand daM)

This permits surface water to pass through the bunker sand, get into the bunker liner, and then flow through the sand-filled grid to the drain line at a rate too slow to cause erosion of the bunker sand. I have personally observed 12-foot-high, very steep bunker faces go through a hurricane that dumped 11 inches of rain in 36 hours without having a bit of sand erosion.

Whether bunker liners are used or not, after edging the bunker and carefully compacting and smoothing the bottom to a smooth bowl shape, and after hauling away the excess spoil, attention should be given to the drainage system (see Figure 5-56). This means assuring oneself that the drainage is in the lowest places, that the gravel or sand bedding is clean of all silt and contamination, and that the drainage tubing is functioning and not damaged. Personally, I would recommend that the gravel covering the tile line be one inch above grade on either side of it so that a thin layer of silt or clay could not seal off the gravel. This one-inch high mound of gravel would require at least an inch of contamination before it would cease to function.

Finally, it is time to place the laboratory-tested sand (see Chapter 6 for discussion of lab testing) into the bunker cavity. Assuming the vertical edge of the bunker is six inches, then several grade stakes should be placed throughout the bunker every 10 to 12 feet, and marked to the same depth, *plus* an allowance for sand settling. If the vertical edge is six inches, we would recommend setting the level on the grade stakes at eight inches. This eight inches of loose sand will settle 15 to 20 percent of its volume, or in other words, compact to about six inches. The sand should be dumped into the cavity along the edge and then pushed out to the grade stakes by a small piece of equipment of high floation, or hand placed. Avoid running equipment on the bunker bottom, as that can cause deep tracks in these areas that will hold water, become soft and difficult to maintain, or become a source of contamination.

After the sand is evenly spread to the grade stakes, pull the stakes, and wet down the sand so it will not blow out. Some contractors try to compact the sand by running a sand trap rake over it, or by using a vibrating platform compactor or a small roller. Compaction will happen over time naturally, but it is a good idea to stabilize the profile and compact it well before golfers find it with their errant shots. Soft sand produces fried egg lies, and angry golfers. Some tournament-sanctioning bodies suggest that the bunker sand be in place for at least two years before a competition, but compaction can easily foreshorten that process.

Some sands have mostly rounded particle shapes, and these sands will resist compaction, to the point of having almost every lie be a buried one. There is nothing that can be done to rectify that problem fully, but often blending in a more angular sand can reduce it somewhat. Of course, as the sand becomes contaminated with silt and clay particles, it will begin to set up more firmly, but that could take years and by then the drainage would be slowing down, requiring new, clean sand. In the Midwest, it takes about five to seven years of normal bunker edging, freeze/thaw cycles, and wind-blown contamination before a total bunker renovation may be needed. With some calcareous sands, the time before slow drainage and compacted bunker surfaces may be as short as three to five years. Choosing and placing sand should be done with care by whatever means assures proper placement, cleanliness, and minimal damage to young turf.

The extreme example of bunker sand placement was our Westwood Plateau project near Vancouver, Canada. Because of the steepness of mountainsides, narrowness and twisty nature of the cart paths, and the environmental requirement to limit postconstruction traffic, a helicopter and a bottom dumping cement bucket were used to place the sand in the bunkers (see Figure 5-57). The helicopter would pick up a loaded cement bucket with a hook and cable set up, fly to the bunker, hover, then drop the sand into the bunker, where it was spread by hand.

Figure 5-57: In extreme conditions, a helicopter with a dumping cement bucket can be used to fill bunkers with sand.

Lately in less extreme circumstances, it has become more popular to use high flotation trucks or wagons with long conveyor belts or chutes to haul the material to the bunker, place the sand with the chute, then spread and compact it. Without question, this is the cleanest way to fill bunkers, but it is a bit more costly, and it doesn't work well in steeply sloped ground.

SUMMARY

Although the grow-in process has been touched upon, there is no magic procedure that works well on every site, every time. Each site has enough unique characteristics, such as soils, microclimate, water quality, turfgrasses, growing weather, maintenance budgets and materials, environmental restrictions, and golfer expectations, so that no two grow-ins are alike. The only common denominator is that the goal is to get young germplasm and tissue to establish itself, then have the greenkeeper nurture it through successive growth stages so it is healthy and can vegetatively heal wounds and injuries from golfers and pests. That period of time is 10 to 12 weeks of good growing weather. After that the next task is to develop the mat layer and then maintain it at the one-quarter to one-half inch level. After the mat layer is well established, only then should topdressing and hollow tine aerification be necessary, and then only to control the depth of the mat.

This chapter has outlined a textbook procedure for properly building a green. There are other techniques that work equally well as long as they accomplish the same goals. There is some flexibility—but not much—in the arrangement of steps in the process, and most of those options have been identified. However, only after the builder has a complete understanding of the why and how of ideal green construction should many deviations from the ideal be allowed, for one mistake can ruin the entire project. For example, irrigating with silt-laden water can immediately and negatively produce a rootzone surface layer that can only be fixed by major renovation.

Building golf greens should not be a problem to a reader of this chapter.

Rootzone Sampling, Testing, and Evaluation

THE TEST RESULT NUMBERS GAME

Enormous importance is placed on test results of rootzone material and blends. Actually, some would say too much emphasis is placed on lab results, for there are many factors that can influence the values, even on the same sample. However, as sound or flawed as the testing process is, it is still the best indicator of rootzone performance, and should be part of any green construction activity. The problem is not in the variability between labs; rather, the real problem is the false and empirical criticality placed on the numbers that those labs produce (see Figure 6-1, color insert). A thorough understanding of the testing process, and of its possible sources of error, will allow for a more intelligent and flexible application of lab results.

Before 1993, each soil-testing laboratory was free to generally interpret and implement procedures for testing rootzone materials, as long as they based their approach upon some original methods developed in the early 1960s by a few select labs endorsed by the USGA. There was no strict manual of protocols, because no one believed they were needed. However, golf course architects and golf course builders knew that one could submit the same sample to three separate labs and get three widely varying results, sometimes varying by a factor of two to three. The author once did that, and two of the labs were within a percentage point or two of each other while the third lab was off by over 100 percent from the other two. When the out-of-sync lab was told about the discrepancy, the attitude was, "The other two groups are wrong and I'm right." Some labs tended to be very parochial and demonstrative in their results, and it was their way or no way. Folks out in the field did not know what lab to trust.

ACCREDITED LABS FOR ROOTZONE TESTING

Along with the 1993 revisions to the USGA green construction recommendations (see Figure 6-2) came a more defined protocol for testing, a protocol that was codified into a manual that spelled out in detail how to conduct the tests. To assure that all laboratory personnel performing the standard test procedures were performing them exactly the same way, arrangements were made with the American Association for Laboratory Accreditation (A2LA) to accredit rootzone-testing labs. This was a time-consuming and costly procedure for the individual labs, so it was completely voluntary, but only those labs that became accredited would appear on the USGA's list of testing facilities. There are eight labs around the world (see Figure 6-3) that have applied for accreditation, met the rigid qualifications, and are maintaining their status. The accreditation folks periodically submit known samples to the labs to test their ability to produce known results; they also conduct site visits to observe and inspect the facilities.

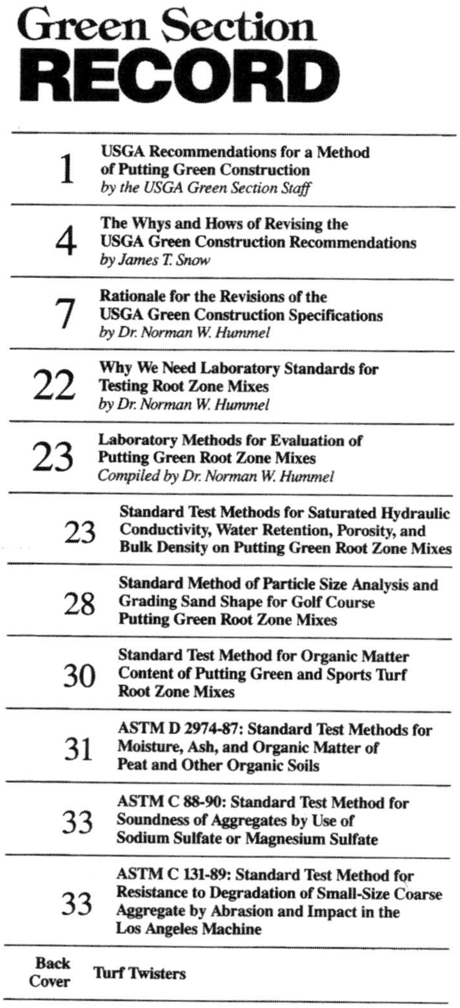
Green Section
RECORD

1	**USGA Recommendations for a Method of Putting Green Construction** *by the USGA Green Section Staff*
4	**The Whys and Hows of Revising the USGA Green Construction Recommendations** *by James T. Snow*
7	**Rationale for the Revisions of the USGA Green Construction Specifications** *by Dr. Norman W. Hummel*
22	**Why We Need Laboratory Standards for Testing Root Zone Mixes** *by Dr. Norman W. Hummel*
23	**Laboratory Methods for Evaluation of Putting Green Root Zone Mixes** *Compiled by Dr. Norman W. Hummel*
23	**Standard Test Methods for Saturated Hydraulic Conductivity, Water Retention, Porosity, and Bulk Density on Putting Green Root Zone Mixes**
28	**Standard Method of Particle Size Analysis and Grading Sand Shape for Golf Course Putting Green Root Zone Mixes**
30	**Standard Test Method for Organic Matter Content of Putting Green and Sports Turf Root Zone Mixes**
31	**ASTM D 2974-87: Standard Test Methods for Moisture, Ash, and Organic Matter of Peat and Other Organic Soils**
33	**ASTM C 88-90: Standard Test Method for Soundness of Aggregates by Use of Sodium Sulfate or Magnesium Sulfate**
33	**ASTM C 131-89: Standard Test Method for Resistance to Degradation of Small-Size Coarse Aggregate by Abrasion and Impact in the Los Angeles Machine**
Back Cover	**Turf Twisters**

Figure 6-2: The 1993 revision to the USGA Specifications also gave a more defined protocol for labs doing the testing.

This doesn't mean that nonaccredited labs are incapable of doing fine analytical work and then making appropriate recommendations, but rather that their results or numbers may be very different from those of an accredited lab. Given a choice of labs, it is strongly recommended that you use an accredited lab, and if possible use that same laboratory throughout the entire construction process for the most consistent test results.

Although all eight of the accredited labs have passed the test, remember that 50 percent of them are in the bottom half of the ranking (as in any profession), so do not assume they are all equal. They are all competent, but finding the best one for a particular project requires some additional investigation. Ideally, the testing facility should have a thorough and open-minded approach to all methods or modified methods of green construction. I would not mention this except that I know there are some accredited labs that do not understand or support any method of green construction except the USGA one. To send such a lab a sand sample that may be used in a California type green is a big mistake. Similarly, many sand or

About   What's New   Programs   Archives   Publications   Construction   Links   Home

▶ **HOME**

THE USGA STORY

JOIN THE USGA

CHAMPIONSHIPS

RULES OF GOLF

AMATEUR STATUS

HANDICAPPING

EQUIPMENT

GRANTS

GREEN SECTION

HISTORY

INT'L GOLF FED.

CATALOGUE

ASSOCIATIONS

NEWS

CONTACT US

DIRECTIONS

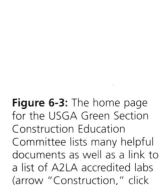

Search ▶

USGA GREENS

For more than 30 years the USGA recommendations for green construction have been the most widely used method for green construction throughout the United States and in other parts of the world. When built and maintained properly, USGA greens have provided consistently good results for golf courses over a period of many years.

Listed below are links to various articles about USGA greens that should prove helpful to those considering the construction of new greens, the renovation of existing greens, or those needing help in the management of greens already constructed to the method recommended by the USGA Green Section. (By the way, the USGA's *Green Section* is the agronomic branch of the USGA and deals with much more than just greens. For more information about the Green Section and the USGA, browse your way to the USGA's Homepage.)

▶ Quality Control Sampling of Sand and Rootzone Mixture Stockpiles

▶ USGA Greens Construction Guidelines

▶ Confidence Intervals

▶ Physical Soil Testing Laboratories

▶ History of USGA Greens

▶ Quality Control Guidelines

▶ Determining the Need for Reconstruction

▶ Helping Your Greens Make the Grade - A Report Card

▶ ASTM Procedures Required for Testing Putting Green Materials

▶ Troubleshooting Checklist

▶ Research Summaries

The USGA Story | Members Program | Championships | Rules | Amateur
Handicapping | Equipment | Grants | Green Section | History
Golf Shop | Associations | News | Contact Us

Figure 6-3: The home page for the USGA Green Section Construction Education Committee lists many helpful documents as well as a link to a list of A2LA accredited labs (arrow "Construction," click "Greens," arrow and click "Physical Soil Testing Links")

organic sources are regional and have their own peculiar characteristics of performance. A lab that has previously tested and observed these materials in use may make different recommendations than a lab unfamiliar with them. Another example is to find out if the laboratory has any experience with the interaction of rootzone materials available to your project with the type of turf being considered *and* the quality of the irrigation source. All of these examples and more can influence the success of the project, and they go beyond simply producing a test number or value. The point is to feel confident that the lab selected fully understands and is sympathetic to the real-world constraints and limitations of your situation. If there is any doubt, keep looking for the right fit.

AMERICAN SOCIETY FOR TESTING AND MATERIALS

Most laboratories now generally follow standards for testing established and published by the American Society for Testing and Materials (ASTM) (phone 610-832-9585 or visit their website at www.ASTM.org). There are at least 11 standards that are directly applicable to rootzone testing, ranging from sand particle size and shape to testing aggregate samples. However, even with accredited labs running tests to very exact and precise procedures, different labs can produce different results. The sources of those differences can be attributed to major areas: (1) slight variability in testing apparatus and procedures and (2) slight variability in methods used by different lab technicians. Generally, the results within a lab are much more repeatable or consistent than results between labs. This further supports the advice to stick with one lab throughout the entire project; don't expect samples sent to different labs to have results that necessarily agree.

The USGA, ASTM, and others have recognized that it is nearly impossible to remove all variability, nor is it necessary, if one doesn't hone in on specific numerical values, but rather sees test results as a general indicator.

CONFIDENCE INTERVALS

To this end, the USGA has published a list of confidence intervals (c.i.) that should be applied to any test result. These confidence intervals simply mean that there is a bracket of values on either side of the reported test number, within which the sample values could fall and still be treated as equal. For example, assume the lab test shows a value for fine sand size particles to measure at 10 percent. The established confidence interval for fine sand measurement is 15 percent. Fifteen percent of 10 percent is 1.5 percent, so the value for fine sand can vary plus or minus 1.5 percent. This means that, although the measured value for fine sand was 10 percent, that sand is still acceptable at any value between 8.5 and 11.5 percent, which is the acceptable confidence interval. In other words, even though the designer's specifications state the fine sand component should be 10 percent, the sand should not be rejected if the component is within the range of 8.5 to 11.5 percent.

The complete list of USGA confidence intervals for quality control testing of rootzone materials is shown in Table 6-1.

It would seem that, with A2LA, ASTM and c.i.s., rootzone testing should be without controversy, but that is far from the case at this time of writing. The reason is ignorance or lack of education, depending upon your point of view, on the part of whomever has final authority to accept or reject a rootzone based upon test results. Specifically, the problem is mostly with values for saturated hydraulic conductivity (Ksat), which is measured with a permeameter (see Figure 6-4). The c.i. for Ksat is shown to be 20 percent, which means that, if a spec calls for a rootzone perc rate of 20 inches per hour, that rootzone should be acceptable if it is measured anywhere within the range of 16 to 24 inches per hour. The real problem is that, if the designer's specs call for 20 inches per hour, someone may reject that rootzone if it tests only 16 inches per hour, either before or after it is placed in the green cavity, or if one quality control sample tests 24 inches per hour and the next 16 inches per hour. In theory, there may be no functional difference in performance between the rootzone samples, but you cannot convince some people of that.

Table 6.1
USGA CONFIDENCE INTERVALS FOR QUALITY CONTROL TESTING OF ROOTZONE MATERIALS

TEST PARAMETER	USGA CONFIDENCE INTERVAL (%)
Fine gravel	50
Very coarse sand	50
Coarse sand	10
Medium sand	10
Fine sand	15
Very fine sand	30
Silt	25
Clay	25
Total porosity	10
Air-filled porosity	10
Capillary porosity	10
Saturated conductivity	20
Percent organic matter of mix	0.2

[a]The confidence interval for percent organic matter is not represented as a percentage. Thus a reported value of 0.7 percent organic matter could range from 0.5 to 0.9 percent.

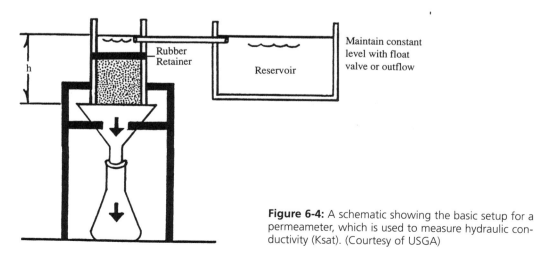

Figure 6-4: A schematic showing the basic setup for a permeameter, which is used to measure hydraulic conductivity (Ksat). (Courtesy of USGA)

KSAT CONTROVERSY

On top of that, some independent research has shown that the confidence interval for Ksat should be more like 50 percent, which expands the range for a targeted Ksat of 20 inches per hour to one of 10 to 30 inches, and that seems to defy prudent logic.

There are several theories as to the source of error that can cause such widely varying Ksat values: the actual material composition of the testing equipment; the effect of steel versus plastic versus copper cylinders; and/or the moisture percentage of the rootzone when tested. For example, the same rootzone, when tested at 10 percent soil moisture, gave radically different values than when tested at 2 percent, even though the tests were conducted by the same lab and the same technician, using the same equipment. In some instances, the range of Ksat varied well over 100 percent as moisture varied between 14 and 2 percent. Intuitively, it should be simple enough to simply specify a standard cylinder made by one company using precise manufacturing standards and to set an ASTM standard for moisture content. Granted, the cylinder problem can be solved with just a bit of money, but controlling soil moisture is a far more difficult problem, one that would significantly add to the time it takes for a lab to receive a sample, process and test it, and report results. Since no blending should take place between quality control testing, this means construction downtime, and with the sand to be blended also possibly changing soil moisture content, and hence the blend. And even if someone were to solve these two problems, most lab technicians believe that just the differences in the water sources used for the tests could cause varying results. Certainly, one could use distilled water, but few golf greens are irrigated with distilled water, so the rootzone test result may be meaningless.

This Ksat problem has led to a schism between USGA accredited labs and the Golf Course Builders Association of America, supported by the American Society of Golf Course Architects. The labs insist that it is a necessary test to assess the performance characteristics of a rootzone, with the Builders seeing it as a meaningless number that subjects them to potential extra costs in time and money, as well as liabilities in workmanship. The Builder's claim seems valid, for far too much emphasis is placed on achieving some magical yet questionable Ksat number.

In 2003, the Golf Course Builders Association of America issued a policy statement, endorsed by 90 percent of their membership, that states:

Verbiage for Ksat Testing in Specifications

Testing and/or performance requirements, specified in this contract not withstanding, pertaining to samples used in the construction of greens and tees should not be tested for Saturated Hydraulic Conductivity (Ksat).

> The term Ksat shall include, without limitation; percolation rate, infiltration rate, saturated conductivity as that term which is utilized within the United States Golf Associations [sic] Recommendations for Putting Green Construction.
>
> The Ksat is not recognized for a requirement of this contract. All other physical properties as described by the current USGA Recommendations of the rootzone mix will be sampled at the location wherein the rootzone mix is mechanically soil blended and tested prior to installation into green or tee cavities. Once the approved root zone [sic] mix is removed from the said stockpile, it is deemed acceptable.

The USGA is caught in the middle between the Builders and Architects on one hand, and the labs accredited by A2LA on the other, who insist on keeping the test. Perhaps by 2004 or 2005, when revised USGA recommendations for green construction are published, the Ksat value controversy will be a moot point, but for now it is not. The teaching point of this discussion should be that testing of rootzone materials is important and highly regulated, but not perfect.

PROPER SAMPLING TECHNIQUES

Once the "right" lab is identified, the next critical step is to properly take samples for testing. The old "scoop a baggie full off the surface of the pile" method assumes the exterior reflects the interior and that often is far from true. Rootzone materials on the surface of a stockpile have been subjected to the forces of wind, water, gravity, contamination, perhaps freeze/thaw cycles, or extreme temperatures. The best method is to make a composite sample of many mini samples, taken throughout the stockpile. This is so important that the construction education committee of the USGA Green Section has published a booklet on the topic titled *Quality Control Sampling of Sand and Rootzone Mixture Stockpiles* (available from www.usga.org/green/coned) (see Figures 6-5 and 6-6).

The essence of their recommendations is to use two levels of sampling and testing. The first level should take place at the source of the materials to be used, and the second level once the materials are selected, purchased, delivered, or blended. The idea of this two-stage approach is to detect any differences that may have occurred during the handling and shipping, and perhaps blending, process.

Figure 6-5: Cover from USGA booklet on how to properly sample for rootzone testing. (Courtesy of USGA)

Figure 6-6: The correct way to sample, as shown in the USGA booklet on sampling shown in Figure 6-5.

The first level of tests could be called "selection testing" and the second is "quality control" testing, which compares the baseline results of the selection tests against what is installed in the green cavity.

Selection testing may involve taking multiple samples from multiple sources and sending them to the accredited lab for evaluation. The sample is tested as received by the lab, except perhaps for air or oven drying, and it generally only involves particle size analysis, which is quick, inexpensive, and is a reasonable predictor of performance. Once promising samples are found by physical analysis, they can then be tested for their performance characteristics, which takes more time and money but gives the best indication of rootzone quality.

Generally, sands are degradation products of stone, degraded through either weathering or crushing. As would be expected, natural deposits of weather-derived and sorted sands can be highly variable, especially when associated with deposits influenced by the dynamic forces of wind, water, or gravity. To reduce this naturally wide distribution of particle sizes and shapes, sand mining operations usually wash and screen to separate the deposits into their various products, such as mason sand, filter or septic sands, or concrete sand. By simply changing the screen size, conveyor speed, wash cycles, and a few lesser variables, the producer can alter the properties of the sand. Historically, golf courses have not been target markets, simply because so few golf courses are built compared to the demand for sand suitable for other uses like concrete or cement. So, when a golf course wanted to buy sand, it usually had to choose among the standard products available in the surrounding area, or pay the sand producer an extra fee (often 100 percent more) to produce a sand that was theoretically better suited to golf courses. Some large sand companies simply have no interest or incentive to produce a small quantity (7,000 tons) of high quality rootzone material, as opposed to the huge tonnages of widely varying sands suitable for other uses. There have been a few sand producers who have found a niche selling golf course sands for green construction and topdressing, but not many. This means that, unless one arranges with the sand producer to isolate and save the stockpile of sand from which the sample, that is being subjected to level one testing was drawn, that tested sand will be long gone, and a new sand stockpile in its place when one goes to purchase sand. Time can be of the essence in selection testing, and once selected, that sand pile should be purchased immediately and preserved with tarps and covers if possible. Otherwise, there could be some big surprises once quality control (q.c.) or level two testing begins.

The most common problem with purchasing sand from a major sand producer is that tolerances to past rootzone standards are too demanding, especially when it comes to percentages of very fine sands, silts, and clays. To remove or reduce the percentage of these textural classes means running a final screen with smaller openings, which clog more easily, using a slower conveyor speed, and applying a good deal more clean wash water. It is surprising how effective even a second washing can be in improving sand for rootzone material.

To properly take a level one test requires a four-foot long sampling tool made of two-inch PVC pipe with one end cut at a 40° angle, and the other end fitted with a "tee" as a handle (see Figure 6-6). Using duct tape or a permanent felt tip pen, mark the pipe at two feet from the sampling end to reference sample depth.

The USGA recommends taking a minimum of eight samples from one-third and two-thirds up the stockpile from the bottom, and from all four sides of the pile.

Dig a hole about 12 to 18 inches in diameter, and about as deep, into the side of the stockpile as a sample pit. Push the PVC collection tube into the hole as horizontally as possible, and you may need a rubber hammer to drive the pipe in up to the two-foot mark. Carefully remove that sample tube and dump the contents into a clean, dry five-gallon bucket, but do not try to make a composite sample yet. Repeat procedure at all eight locations and mix the samples together. Do this for each 1,000-ton stockpile. Then, on a clean, dry, impermeable surface, such as a sheet of plastic, dump the five-gallon buckets out and blend the samples together. Form a large square with the total sample and then divide it into equal quarters. Select two of the quarters and place the sand into a one-gallon zipper-top type plastic bag. Take the other two quarters, make another square, divide into quarters, and select two quarters to add to the bag. Repeat until one-gallon bag is full, then seal it with duct tape and label it with permanent felt tip pen, double bag, place in a sturdy box, and ship to lab. If possible, also ship the lab about five gallons of identified irrigation source to be used for sand sample evaluation. Ship as quickly as possible and keep a tracking number in case sample is lost or damaged. If test results are favorable, lock down stockpile and protect it.

The previously described procedure works for materials both before and after blending, but once the material is in the green cavity, whether it is a new green or an established one, the process changes slightly. Now the depth of vertical profile is somewhere around 12 inches, and any differences between the top, middle, or bottom of that profile may be meaningful, so disturbing a core sample as little as possible becomes the goal. Again, the USGA has well thought-out recommendations that include using the two-inch diameter PVC pipe, cut to 16 or 18 inches in length, and sharpened with an outside radius using a file or pipe deburring tool. These pipe sections can be driven into the green profile using a block of wood to blunt the blow and shock of a heavy hammer. These cores should be packed with wadded-up newspaper to take up any extra space, capped, sealed with duct tape, labeled as per location, and shipped in a protected box or container. Upon reaching the lab, the technician will cut the sample open the long way to reveal the entire core. Besides being able to visually assess the sample, the lab can also choose to sample by depth below the soil surface, trying to measure the uniformity throughout the column. It is not unusual to find that the top inch or two is substantially different than deeper samples, owing to the accumulation of organic and mineral debris and contamination at the solid surface.

THE LABORATORY ANALYSIS REPORT

Once the lab has received the samples, they will perform only the analyses that they are instructed to do (see Figure 6-7). Since each lab is slightly different, it is a wise idea to contact your chosen lab, and discuss with them what you are trying to accomplish, as well as what services they offer and at what costs. It might not even hurt to contact a couple of labs and ask those kinds of questions, as well as asking about turn-around times, guarantees, and so on, for you are going to base a lot on what they do or don't do. This also alerts the lab to your shipment so they can process it for you in a timely fashion.

As a matter of procedure, if not law, labs will usually send test results only to the person paying for the testing services, unless otherwise instructed. Therefore, the project owner, not the contractor, should take samples, submit, and pay for the tests. This eliminates the possibility that a negative test report gets "lost," or a "Hollywood" sample, not reflective of the stockpile, gets submitted. Typically, the labs will e-mail or fax, or both, the results back to expe-

Figure 6-7: Once the lab receives the samples, it starts a paper trail to document the test procedures and test results requested. Samples are tested as received. (Courtesy of Hummel & Co., Inc.)

dite ongoing operations. Start a file of any and all conversations, notes, letters, tests, or anything else related to the rootzone testing, for it may be very important later. I suggest taking duplicate samples from each stockpile or green, and storing them for later reference if needed.

Reading and interpreting a lab report is not difficult, although at first it just seems like a bunch of numbers. Usually as part of the lab service, a letter accompanies the report that interprets the test results and makes recommendations. Such information is based solely on what was either found by the lab, or told to them in first person. There is no way they can judge if the sample is representative of the total rootzone, or whether subsequent handling of the material will significantly change it. So the lab report should be seen as a snapshot in time, and that is why subsequent quality control or level two testing is important to show a continuum of results or changes.

Since sands are physically and chemically so different, they respond differently to construction activity. In the past, I have seen sands sampled first at their source and again when finally installed in the green and show no changes. At other times, I have observed sands pass all tests at the source, be loaded, hauled, processed and placed in the green, and exhibit as much as eight to ten percent change toward being finer—to the point of falling out of acceptable ranges. There are lots of explanations offered, such as hardness of the sand grains, acid rain, mechanical crushing by construction equipment, and a few

HUMMEL & CO., INC.

#0775-01

Hummel & Co., Inc. • 35 King Street • P.O. Box 606 • Trumansburg, New York 14886 • Phone: (607) 387-5694 • Fax: (607) 387-9499 • Email: soildr1@zoom-DSL.com • Web Site: www.turfdoctor.com

MATERIALS TEST REPORT FOR
Rotten Oaks Golf Club

REPORT TO: Golf Course Superintendent
Rotten Oaks Country Club
P. O. 001
Sunken Forest, PA

DATE RECEIVED: June 17, 2003
TEST DATE: June 17 - 21
REPORT DATE: June 21, 2003
CONDITION OF SAMPLE: Normal

PARTICLE SIZE ANALYSIS (ASTM F-1632)

| Lab ID No. | Sample | Soil Separate % | | | Sieve Size/Sand Fraction Sand Particle Diameter % Retained | | | | | | | |
		Sand	Silt	Clay	No. 10 Gravel 2 mm	No. 18 V. coarse 1 mm	No. 35 Coarse 0.5 mm	No. 60 Medium 0.25 mm	No. 100 Fine 0.15 mm	No. 140 V. fine 0.10 mm	No. 270 V. fine 0.05 mm
125274-1	90-10 Mix	97.5	1.4	1.1	0.0	6.6	26.2	45.0	16.1	2.7	0.9
	USGA Recommendations		≤ 5%	≤ 3%	≤ 3% gravel ≤ 10% combined			≥ 60%	≤ 20%	≤ 5%	

PARTICLE SHAPE/PARTICLE SIZE PARAMETERS/pH

Lab ID No.	Sample	Sphericity/Angularity	pH*	D85	Cu	Grad. Index
15274-1	90-10 Mix	Low to high/angular to rounded	6.5	0.73	2.45	4.8

*ASTM D4972

Page 1 of 3. This report may not be reproduced except in full, without written permission of the lab.

Turfgrass Soil Consulting and Testing Services

Figure 6-8: Labs generally report all of the same information but sometimes in a slightly different format. Therefore, this example should be representative of most labs. (Courtesy of Hummel & Co., Inc.)

lesser ideas. No one, however, has yet adequately explained how to determine and predict such changes before they happen. The fact that such changes do occur should not be alarming if other performance indicators show the rootzone material to be good. Again, the caution is to avoid getting too hung up on test results numbers.

See Figure 6-8 for a sample soil test report whose format is fairly standard among all labs. In this example, the first section identifies the person or company submitting the sample, various dates, and the condition of the sample as received. If the sample had been damaged during shipment, this would have been indicated, in case this influenced the results.

PHYSICAL ANALYSIS

The next section is particle size analysis or what is sometimes called the "physical analysis." Generally, the sample is oven dried according to the ASTM standard, and then the sample is separated into fractions based upon particles being retained on a set of standard screens (see Figure 6-9, and Figure 6-10 in color insert). Notice it is the "percent retained" that is recorded, not percent passing. Nonaccredited labs may use percent passing. For golf green construction, the important information for sand selection is not only the percentage of sand, silt, and clay (see Figure 6-11), but also the percentage of the sand that separates into each of six different fractions, ranging from gravel (2 mm) to very fine sand (0.05 mm). For California green construction, a seventh sieve size of 0.10 mm should be added according to University of California recommendations. The last line in the particle size analysis is usually the target values for either USGA or California recommendations for green construction. Generally, just this size analysis is enough to eliminate some samples from further consideration. Currently, the USGA is considering the need to amend some of the recommended percentages for gravel selection and fine sand (0.15 mm), which may appear in the 2004 revisions. However, as can be seen in our example, all three samples appear to be well within recommended ranges.

The next evaluation section deals with the particle shape, uniformity, and pH. Generally speaking, the more angular sands are preferred because the rough

Figure 6-9: Samples are dried in ovens according to ASTM protocols. (Courtesy of Hummel & Co., Inc.)

Figure 6-11: A hydrometer method is used to determine percentages of silt and clay by measuring the settling out over prescribed times. (Courtesy of Hummel & Co., Inc.)

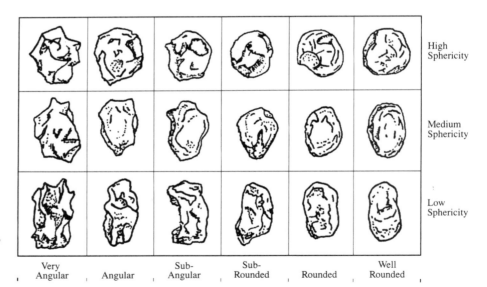

						High Sphericity
						Medium Sphericity
						Low Sphericity
Very Angular	Angular	Sub-Angular	Sub-Rounded	Rounded	Well Rounded	

Figure 6-12: Angularity is determined by microscopically comparing the sample to a standard chart used by all A2LA-accredited labs.

or jagged edges of the particle can interlock more easily and give a firm matrix and surface (see Figure 6-12). Rounded particles, on the other hand, do not form very stable profiles because they are so easily displaced, like walking on a bunch of tiny balls or spheres. Therefore, angularity can be a good discriminator between samples if one is more spherical shaped than the other. Typically, sands deposited by wind or water are more rounded than sand produced by crushing and processing of rocks either by natural or mechanical forces. Rounded particle sands are often called "live sands" because they move so easily under foot or when disturbed by normal construction or maintenance equipment. However, it has been my experience that in some areas there is nothing but rounded sand, so it must be used. New greens built from these sands are very disconcerting to the greenkeeper because they show footprints and mower marks so easily and tend to scalp at transitions in grade, and just feel soft or puffy. After about two years, enough mat layer builds up over the sand surface, and the putting green turf develops enough of a dense root system that these sands settle down. Some greenkeepers have had great success by routine rolling of these greens with lawn rollers, green rollers, or the vibrating rollers that can be fitted to triplex mowers. If one must deal with rounded sands for green construction, every effort should be made to avoid topdressing until at least one-quarter inch of mat layer is developed, or the condition will never be corrected. The point is that, although angular sands are preferred, rounded sands will work as well or better than extremely angular sands, which may become excessively compact.

The pH value for a sample is of interest only in that most putting grasses grow best at a slightly acid to neutral soil solution (see Figure 6-13). Silica sands tend to fall naturally into that range, while sands of limestone origin,

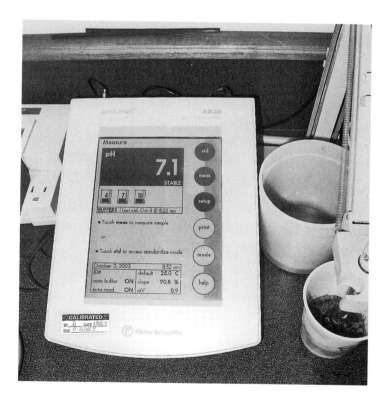

Figure 6-13: For pH measurements, the A2LA protocols call for a standard pH meter. (Courtesy of Hummel & Co., Inc.)

called calcareous because of the preponderance of calcium in their chemical composition, are more basic or of a higher pH value. In the Midwest, calcareous sands with pH values of 8.2 or higher are common. On the face of it, such high pH values seem to spell long-term unsolvable problems, but that is not the case. I believe the reason is that, although the sand particles are very basic, the soil solution is closer to neutral or acidic from applications of common fertilizers and irrigation sources. Whatever the reasons, calcareous sands are not preferred but they do perform well. Generally, it is easier and more cost effective to acidify the irrigation water than it is to find neutral pH or silica sand.

The next column of the lab results shown in Figure 6-8, the one labeled D85, simply refers to the particle diameter of a rootzone sample, where 85 percent of the particles are finer and 15 percent are coarser, which is taken from a graph of the particle sizes and then calculated for the ratio (see Figure 6-14). This number is most important when USGA construction is planned, for it is used to determine if the rootzone sample will successfully bridge or mate to the gravel layer sample, without needing an intermediate coarse sand layer. Since the intermediate coarse sand layer is difficult to source, is expensive to install, and does not contribute to the performance of the green, most designers, contractors, and superintendents avoid it. The easy alternative is to find a gravel sample that matches up to the rootzone D85, and forget the intermediate coarse sand layer. Some old-timers still insist on using the intermediate layer, but very few greens are still built that way.

The Cu value stands for coefficient of uniformity, which is a numerical expression of how uniform the particle sizes are. The acceptable range is two to four, with the optimum being about three or less. The higher the value, the less uniform the sample, and the greater is its potential for packing. Sand with a lower Cu, below two, will not pack at all, resulting in the unstable surface problem discussed earlier for sphericity. The Cu is determined by a formula that compares the particle diameter where 60 percent of the particles are finer against the particle size diameter where 10 percent are coarser, or $Cu = D60/D10$.

A very similar measurement is called the gradation index (GI), and it looks at the middle 80 percent of the particle size range by comparing the particle size where 90 percent are finer against where 10 percent of the particles are coarser. This formula looks like: $GI = D90/D10$. A range of values for GI is three to six, with a lower value indicating an increased chance of surface instability and a higher value showing the potential for excessive packing. A comfortable range is four to five.

With just this information, a rootzone-testing specialist can pretty well decide which samples are worthy of further testing and evaluation. This is helpful when doing level one testing and just trying to find worthy candidates for possible use.

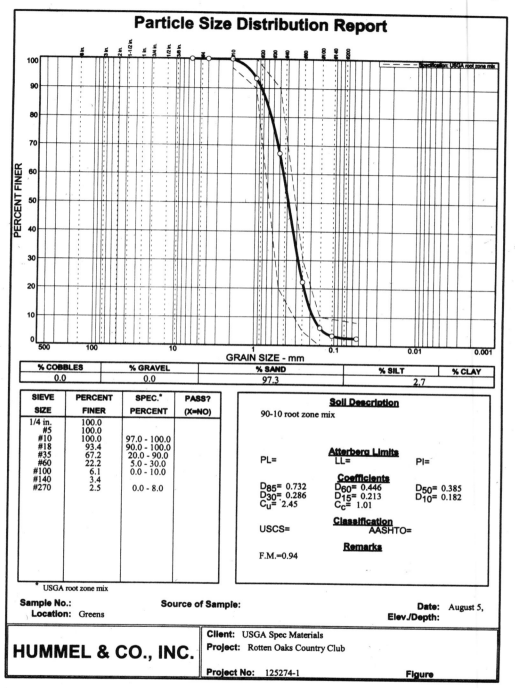

Figure 6-14: Particle diameter of various sand fractions is graphed in order to show the precise relationship between particle size and percent of sample. From this graph D_{85} and D_{15} values can be determined. (Courtesy of Hummel & Co., Inc.)

PERFORMANCE TESTING

The next series of test is commonly called "performance testing," when in reality it is simply a further evaluation of physical properties (see Figure 6-15). The samples to be tested are placed into cores or cylinders according to ASTM F-1815-97. How the technician fills the cylinders, the moisture content of the sample, the material of which cylinder is made, all may be sources of variability among labs (see Figure 6-16). Nonetheless, the following tests, taken together, are considered to be important potential performance indicators.

The cylinder containing the sample being tested is placed in a pan of water and allowed to become fully saturated from the bottom up. Then the cylinder is placed on a tension table to extract excess water at 40-cm tension for at least 16 hours (see Figure 6-17, color insert). The cylinder or core is now compacted using a standard weight dropped 15 times from a height of 12 inches (see Figure 6-18, color insert).

With the sample core compacted and saturated to field capacity, it is now ready for the measurement of saturated hydraulic conductivity or Ksat using a permeameter (see Figure 6-19, color insert). A constant head of water is placed on top of the sample core and passes freely through it for four hours. Then the amount of water that is able to pass in 30 minutes, or some known time period, is measured (see Figure 6-20, color insert). With some calculation, a rate in inches per hour is determined by the lab technician.

To determine water retention or capillarity, the sample is returned to the tension table to once again reach field capacity at 40-cm tension. Then the sample is weighed, dried, reweighed (see Figure 6-21, color insert), and a bulk density is calculated, as is water retention. A more familiar measure for anyone who has taken a basic soil course is bulk density, which, unlike particle density,

---

Rotten Oaks GC
June 21, 2003
Page 2 of 3

PHYSICAL PROPERTIES (ASTM F-1815-97)

Lab ID No.	Sample	Particle Density (g/cc)	Bulk Density (g/cc)	Ksat Infiltration Rate (in/hr)		Aeration Porosity %	Capillary Porosity* %	Organic Matter+ %
125274-1	90-10 Mix	2.67	1.56	19.2	41.4	23.1	18.3	0.86
	USGA Values			6 - 24	35 - 55	15 - 30	15 – 25	

* Determined at 30 cm tension
+ Determined by Method 1 of ASTM F-1647

Figure 6-15: A sample of how "performance test" is reported by most labs. (Courtesy of Hummel & Co., Inc.)

Figure 6-16: The first step in "performance testing" is for a technician to fill a standard cylinder, saturate it from the bottom up, and place it on a tension table. (Courtesy of Hummel & Co., Inc.)

allows for pore space. To determine this value, a standard cylinder is filled with the sample by the technician and compacted according to the ASTM protocols. Again, the result is a ratio measurement of weight to volume (grams per cubic centimeter, or g/cc), which will be later compared to the particle density measurement that is in the same units. The higher the bulk density, or the closer it gets to the particle density, the more dense or compacted the soil.

Particle density is measured in an apparatus called a pycnometer (see Figure 6-22, color insert). Particle density is important in determining the total porosity of a sample, and it is a measurement that assumes that there are no pore spaces at all in the sample. It would be as if one could melt down the sample into a solid block and then weigh a known volume of it. Of course, the labs do not melt down the sample, for that would destroy it for further tests, so an ASTM method is used that places a known weight of sample into a chamber, fills the chamber with an ideal gas such as helium, and then determines the volume of the sample by pressure. For silica sands the particle density is around 2.65 grams per cubic centimeter (g/cc), and for calcareous sands, it is slightly higher. Of course, if the sample has been amended with either an organic or inorganic amendment, the particle density value will change.

Figure 6-23: When undisturbed cores from existing green are received, the lab technician opens them, inspects them, and then does testing as requested by the client. (Courtesy of Hummel & Co., Inc.)

When undisturbed cores from existing greens are received, they are oven dried and the particle density and bulk density tests are usually performed in situ or as received (see Figure 6-23). This obviously takes a good deal more care and skill but can yield valuable information in understanding why the green is performing in a certain manner. Of particular interest is to test the cores in two- to three-inch segments to determine if one level of the profile is negatively affecting levels above or below it.

Of far greater importance to most rootzone specialists are the next three measurements, which are total porosity, aeration porosity, and capillary porosity, which can be calculated from the information obtained from the sample. These values have a much lower and fairly undisputed confidence interval, and are more reflective of how a rootzone may actually perform. Ideally, a rootzone should have a total porosity centered in the range of 35 to 55 percent, as shown, and aeration and capillary porosities in the mid range of 15 to 25 percent. Total porosity is determined by comparing the particle density to the bulk density. To determine the capillary porosity or the amount of water the sample will hold against the pull of gravity, the cylinder or core is placed on a tension table that simulates the pull of gravity on a 12-inch deep profile, which is about 30 cm. This 30-cm tension is for golf greens with 12-inch rootzone, but different tensions should be used to simulate profiles that are not 12 inches. For example, an athletic field or a tee may only use a six-inch rootzone, so less gravitation pull is needed for testing. By varying the tension, a lab technician can sometimes determine that, while a sample is not acceptable for use with a 12-inch deep profile, it may provide acceptable aeration and capillary porosity values at deeper or shallower depths. Sometimes using a less expensive rootzone material at greater depth can save money and perform better than a more expensive material at the standard 12-inch profile.

The ideal rootzone should be around 50 percent pore space that is equally filled with air and water after being drained down by gravity. Remember, these values are a snapshot of the rootzone material sample submitted, with no turf growing in it, no mat accumulation on top of it, and no naturally occurring increases in soil organic matter. Once all this happens, along with roots filling the large pores, compaction from golfers and maintenance procedures, and possible contamination from the irrigation water, wind-blown dust, topdressing components, and so on, there will be dramatic shifts in the tested values. New green construction rootzone lab tests should be looked at as simply a method to select the best *potential* material for the available budget. A written report usually accompanies the test results, giving the lab technician's interpretation of test data (see Figure 6-24). In many areas, it is nearly impossible to find a material that meets the ideal ranges that have been discussed, but understanding those indicators can assist in making an intelligent compromise.

Rotten Oaks GC
June 21, 2003
Page 3 of 3

Comments: The 90-10 root zone mix sample (Lab ID. No. 125274-1) was tested as received and was compared to the USGA recommendations for greens construction. The results of the particle size analysis shows that the mix had a small quantity of silt and clay present, the amounts falling within the range recommended by the USGA. The sand fraction was uniform in particle size, most of the sand falling into the fine through coarse size fractions. The uniformity of the mix particle size is illustrated by the uniformity coefficient (Cu), this value falling into the optimum range of 2 to 3 for construction mixes. The lower the Cu, the more uniform the particle size and the greater the compaction resistance. The mix has a particle size distribution that meets the USGA recommendations.

The sand particle shape was mixed. The pH was acceptable.

The physical properties of the mix, as determined on compacted cores, are found in the table on page 2. The mix had a saturated hydraulic conductivity (infiltration) rate that meets USGA recommendations.

The total porosity was acceptable, as was the distribution of pore space. The aeration porosity is made up of relatively large pores that conduct water under saturated conditions. When drained, they are filled with air providing the oxygen that is necessary for root growth. The capillary porosity is made up of small pores that hold water against the force of gravity, retaining much of it for plant use. Ideally, a root zone mix would contain a nearly equal distribution of air and water filled pore space after free drainage.

You can see from the results that the aeration porosity was acceptable. The water retention, as reflected in the capillary porosity was acceptable as well. The results suggest that greens built with this mix and at the density reported would have good drainage, and after free drainage would have good aeration and water retention. The mix meets USGA recommendations in all regards.

Please let me know if you have any questions on the results. Thank you.

Norman W. Hummel Jr.
President

Figure 6-24: A written report, in letter form, usually accompanies the returned test results, with an opinion of the lab technician on the suitability of the sample as a rootzone. (Courtesy of Hummel & Co., Inc.)

ORGANIC MATTER TESTING

The last value in the sample soil test report is for organic matter. This column would be reported as zero for pure sand, but for a blended sample, it would have a percentage figure based upon weight. Although most folks concerned with green construction still talk in terms of volume-to-volume, percentages such as an 80:20 mix (80 percent sand, 20 percent organic matter), this approach is extremely inaccurate. One reason is that the organic matter may be fluffy or compact, stringy or finely ground, or very dry or moist; lots of other sources of error can also affect the lab's ability to arrive at consistent percentages. However, by using a weight of organic matter to be blended into a volume of sand, more accurate determinations can be made. The range for organic matter under USGA recommendation is from zero to 3 percent, but ideally it should be about 2 percent by weight and still yield desirable performance numbers for porosity and Ksat.

To determine the best percentage of organic matter for any given sand, samples of both should be submitted to the lab for testing (see Figure 6-25). The lab will test each component independently, and, if both are acceptable, they will mix together various ratios for evaluation and subsequent recommendation. Once an ideal blend is determined, these test values should become the baseline against which quality control samples are compared. This procedure is the best approach to having a consistent rootzone blend within the entire project.

Organic matter is widely variable and is discussed later. To evaluate which type might be best, the lab begins by assessing the moisture content, ash content, and amount of organic matter. Moisture is determined by weighing the sample, drying it under standard procedures, and reweighing (see Figure 6-26). Ash content can be measured by burning away the organic matter in a 440° muffle furnace (see Figure 6-27, color insert). From these measurements the organic matter content can be calculated (see Figure 6-28, color insert).

Testing of blends of inorganic amendments would be done in a similar fashion as for organic products. A difference would be that, depending upon the relative particle density between the inorganic amendment and selected sand, a ratio of volume-to-volume may be used instead of weight to volume as for lighter weight organics.

Testing is done for gravels to be used in green construction, especially when the USGA method, which uses a gravel drainage blanket, is to be followed. Generally, gravel tests are confined to particle size analysis so the lab can calculate a coefficient of uniformity and a D15 calculation, whereby 15 percent of the gravel particles are finer and 85 percent are coarser. An *acceptable* value for Cu should be 2.5 or less, and the D15 is compared to the D85 of the rootzone sample to determine if an intermediate coarse sand layer is needed. The formula is that five times the D85 of the rootzone is equal to or less than the D15 value of the gravel. For example, if the D85 of the rootzone equals 0.66, then five times that is $0.66 \times 5 = 3.30$, which is less than the D15 of gravel, which was calculated to be 4.9. Therefore, no intermediate coarse sand layer is needed to keep the rootzone material from migrating down into the gravel layer. Currently, the USGA is considering revising this guideline to allow for a slightly coarser gravel component.

Although there are differences in opinion about the requirement and value of blending organic matter into a rootzone, there is no disagreement that there

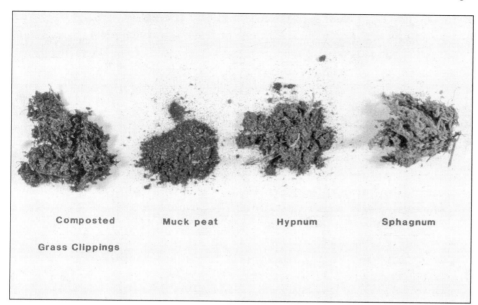

Composted

Grass Clippings

Muck peat

Hypnum

Sphagnum

Figure 6-25: When selection testing is done, clients often want to know how to amend the sand sample with organic matter. They often submit various sources of organic matter to allow the lab technician to make various blends. (Courtesy of Hummel & Co., Inc.)

Figure 6-26: Organic matter testing includes measuring moisture content by weighing, drying, and reweighing. (Courtesy of Hummel & Co., Inc.)

are good and bad sources of the material. This is especially true of composts, whose properties are direct reflections of their parent materials, as well as of the composting process. In other words, there is great variability among organic sources, and often laboratory testing is helpful in finding the best choice.

SELECTING ORGANIC AMENDMENTS

Dr. Norman Hummel, Jr., of Hummel & Company, Inc., conducts all sorts of rootzone material testing and offers some advice on how to find a high quality organic amendment. He suggests, "There are several characteristics of organic sources that can be used to identify quality," namely:

- Percent organic matter
- Ash content
- Fiber content
- Water holding capacity
- Moisture content
- Density
- PH
- Carbon-to-nitrogen ratio

A closer look at these characteristics may prove useful.

The various organic sources are usually categorized as to their age, type of parent material, and amount of organic matter. The USGA recommends that a peat have a minimum of 85 percent organic matter as determined by loss on ignition, but most labs believe this number should be closer to 90 percent organic content. Generally, what is left from the ignition procedure is called ash content, and typically this is a mineral-like silt or clay (see Figure 6-28). The amount of actual organic can vary widely, especially for composts, which can have as little as 50 percent actual organic content.

The fiber content of organic matter can vary by the plant material they were derived from as well as by their age. For golf green construction, some fibrous nature of the material is very desirable, as that enhances water-holding capacity, but materials that are too stringy are a little more difficult to blend. The fibrous nature of peats is usually lost as they age and decompose, so old peat holds a little less water. If the sand has excellent water-holding or capillary porosity on its own, perhaps one should lean toward selecting an older, more stable but less fibrous peat. Conversely, more droughty sand may benefit from a younger, greener, more fibrous material. Fiber content is more of a visual assessment that a hard line scientific test, for there are no reliable, reproducible tests for measuring fiber content.

On the other hand, the water-holding capacity of an organic source can be measured by blending a known quantity into a sand previously measured for capillary porosity, rerunning the test with the organic, and comparing the results for differences. This is the best method to see exactly what water-holding capacity any particular organic source would have on any particular sand.

The moisture content of the organic sources can influence both the performance and blending. If the organic materials are too wet, they tend to stick together in lumps or clods, while if they are too dry, they are fluffy and want to "float" during blending and subsequent handling. In addition, if organic matter gets too dry, it can become hydrophobic, which will negatively affect all characteristics of the rootzone blend, not to mention the problem of trying to rewet the stuff. Ideally, the moisture content of the higher quality peat is in the range of 35 percent to 55 percent, which can be easily checked by weighing, drying, and reweighing. Oftentimes labs will specify the moisture content and weight of an organic source to be blended, such as 17.0 pounds of specified organic matter at 50 percent moisture content per cubic yard of sand. This type of precise description assures a consistent blend but puts a great deal of pressure on the blender to continually monitor moisture content.

The pH of most organic sources is quite variable, and since hydrogen is a cation and organic matter has a fairly high cation exchange capacity (CEC), even a small amount of organic matter can have a big influence on the pH of the final blend. Typically, if organic matter represents about 2 percent by weight of the blend, the CEC might be expected to be about 2 to 4 milliequivalent per milliliter (mEq/ml). Even in a California style green, organic matter will naturally be produced by the turfgrass and can easily reach 2 percent with two growing seasons. The CEC of a rootzone blend can easily be determined in the lab.

CARBON-TO-NITROGEN RATIO

One final measure of the quality of an organic source that is frequently tested is the carbon-to-nitrogen ratio or C:N. Basically this is a measure of the state of degradation or decomposition of the organic material (see Figure 6-29). A new plant material like straw might have a C:N ratio of 150:1 to 200:1, but as the straw is broken down by organisms, that ratio may fall quickly to 50:1 to 70:1, then slowly be reduced to 20:1, which then makes the material fairly stable. The reason for this measurable shift has to do both with the reduction in the number of carbon atoms being consumed by the organisms, and with the demand by these microbes for nitrogen, which is taken from the surrounding soil, water, and air. The more nitrogen is available, generally, the larger the population of organisms, and the faster the decomposition takes place. As the carbon energy sources are diminished, there is a diminution in the number of live

SAMPLE CARBON-TO-NITROGEN RATIOS

MATERIAL	C:N
Blood meal	3:1
Cottonseed meal	7:1
Sewage sludge	10:1
Seaweed	12:1
Turkey and chicken litter	16:1
Humus	20:1
Compost	20:1
Coffee grounds	21:1
Grass clippings	21:1
Other animal manures	65:1
Oat straw	75:1
Peat moss	75:1
Corn cobs	100:1
Wheat straw	125:1
Sphagnum peat	150:1
Rotted sawdust	150:1
Paper/cardboard	400:1
Green sawdust	600:1
Hardwood chip	600:1
Softwood chips	800:1

Figure 6-29: Some sample values for various organic materials. Ideal is to reach a C:N of 20:1 to avoid tying up nitrogen needed for plant growth.

microbes, and a small release of nitrogen. Ultimately, the organic sources will be completely consumed by a process called "mineralization," which becomes the dominant activity when C:N ratio gets down to about 10:1 or so. Of course, the more lignin and cellulose the organic matter has, the slower the decomposition. For example, it might take hardwood sawdust high in these cell wall materials at least five years to reach a state of C:N where it can contribute positive attributes to a rootzone, while seaweed with little lignin and cellulose can decompose in a matter of days. Although few labs do C:N, lignin, and cellulose analyses, if there is any doubt, either find someone to do the test or get an organic source with a proven tack record of performance, if one is to be used.

There are many different types and classes of organic and inorganic amendments, so many, in fact, that almost a complete book could be written about them, and newer ones are coming on the market every year. The success of California pure sand greens demonstrates that none of these are critical or imperative, but the right one(s) could make the greens perform more predictably while immature. Once the turf and rootzone are established, their positive impact is less noticeable, for then the emphasis is controlling the amount of naturally occurring organic matter.

I can speak with some authority, for I have personally used and observed in rootzones just about every type of organic material that is cheap and plentiful in the United States. Clearly, some work better than others, but I was never sure in a particular instance if better performance was because of the organic material, the irrigation water quality, weather or microclimate, the turfgrass being grown, the sand and/or soil component of the rootzone, or the management treatments given by the greenkeeping staff. None of the greens in question failed, for in every case the golf course superintendent simply figured out how to manage the situation and made the appropriate adjustments. I constantly read comments that attribute easier grow-in to the turf if organics are part of the blend, but I have never seen any definitive study that showed that adding any organic source can compensate for poor water quality, a marginal growth environment, cold weather, excessive rain, and so on. The point is that the only magic material in golf green construction is the gray matter between the ears of a superintendent who is a keen observer and who fully understands how to manage plant growth. Rather than gamble on some rootzone amendment, I always encourage owners, if they truly want great greens, to hire the most experienced and talented superintendent they can find and afford, and give that person the necessary tools.

However, a few of the more common materials or classes of materials are worthy of comment. Sphagnum moss peats are one of the most readily available classes because there are so many producers, particularly in Canada, and surface harvesting is relatively easy (see Figure 6-30). These materials are relatively young, which means they have a high C:N ratio, the pH is medium low to low, and they are very fibrous. Their organic content is in the mid to high 90

SPHAGNUM MOSS PEAT

REED SEDGE PEAT

Figure 6-30: Two popular sources of organic mater are sphagnum moss peat and reed sedge peat, which may look similar but perform differently. (Courtesy of Hummel & Co., Inc.)

percent range, and they can hold 10 to 14 times their weight in water. They are low cost, low density, and lightweight, and so incorporation rates may be slightly higher than for more mature and stable alternatives. Since they have a higher C:N ratio, they may require a couple of extra pounds of nitrogen per thousand square feet so as not to starve the turf seedlings or plantings. Frequent soil testing will indicate if any pH adjustment is required once grow-in begins.

A little older and more stable form of peat is reed sedge, which is mostly harvested in the north central United States, particularly North Dakota and Minnesota (see Figure 6-30). Rather than coming from moss like sphagnum, these materials, as the name implies, come from reeds and sedges, and are generally 85 to 92 percent organic. These plants are finer textured, giving them moderate water-holding capacity of four to six times their weight, and since they are heavier or denser, less is needed by volume to amend the characteristics of sand. Their C:N ratio is lower and their pH tends to be higher than sphagnum peat, and overall they are a little longer lasting in rootzone blends.

Many designers and superintendents prefer the even more stable influence of peat humus in rootzone blends. Generally, these materials are much older, are mined rather than surface harvested, and are decomposed to the point that their parent material is not identifiable. They also tend to have lower total organic content, perhaps 82 to 85 percent, with the remaining ash often having significant silt and clay content. Peat humus is very dense and so a smaller volume can have a fairly large impact. Their water-holding capacity is three to five times their weight, they are neutral to slightly acid, and have C:N ratios of 20 or less. These materials can be finely ground, which makes them desirable as a topdressing constituent, if organic topdressing is warranted.

Figure 6-31: Composts are highly variable depending upon their parent material and how they were composted. Some composts are low ash, low C:N, and high organic, while another sample may not only look different, but also perform differently. Only testing can help select the best one. (Courtesy of Hummel & Co., Inc.)

Composts are the most ill-defined class of organics because they are so variable in their sources, composting procedure, age, consistency, and chemical makeup (see Figure 6-31). A few reliable companies that use predominantly sewage sludge mixed with softwood sawdust, and that professionally manage the material throughout the composting process, have won high praise from golf courses. On the other hand, composts derived from any organic waste may produce negative results because they are so unstable and may contain phytotoxic compounds. As a general rule, the compost should be as old as possible, which means near peat humus degradation, and should be screened to the smallest size particle practical. It should be tested for as many of the aforementioned quality characteristics as possible. Since composts can bring a premium price, they should be checked to insure they deliver superior benefits. There is some anecdotal observation that using composts helps reduce the need for pesticides by natural antagonism of pest organisms. Without question, the fewer pesticides that must be used the better, but I am not aware of any peer-reviewed study that assures that compost will suppress pest organisms. Again, it is a case of buyer beware.

All efforts should be made to avoid any organic source with less than 80 percent organic matter, for generally the ash content will cause more harm than the organic can provide in benefits. The legendary "rich black earth" may in fact be nothing more than soils that are texturally classified as silts, clays, or silty clays. "Better than nothing" is another phrase that does not hold true with such materials, for they will be nothing but trouble.

INORGANIC AMENDMENTS

Inorganic amendments can be generally reduced to three or four categories based upon their source. Calcined clays are simply naturally occurring or blended clays that have been made into aggregates and then heated a time or two to make them as stable as pottery (see Figure 6-32). Some are dense particles while others are open or porous, and hence some have ability to hold air or water in their structure. They are touted as being able to increase total porosity as well as capillary porosity, and without question these influences are measurable in the lab. However, whether these benefits are available to the plant or are just too tightly bound to the particle is widely debated. Another measurable claimed benefit is that these materials increase CEC, and they seem to be effective in holding monovalent cations against leaching. However, when the magnitude of this benefit is weighed against the cost of using the materials, the picture is less attractive.

Diatomaceous earth refers to deposits of single-cell organisms that accumulated in significant layers on ancient seabeds. With upheavals in the earth's crust, these deposits were made available for mining. They are fairly porous materials that can be naturally hard or that may require calcining or heat hardening to have any real utility or contribution to amending a rootzone. Test results show adding calcined diatomites does increase the total porosity and capillary porosity with minimal influence on infiltration rates. Although these materials can be shown to hold water, there is some conjecture about whether that water is plant available or not. Again, it is a matter of doing a proper cost-to-benefit analysis and not just accepting advertising claims.

The third class of inorganic materials is the zeolites, which are naturally occurring porous materials with very high cation exchange rates and low bulk

Figure 6-32: Inorganic amendments differ much more in their properties than just color, so investigate benefits and costs carefully. On the right is calcined clay, middle is diatomaceous earth, and on the left is zeolite. (Courtesy of Hummel & Co., Inc.)

densities. The National Aeronautic and Space Agency (NASA) did quite a bit of research on these materials as a growing medium for plants in space stations. Again, research has shown some excellent results with some types of zeolites, but they are quite variable depending upon their source. The best ones do increase total porosity and capillary values, and although there seems to be less total water held than with the calcine clay and diatomaceous products, more of it is available for plants.

The fourth class of material is polyacrylamide gels, which are also called PAM or hydrogels and which have been around since the early 1950s (see Figure 6-33). These are manufactured materials made by cross-linking long chain polymers of acrylamide and potassium acrylate or other such materials. There are some organic hydrogels, usually composed of starch, gelatin, or agar, but these have a short functional life similar to other organics, while the inorganic hydrogels may last five to seven years. These materials have tremendous water-holding capacity, perhaps as much as 400 times their weight, and some have fairly high CEC. They have been shown to be effective in conventional agriculture but when used in golf course applications, such as tee and green construction, no discernible benefits were observed. Conversely, when excessive amounts (greater than 10 percent by volume) of these materials were used in error, the soil surface became an unstable, gelatinous mass. In addition, there have been some stated concerns that, when these gels break down or depolymerize due to actions of microorganisms or in the presence of soil salts, the resulting degradation product is acrylamide, which has been suspected of causing cancer in lab animals.

Figure 6-33: Polyacrylamide (PAM) gels have proven highly effective in agriculture and horticulture, but not yet in golf course maintenance. Perhaps when water is less available their benefits will be more evident. Shown are dry crystals and crystals after being soaked in water.

The value of building test greens using various lab-tested materials and observing the long-term results will not only help advance the art and science of greenkeeping, but will also provide greenkeepers with intrinsic information about growing fine putting turf.

BUNKER SAND

Currently, there is almost a fetish in North American golf to provide improved, consistent playing qualities of bunkers. Golfers want—no, demand—that bunkers be well drained and firm, produce no "fried egg" lies, be uniformly colored, and be of such playing quality as to be able to advance the ball to or toward the hole. Consequently, North American hazards look pretty and do not carry the penal qualities associated with bunkers in other parts of the world. To achieve this bunker sand perfection, great sums of money and blocks of time are invested, to the point that some sand sources of desirable qualities are specified by American architects and are shipped nearly around the world to their projects. Therefore, bunker sands often cost more than rootzone sand and undergo nearly equal evaluation by labs. However, unlike rootzone material, with its very clear guidelines, bunker sand has none, so each lab or golf course architect or superintendent or vocal golfer offers his or her own standards.

Sand selection for bunkers generally is most concerned with at least three physical analyses consisting of particle size gradation, particle shape, and the more subjective analysis of color. In addition, there are at least two performance measures that are made, namely, hydraulic conductivity (Ksat) and resistance to plugging as indicated by penetrometer readings.

The ideal bunker sand would have a wide distribution of particle sizes nearly equal to a USGA rootzone sand, so it would set up well, yet when blasted onto the putting surface not cause an incompatible textural layer. The particles should be as angular as possible so they will interlock or stack well upon one another. Although color is an individual choice, most prefer cream color sand as opposed to a harsh, glaring white. The ideal bunker sand should drain as rapidly as the rootzone sand, and contain less than three percent silt and/or clay.

Last—and most imprecise—consider the penetrometer reading. A penetrometer is usually not much more than a spring-loaded depth gauge, inserted into a golf ball that is marked at its mid point or equator (see Figure 6-34, color insert). The golf ball is pushed into a four- or six-inch depth bunker sand sample until the ball is half buried, and then a reading is taken on the spring-loaded gauge or penetrometer. This process is repeated three to five times and readings are averaged. Penetrometer readings of 2.5 or greater will produce very few "fried egg" lies. Rarely will penetrometer readings reach 4.0, so the working range seems to be 2.5 to 4.0.

The safest way to select bunker sand is to build one or more test bunkers and fill it or them with each different type of sand being considered. Then have golfers hit shots out of the bunkers. Keep a record of their preferences and use this as a final determinant of what sand to purchase and install.

Bunker sand will naturally become contaminated over a four- to seven-year period and will need to be pulled out, washed, and reinstalled, or simply replaced with fresh sand. Properly built bunkers do not get dirty from the bottom up, so bunker liners will not keep sand clean. Bunkers get dirty or contaminated from the bunker edges by native soil breaking down due to traffic or excessive edging. Generally, sand is washed off the faces or high places, exposing soil that erodes. In northern climates, the freeze/thaw cycle causes soil to fracture and roll down the frozen slopes.

Selecting Turfgrasses or Artificial Turf for Greens

A HISTORICAL PERSPECTIVE

Probably from the time that golf was first played on land instead of ice, golfers recognized that some vegetative surfaces played differently and better than others. Although there are no written records to indicate it, from the early paintings of golfers, one would assume that short, dense grasses were preferred, especially grasses that were found in natural grassy hollows of the links (see Figure 7-1). Since very little maintenance was done, the most sought-after places for greens was where the grasses were thin bladed, because of low fertility, but were also dense, because of adequate natural moisture and protection from winds, as well as being kept short by grazing animals, both wild and domestic (see Figure 7-2). Often golf was only played in the late fall, winter, and early spring, because once these native grasses started their annual cycle of rapid top development in late spring and early summer they became unplayable. The summer would slow this top growth, a few months of grazing would nibble the grasses short, and they were again suitable for golf. This seasonal nature of golf was true for most sites.

At some point, the desire to play golf all year long led to efforts at keeping the grasses short even during times of active growth, which meant mowing, or more accurately cutting, was necessary. Early "greens" were cut with scythes and finished off with sickles until fairly late into the 1800s, which meant the surfaces were often uneven and bumpy. Later, when mechanical mowers became well enough developed to be efficient and cost effective, they were

Figure 7-1: When golf was played on unaltered and minimally maintained linksland, protected hollows with fine-bladed grasses were selected for "greens."

ON THE LINKS AT THE NORTHFIELD--EAST NORTHFIELD, MASS.

Figure 7-2: Early golf courses often maintained herds of grazing animals to keep grasses trimmed short.

RANSOMES' LAWN MOWERS.

THE BEST FOR GOLF LINKS.

SUPPLIED TO ALL THE PRINCIPAL GOLF CLUBS.

SENT CARRIAGE PAID ON A MONTH'S FREE TRIAL.

THE "PATENT" AUTOMATON. GEAR OR CHAIN.—The best general purpose machines in the world, with numerous special patented improvements possessed by no other makers' machines.
"ANGLO-PARIS" AND "LION."—The best small machines.
"HORSE AND PONY."—The best large machines; new patterns; new adjustments; new Patent Spring Handles preventing vibration.

RANSOMES, SIMS & JEFFERIES, LTD., IPSWICH.

Figure 7-3: Although early mowers were crude and could not mow much below one-half inch, they produced greens vastly improved over using grazing animals to control turf height.

favored over the scythe and sickle methods, because they could cut uniformly at or below one-half inch, which provided superior putting surfaces (see Figure 7-3).

SEED FOR GREENS

It was also recognized early that some finer textured grasses, such as fine fescues, redtop, brown top, and meadow grass, could provide better playing surfaces than more coarse textured grasses. Thus, when new golf greens were built or older ones were being heavily topdressed and required overseeding, planting these fine-bladed grasses was logical and practical. Of course, with demand comes supply, and soon seed companies starting harvesting seed from desirable grasses and blending them for putting greens (see Figure 7-4). There were no laws back then to guarantee seed types, purity, germination, or weed seeds as there are today, so the only way to be assured of good seed was to trust the reputation of the seed company. We also recognize today that the same seed blend

Figure 7-4: In the 1910s and 1920s, seed companies offered wider varieties of grasses, and since there were no regulations on seed blends, they offered whatever they had or thought best.

can perform differently based upon the microclimate of the site and the cultural practices to which it is subjected, so that what works well in one location might be marginal in another, regardless of the seed quality. However, since a variety of species were being used in those early seed blends, it could be expected that one or two or more types would emerge as the dominant type(s), and provide adequate results. There were no thoughts of monoculture for greens simply because turfgrass science had not evolved to that point of sophistication. Once Charles Piper and Russell Oakley were hired by the United States Department of Agriculture (USDA) in the early twentieth century, the movement toward a more uniform and less patchy putting surface began.

SOD FOR GREENS

Because of the variability of seed performance in the 1800s and early 1900s, especially when not irrigated and thus reliant on natural precipitation for establishment and sustainment, sod was used. Sod for greens was cut from plots or areas near where it was to be laid, from grass swards that were well established (see Figure 7-5). These "turves," as they were called, were often several inches thick, so what was being moved was both rootzone and root mass, as well as the leafy stuff. Naturally, these sod slabs were heavy, so they were only a couple feet square, thus many seams resulted that would require much topdressing and rolling to produce a smooth putting surface. The newly laid sod would be stimulated with organic type fertilizers, and had a fairly high rate of survival. Although a bit more costly than seeding a putting green, sodding had a much higher success rate of producing "first rate" greens in a much shorter period than seeding.

OTHER PLANTS FOR GREENS

Not all greens were planted with grasses, for there are references in the older magazines and books of greens being planted to yarrow, clover, mosses, mints, and anything else that could grow close to the ground, take traffic, and play reasonably well. Over time, however, fine-bladed grass greens became the choice of golfers.

TURF GARDENS DEVELOP

Due to the fact that golf never really got established in the United States until the 1880s to the 1890s, no concerted search for superior grasses for greens was

LAYING TURF FOR A PUTTING GREEN.

Figure 7-5: Cutting sod for greens was often done by men using sod knives. It was usually cut very thick.

made in North America before that time. A few amateur gardeners, like James Olcott in Connecticut, did make a hobby out of collecting grasses and subjecting them to low mowing heights (see Figure 1-34). But since there was no commercial incentive to market grass seed for golf courses, seed companies focused mostly on pasture grasses. By 1900, however, the golf boom was on in America, and with it came the need for more knowledge about grasses best adapted to golf courses, especially greens. Enter Piper and Oakley, trained botanists who could identify different genera and species of grasses, and they were hired by the USDA to research turf for golf. They established the Arlington Turf Garden and began selecting plant materials to establish there what had proven to perform well on North American golf greens. In Europe, bentgrasses were not considered best suited for golf courses, as is still true today, but in America several genotypes of creeping bentgrasses were producing superior greens, especially under the then state-of-the-art maintenance procedures. So Piper and Oakley selected plants from these greens, and vegetatively propagated them, which assured that they maintained their genetic purity (see Figure 7-6). The process involved nothing more than planting the

Figure 7-6: Piper and Oakley, while working on grasses for the USDA, established the Arlington Turf Gardens in Maryland in about 1910.

Stumpp & Walter Co.'s GOLF TURF

GRASS SEEDS OF KNOWN PURITY AND PROVED VITALITY

Variety	Description** Helps you to distinguish varieties in your turf	Period of Maximum Development-†	Use	Soil Suitable	Height Ins. if Uncut ‡	Weight Per Bushel	Price per 100 lbs. *
AGROSTIS VARIETIES OR BENTS (1 lb. contains about 4,000,000 live seeds)							
Creeping Bent, South German Bent, European Agrostis, Fiorin (*Agrostis species*).	"Creeping Bent," a name used for many years for seed collected in Central Europe; and consisting of a mixture of *A. vulgaris*, *A. canina*, *A. palustris*. Blades wide; creeping.	Early fall	Makes velvet-like, thick, beautiful, soft putting-greens and lawns; used largely in conjunction with Red Fescue.	All; especially moist land.	12		
			Superfine Quality.........	....			24
Cocoos Bent (*A. maritima*).			Fine Quality...........	....			16
Rhode Island Bent (*A. tenuis; A. vulgaris*); **Colonial Bent**).	Blades very narrow, flat. Slightly creeping. Forms a brownish green velvety turf. Leaves are rolled in the bud.	Early fall	Makes mat-like, uniform turf. Splendid for putting-greens and fine lawns. Rhode Island and Colonial Bent are identical.	Moist All soils.	12	18	
					18		
			Superfine Quality......	....			24
Rhode Island Bent, Washington Strain (*A. tenuis*).	As above; domestic grown.	Early fall	Fine Quality...........	.... All soils.	18	20	18
Red Top (*A. palustris; A. alba*).	Leaf-blades narrow, becoming very narrow with turf cultivation; plants slightly creeping. The young leaves are rolled in the bud. Prominent ligule.	Early fall	Valuable for fairways and tees.	All soils.	24		
			Superfine Quality.........	....			36
			Recleaned Quality......	....			32
			Ordinary Good Commercial Quality (unhulled)..	....			18

Figure 7-7: During the period 1900–1930, only a couple of seed blends of bentgrass were offered.

aboveground stems or stolons from chopped up sod. These varieties were planted in plots for evaluation and given experimental numbers for record keeping. The ones with the greatest potential for putting green turf were given names before being released to growers, who then produced clean sod to produce more stolons. No seeded varieties can claim such purity and so no serious effort was made to develop them. Now greens could be a monoculture of just one type of grass, vegetatively propagated, that should produce the most uniform putting surfaces and be the most predictable to maintain. In all, Piper and Oakley released many varieties over about a 20-year period, with names like Cohannsey (C-7), Toronto (C-15), Arlington, Washington (C-50), and Congressional (C-19). Similar work on warm-season grasses was also being done but no named varieties were produced.

For those in northern climates who could not afford to vegetatively plant greens, the seed of choice was south German or Seaside creeping bents (see Figure 7-7), and in southern regions common Bermuda grass was used. These seeded greens were often patchy when the individual contributing members to the blend segregated out or became invaded with weeds like *Poa annua*, became off-types of warm-season grasses. These grasses also tended to become grainy and might even have different daily growth rates, so the art of putting was complicated by the necessity to "read" the grasses.

Figure 7-8: Penncross was developed and released by Penn State University as the first genetically stable, seeded creeping bentgrass. One of the first ads for it ran in late 1957.

NEW GENERATIONS OF GRASSES FOR GREENS

Piper died in 1926, and Oakley carried on their research until his death in 1931. Their deaths and the great economic depression of 1929–1934, followed closely by World War II, ended all research for about 15 years. However, after the war, there was renewed interest in plant breeding, and in 1953, Penncross creeping bentgrass was introduced into test plots as an improved, seeded, creeping bentgrass (see Figure 7-8). It was less patchy than the other seeded bents and came from a tightly controlled and consistent germplasm, although it had 21 original parents. It was made available in 1957. Even today, Penncross may be the first choice to provide the best putting surfaces in selected locations.

Vegetatively propagated putting greens remained popular well into the early 1980s until a catastrophic, mystery disease wiped out greens almost overnight at Butler National before the 1980 Western Open. The disease was called C-15 (Toronto) Decline, and was later determined to be a bacterial wilt that was peculiar to this vegetative strain. Soon other golf courses in the Midwest that had Toronto greens started seeing the disease, and the best alternative turf seemed to be Penncross. Soon other creeping bentgrass varieties were introduced that were developed by either selecting plants shown to produce superior turf qualities, or breeding among plants with desirable characteristics. In the 1990s, genetic engineering became popular, and superior varieties were created by selecting and transplanting genes from one plant to another.

SELECTING THE "RIGHT" VARIETY

Today there are dozens of seeded creeping bentgrass varieties, and selecting the potentially best one for a golf course is often based on a less than methodical process. There is no sure way to select the best variety, and newer improved cultivars are being continually introduced. Then there is the confounding problem that the turfgrass one selects may be in such high demand that the available supply is sold out when needed. Producing a seed crop is highly regulated and can be highly risky because it is so weather dependent. Seed growers are usually independent farmers who contract with seed companies to grow a certain variety on a certain acreage of fields that have met certain standards of cleanliness for noxious weeds. If regulations get too strict, the farmer/growers can simply choose to grow another variety that has fewer restrictions, and perhaps higher yields. So seed supplies can vary significantly from year to year.

Another problem is that no one can precisely predict which variety is best adapted to any particular set of site conditions, such as microclimates, rootzone composition, water quality, and endemic pests. On the other hand, a variety may be well adapted to a site and produce excellent putting surfaces but require such intensive and aggressive maintenance that it is impractical to maintain with the budgets available. So sorting out which variety is best for a particular site requires some study. This is true for both warm season and cool season putting green turf.

NATIONAL TURFGRASS EVALUATION TRIALS

The place to start is with the National Turfgrass Evaluation Trials (NTET) at www.ntep.org (see Figure 7-9). This is a collaboration of independent research facilities in 40 U.S. states and 6 Canadian provinces to cooperatively evaluate 17 turfgrass species for quality, color, density, pest resistance, tolerance to heat, cold, traffic, and drought. The entire process is administered by the National Turfgrass Federation, Inc. with funds from the seed industry, sports and golf organizations, and the United States Federal Government. The process is to take a single seed lot of a turfgrass submitted for testing, then send a portion of that specific seed lot to each station participating in the evaluation for planting. This seed lot is assumed to be genetically representative of the variety being evaluated, although it may express its genetic potential differently at each site because of reasons previously discussed. Therefore, although the NTET trials are the place to start, they should not be looked at as the final answer. What follows is a personal method for evaluating NTET data.

First, I might check data for the state nearest the golf course project to see if a test site is nearby. Then I would click on "Latest data" and select the turf type I am most interested in; for example, I might choose "Bentgrass (putting green) test," and then choose "Location/entry info." Once you get the location code for test sites near the proposed project, I suggest reviewing the information on "Locations, site descriptions and management." The intent is to find the test site that is closest, not only in terms of the location, but also in the management to be given on the proposed green sites. The next click is "Data by locations."

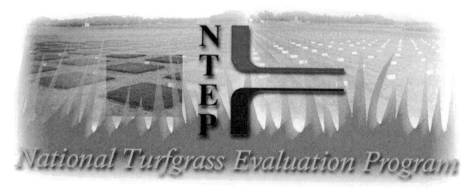

"Providing Results of National Testing of all Major Turfgrass Species"

Figure 7-9: National Turfgrass Evaluation Trials are a good place to begin researching the performance of a variety. Be careful not to believe the highest rated one will be best for any particular site. (Courtesy of NTEP)

Figure 7-10: Selecting the best variety for a site should consider the irrigation water quality and quantity, microclimates, soils, environmental restrictions on pesticides and fertilizers, maintenance budgets, and golfer expectations, for each golf course and green site is unique.

Now you will see lots of turf varieties and the ratings they were given over the evaluation period. But do *not* just assume that the highest rated varieties are best, for at the bottom of the rating chart is something called "LSD value," which stands for least significance difference, and there is a number. This LSD value means that there is no statistical difference between any turfgrass variety in the test that is within that range. For example, if the LSD is 1.5 and the top rated variety is 7.5, then every other variety with a rating of 6.0 (7.5 – 1.5 = 6.0) or higher is statistically the same. It is not unusual to find that, if there are 30 varieties in the test, 24 or 25 will fall within the LSD of the top-rated variety—meaning there is no statistical difference. This doesn't mean there are no differences, for chances are there are huge differences in the performance between varieties. It simply means no statistically significant difference was measured in this evaluation, under the conditions of the site, weather, and management, for this particular period (see Figure 7-10). The value of this information is that the higher the numerical rating of the variety, the better potential it has to perform well for your project.

Now you must factor in your site conditions, the foremost of which is water quality. If your irrigation source is of excellent quality (low salts, neutral pH, no heavy metals, etc.), then the test site data may be relevant. But if your irrigation water quality is marginal to poor, that NTET data is less valuable. If there is any doubt about the similarity between your irrigation water quality and that used at the evaluation site, I would contact the principal researcher at the site, and ask his or her opinion on the best variety for you and your site condition.

Once I start to zero in on a couple of possible varieties, I contact suppliers' representatives for those grasses, and ask for names and places near me where they are being used. Obviously, the next step is to follow up and visit each location, and talk with the greenkeeper or superintendent about his or her experiences. Be sure to inquire about the quality of the location's irrigation water and compare it to yours. Similarly, compare rootzones, fertility philosophies, pest management practices, budgets, and so on. The idea is to select the very best turfgrass variety for your conditions, with the least chance of failure and the best chance of success for the management practices it will receive.

SEED BLENDING

Oftentimes, the search for the perfect putting green turf becomes a dead heat between a couple of varieties. Then the choice becomes choosing one and living with that choice or, if the varieties are compatible, blending them. In the period from 1960 to about 1985, few people would recommend blending for putting green turf, for fear of patchiness outweighed the value of genetic diversity. But as new varieties came to the markets that were more closely related, the idea gained more favor. Today, very few people would resist blending if—*if*—it is done in a very deliberate way. (Blending of vegetatively propagated varieties, however, is not, and never has been, an accepted practice, so this discussion refers only to seeded varieties.)

The major consideration when blending seed for putting green turf is the compatibility of the individual varieties to each other. The more closely matched the cultivars are for color, growth habit, blade characteristics, growth rate, maintenance requirements, and site adaptation, the better will be the result (see Figure 7-11). If care is not taken to match these phenotypic characteristics, then the results could be disastrous. Generally, cultivars from the same

Figure 7-11: Blending of seeded putting green turf varieties is becoming more popular for closely matched cultivars.

plant breeder will blend better together than cultivars from various breeders. For example, it is not uncommon in the mid-South to see A-1 and A-4 blended together because they look so similar but have different enough qualities that superintendents feel there is security in having them both during summer stresses.

Another sort of seed blending for greens is when only a few older greens are being rebuilt on an established golf course with old patchwork greens, and the membership wants the new to play like the old. Then just about anything is fair game as long as the requirements for water, fertilizer, and pest control are well matched. Blending fine textured or extreme upright growth habit types with prostate or semiupright growers will give a new green an old appearance almost immediately. Another technique is to use either 100 percent creeping blue (*Poa annua* spp.) or *Poa trivialis,* which will segregate over time, or add in some creeping blue with the bentgrass.

Blending bentgrass seed with other varieties that can serve as a nurse crop is also an accepted practice that makes sense in some situations. For example, fine fescues, which weakly tiller, can stand putting green height mowing but cannot compete against stronger vegetative spreaders like creeping bentgrass when growth conditions are wet and favor bentgrasses (see Figure 7-12). This means that sowing the bunch grass with the creeper does not significantly retard the creeper's establishment. Of course, the question is, why would you want to? One reason might be that the preferred cultivar for that particular project is in short supply that year, and hence very expensive. This was the thought process at the Sand Barrens golf courses in southern New Jersey. The decision was made to buy as much of the preferred cultivar L-93 as available, seed it half rate (three-quarters of a pound per thousand square feet), and then

Figure 7-12: Mixing or overseeding with a nurse crop, such as fine fescues on bentgrass putting greens, is often a smart strategy, such as when irrigation water is severely limited. All of the Sand Barrens courses in Avalon, NJ, were seeded in that manner.

overseed it with a half rate (two pounds per thousand square feet) of chewings fescue. This worked wonderfully, for the speed of germination between the grasses were about the same, as was their seedlings development, and where there was plenty of water the bentgrass dominated, and where water was in short supply, the fescue persisted. In either case, the turf looked and played the same, and over time became all bentgrass.

The topic of availability of seed when it is needed is obviously important, and as explained earlier, there can be wild market fluctuations. The only way to avoid these market swings is to deal with a reputable seed supplier and place the order early, and even guarantee it with a deposit if necessary. This process of getting what you want begins about one year earlier when, after having determined the most desirable variety(s), you ask the supplier to forecast the next year's supply. Then watch the spring weather in the seed production areas, for weather can have a devastating effect. It is also a good idea to check with the supplier periodically as the season goes on. Things happen fast in the seed business, so the best idea is to place your order as early as possible.

SEED QUALITY

Seed for putting surfaces should be of the highest quality practical, and this means purity and pure live seed (PLS). I believe that the PLS issue is a bit overblown when one considers the sheer numbers of seeds that are planted. For example, if the seeding rate for a bentgrass green is one and one-half pounds per thousand square feet, and if there are 8 million bentgrass seeds per pound, then the seed rate is 12 million seeds per thousand square feet. In 1,000 square feet, there are 144,000 square inches. So the number of seeds per square inch equals 83 seeds, so even with 90 percent PLS, this is 72 viable seeds per square inch! A sod grower would use less than half that rate to seed a sod production area, because he or she wants the plants to quickly reach a stage of vegetative growth to knit into a sod that can be harvested. Yet time after time I see seeding specifications, written by uneducated designers and greenkeepers, that call for four or five pounds per thousand square feet for greens. The negative effect of too heavy a seeding is that the plants never reach a level of vegetative tillering that allows the green to recover from traffic and ball marks. Oftentimes, the effects of greens seeded too heavily are still discernible even after five or six years.

Now the issue of purity cannot be stressed strongly enough, because even a seemingly small percentage of weed grasses can ruin the looks of an excellent turf. To guard against this, the seed growers, harvesters, processors, and suppliers take extreme precautions to keep every step of seed production free of contamination. It costs lots of time and money to accomplish this, and there are equally stringent and costly standards for testing to ensure weed-free seed for putting greens (see Figure 7-13). Yet every year there are cases where supposedly clean seed produces a weedy turf. The best assurance is to deal with the most reputable seed supplier. Reading a seed tag can be very informative, and Dr. Leah Brilman published an excellent article on that topic in the May 2003 issue of *Golf Course Management* magazine. It is also a good idea to keep all seed tags or copies of them in a historic file for later use.

The way that impure seed reaches the market, although there are well-written and effective methods for certifying seed, is more through deceit than an honest mistake. For example, a seed supplier has a seed lot of 10,000 pounds and he submits 25 samples for testing of one-quarter of a gram each (0.25 g). Suppose 24 tests show weed grasses, and one does not. A reputable seed supplier would reject the entire lot of seed, whereas a dishonest supplier would use the one acceptable test to certify the entire 10,000 pounds, and hope not to get too many complaints. Chances are the dishonest supplier will not get caught and will not have to go through the difficult task of trying to sell a substandard seed lot.

The only way to guard against this mess is to write the specifications for seed purity as tightly as possible, then reserve the right to retest the seed upon delivery to the jobsite. The sample size should be quite large, such as 25 grams as

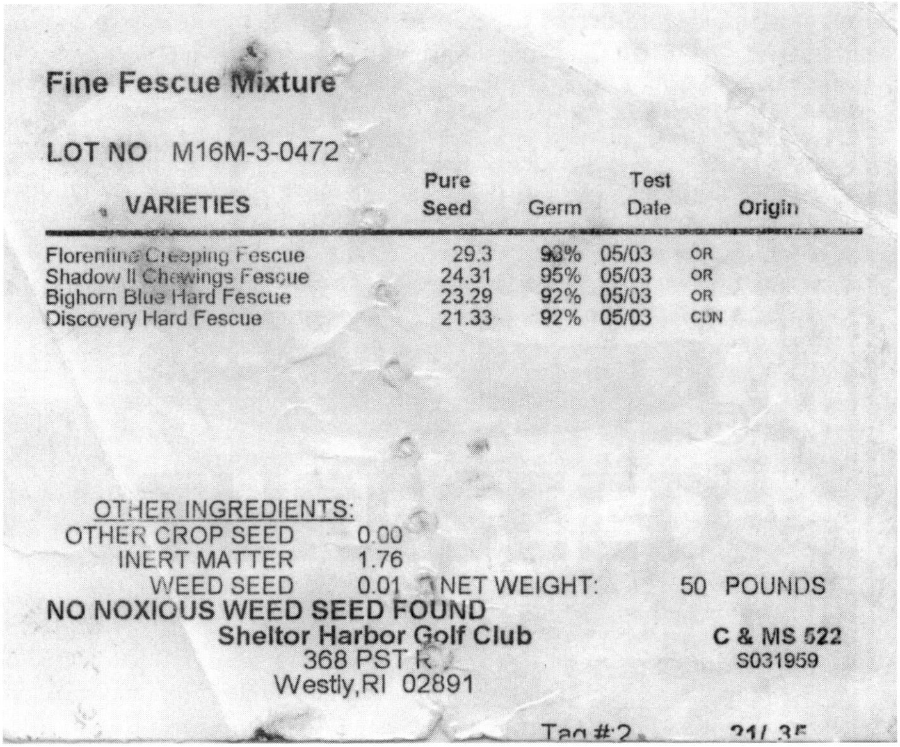

Figure 7-13: Each bag of seed should have a certification of the purity and measured germination rate of seed it contains, as well as percentages of impurities or weed seeds.

Fine Fescue Mixture

LOT NO M16M-3-0472

VARIETIES	Pure Seed	Germ	Test Date	Origin
Florentine Creeping Fescue	29.3	93%	05/03	OR
Shadow II Chewings Fescue	24.31	95%	05/03	OR
Bighorn Blue Hard Fescue	23.29	92%	05/03	OR
Discovery Hard Fescue	21.33	92%	05/03	CDN

OTHER INGREDIENTS:
OTHER CROP SEED 0.00
INERT MATTER 1.76
WEED SEED 0.01 NET WEIGHT: 50 POUNDS
NO NOXIOUS WEED SEED FOUND
Sheltor Harbor Golf Club   C & MS 522
368 PST R.   S031959
Westly, RI 02891

Tag #2   21/35

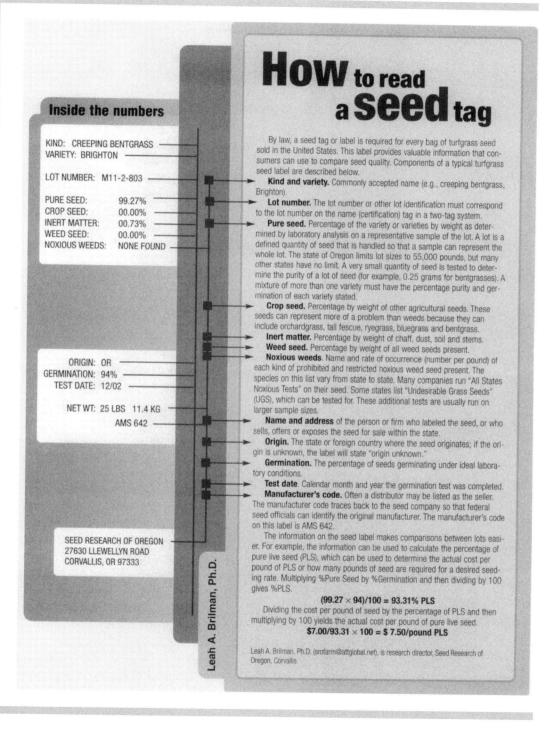

Inside the numbers

KIND: CREEPING BENTGRASS
VARIETY: BRIGHTON

LOT NUMBER: M11-2-803

PURE SEED: 99.27%
CROP SEED: 00.00%
INERT MATTER: 00.73%
WEED SEED: 00.00%
NOXIOUS WEEDS: NONE FOUND

ORIGIN: OR
GERMINATION: 94%
TEST DATE: 12/02

NET WT: 25 LBS 11.4 KG

AMS 642

SEED RESEARCH OF OREGON
27630 LLEWELLYN ROAD
CORVALLIS, OR 97333

Leah A. Brilman, Ph.D.

How to read a seed tag

By law, a seed tag or label is required for every bag of turfgrass seed sold in the United States. This label provides valuable information that consumers can use to compare seed quality. Components of a typical turfgrass seed label are described below.

Kind and variety. Commonly accepted name (e.g., creeping bentgrass, Brighton).

Lot number. The lot number or other lot identification must correspond to the lot number on the name (certification) tag in a two-tag system.

Pure seed. Percentage of the variety or varieties by weight as determined by laboratory analysis on a representative sample of the lot. A lot is a defined quantity of seed that is handled so that a sample can represent the whole lot. The state of Oregon limits lot sizes to 55,000 pounds, but many other states have no limit. A very small quantity of seed is tested to determine the purity of a lot of seed (for example, 0.25 grams for bentgrasses). A mixture of more than one variety must have the percentage purity and germination of each variety stated.

Crop seed. Percentage by weight of other agricultural seeds. These seeds can represent more of a problem than weeds because they can include orchardgrass, tall fescue, ryegrass, bluegrass and bentgrass.

Inert matter. Percentage by weight of chaff, dust, soil and stems.

Weed seed. Percentage by weight of all weed seeds present.

Noxious weeds. Name and rate of occurrence (number per pound) of each kind of prohibited and restricted noxious weed seed present. The species on this list vary from state to state. Many companies run "All States Noxious Tests" on their seed. Some states list "Undesirable Grass Seeds" (UGS), which can be tested for. These additional tests are usually run on larger sample sizes.

Name and address of the person or firm who labeled the seed, or who sells, offers or exposes the seed for sale within the state.

Origin. The state or foreign country where the seed originates; if the origin is unknown, the label will state "origin unknown."

Germination. The percentage of seeds germinating under ideal laboratory conditions.

Test date. Calendar month and year the germination test was completed.

Manufacturer's code. Often a distributor may be listed as the seller. The manufacturer code traces back to the seed company so that federal seed officials can identify the original manufacturer. The manufacturer's code on this label is AMS 642.

The information on the seed label makes comparisons between lots easier. For example, the information can be used to calculate the percentage of pure live seed (PLS), which can be used to determine the actual cost per pound of PLS or how many pounds of seed are required for a desired seeding rate. Multiplying %Pure Seed by %Germination and then dividing by 100 gives %PLS.

$$(99.27 \times 94)/100 = 93.31\% \text{ PLS}$$

Dividing the cost per pound of seed by the percentage of PLS and then multiplying by 100 yields the actual cost per pound of pure live seed.

$$\$7.00/93.31 \times 100 = \$ 7.50/\text{pound PLS}$$

Leah A. Brilman, Ph.D. (srofarm@attglobal.net), is research director, Seed Research of Oregon, Corvallis.

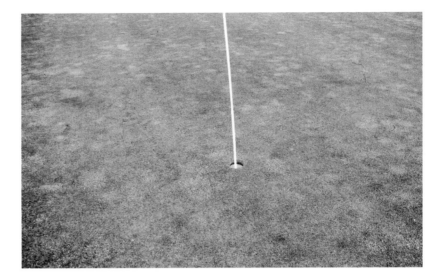

Figure 7-14: It only takes a few seeds of a weed grass like *Poa Trivialis* to show up as bright patches in a newly seeded bentgrass area. Left alone the result can look like this photo in a couple of years.

opposed to the more normal 2- or 5-gram samples. Then the seed test results cannot be hidden or corrupted, and bad seed can be found before it is planted. Even if that procedure is followed, it is still a good idea to keep a small sample (a cup or two) from each bag of seed, in a sealed container, until after the turf is grown in and everyone is satisfied with the quality. This provides the contractor, the project owner, superintendent, and supplier with an inexpensive source of protection.

Years back I observed some new greens that just after grow-in had conspicuous patches of *Poa annua* on them. A test of some saved seed showed that there were about 20 live *Poa annua* seed per pound or 8 million seeds of bentgrass, and at a rate of one and one-half pounds per 1,000 square feet, this amounted to 30 *Poa* plants per thousand square feet, or 12 million bentgrass seeds. So the task of the seed test lab was to find one *Poa* seed among 400,000 bentgrass seeds. In the lab, this is difficult, but on the green, it was obvious. The story had a happy ending only because the seed had been purchased from a reputable dealer who accepted responsibility and agreed to pay for the hand removal of the patches, as well as for two years of chemical treatment for *Poa*. The same problem often happens with *Poa Trivialis* in areas seeded to bentgrass (see Figure 7-14).

Assuring purity of vegetative material is a little more difficult because it means having someone approve the source of the vegetative material before it is harvested, then being there at harvesting and again at delivery to the site. This will assure the purity of the turfgrass but not its viability or vigor, for vegetative material can deteriorate during shipment. Typically, the greatest enemy is heat stress, so often shipments are only done in the cool of night, or packed with dry ice, or shipped in a refrigerated container. Then the key is to plant the turf quickly and get water on it immediately. If a shipment comes in the morning, it should be planted and irrigated by noon. Of course, if the weather is cool, or even cold, then there is less reason to be so fast. Also, some states prohibit shipment of vegetative materials across state lines in an effort to curb nematodes and other pests. This can add to delays in planting and hence vigor of the sod or stolons.

EXPERIMENTAL GREENS

One of the most fascinating things for me is to visit an experimental green that may contain different rootzone mixes, and/or is planted to various cultivars of turf. The USGA has sponsored a wonderful program for such greens, but even without sponsorship, superintendents and greenkeepers should try to get one built (see Figure 7-15). Some build them as small square or rectangular test plots, others like a pie, with each slice being a different turf or rootzone. Naturally, the various tests are permanently marked, either above or below ground, or both, and mapped so that observations can be identified as per cultivar. If possible, this green should receive as much golfer traffic as the rest of the golf course, so a practice green is a good place for one. The responses among the treatments or entrants is of interest, but this can also become an indicator green that can warn of possible disease or insect pressure. Since various cultivars have different sensitivities to stresses, by correlating a response on the experimental green of one turf to the delayed reaction of a similar response on the golf course can prove valuable. For example, if one section of the experimental green is susceptible to, say, brown patch, and would show those symptoms a few days earlier than on the course, a preventative action could be taken instead of a curative one.

To call these greens "experimental" is a bit of a stretch, for more correctly they should be called "observational." The difference is that a true experimental design would call for a random statistical design, a requisite number of repli-

Figure 7-15: An experimental or observational green planted to several cultivars can provide lots of useful information to a keen observer, such as a predictor of possible disease activity. This is a photo of one taken in 1920.

cations, and some definitive markings and record keeping. This is not to suggest that these greens are not valuable contributors to our knowledge about turf-grasses and differences between cultivars, but rather that one should not try to compare those results to those obtained on other such observational greens. There are far too many variables in site conditions and cultural practices to draw any conclusions other than for that particular green. In other words, don't base any final decisions on turfgrass selection on the basis of what you observed on this trial green unless it is yours. What you do learn, however, will certainly help you make an informed and intelligent decision. My advice would be to build one and learn.

Those interested in golf history are often heard to remark, "There are no new ideas in golf, just new materials." A case in point is a 1926 catalog from an American seed company specializing in golf; Stumpp & Walter Co. offered a kit for making an experimental test green of various grasses (see Figure 7-16). In their *Collection of Grass Seeds,* there was sufficient seed to make 20 plots, each 36 square feet. There were:

> 20 varieties in this collection, one half pound each of: south German bent, creeping cocoas bent, colonial bent, Washington Rhode Island bent, red top, Canadian blue grass, Kentucky blue grass, bird grass or rough-stalked meadow, wood meadow grass, hard fescue, chewings New Zealand red fescue, European red fescue, fine-leaved fescue, various-leaved fescue, Pacey's perennial rye grass, Italian rye grass, Bermuda grass, carpet grass, crested dogs tail, sweet vernal.

New grasses are introduced frequently, and what may be best for a particular set of conditions may not have much of a track record in the field. This does not mean you should shy away from a new variety, for before it was released to the market it had extensive evaluation by the plant breeder and probably by the seed supplier. Using a new product may require an even more diligent search for information, however, and there are always risks in being on the cutting edge. There should be lots of folks to help you, though, and the results may be fantastic.

SYNTHETIC TURF

Throughout this book there have been references to nontraditional putting surfaces, and nowhere in the rules of golf is there a requirement for golf to be played on plush, green turfgrasses. As previously discussed, the reasons for these nontraditional greens can be lack of an irrigation source, extreme envi-

Figure 7-16: In 1926 the Stumpp & Walter Co. offered a kit for planting an experimental green.

The Eighteenth Green at the Garden City Golf Club, Garden City, L. I., where the Metropolitan Amateur Championship for 1920 was played. Grass seed for this course supplied by the Stumpp & Walter Co.

Experiment with Grasses

Many clubs desire to experiment with special varieties of grass seeds and determine for themselves the suitability or otherwise of these varieties to their soils. We offer for this purpose a Collection of Grass Seeds, sufficient to take care of 20 plots, each 36 square feet. There are 20 varieties in this Collection, one-half pound each of:

South German Bent, Creeping Cocoos Bent, Colonial Bent, Washington Rhode Island Bent, Red Top, Canadian Blue Grass, Kentucky Blue Grass, Bird Grass or Rough-stalked Meadow, Wood Meadow Grass, Hard Fescue, Chewing's New Zealand Red Fescue, European Red Fescue, Fine-leaved Fescue, Various-leaved Fescue, Pacey's Perennial Rye Grass, Italian Rye Grass, Bermuda Grass, Carpet Grass, Crested Dogstail, Sweet Vernal.

A good scheme is to prepare a piece of typical soil measuring 10 by 8 yards, mark along each side at 2-yard intervals, and bury furring strips on their narrow edge from point to point, marking out twenty small plots. Sow these with each variety, make and keep a plan of the seedings. The collection of twenty varieties costs $8, postpaid.

The experimental plots should be given reasonable care and attention. They need watering when necessary, cutting regularly and rolling from time to time.

What Does It Cost to Build a Golf Course?

Depending on the condition of the soil and the character of the course built, the cost may be between $750 and $4,000 per hole, or from $13,500 to $72,000 or more for an eighteen-hole course. The higher figures enter in when there is much severe green building, clearing, and blasting to be done. This does not include water-supply; the bringing of water on to the property may cost nothing or it may mean the installation of pumps, gravity tanks, etc. Its actual piping to each of the eighteen greens may cost from $2,500 to $5,000. Also they do not include the equipment for the course, concerning which some interesting notes will be found on page 43. While most of the implements to be used on the construction of a course may be hired, the equipment needed for its upkeep requires an investment of from $3,500 to $5,500 or more. The above figures, however, do include the cost of seed. If reasonable quantities of high quality seed, in standard varieties, are selected, their share of the cost will be kept within $5,000. In other words, the seed bill is from about 7 per cent to 35 per cent only of the entire cost; usually it is less than 10 per cent. Is it true economy, therefore, to attempt to save by taking chances with seed? Better to let a firm of specialists supply your requirements and be assured of proper varieties, botanically true, and of the highest quality.

About 120 acres is the minimum area of land upon which a really good eighteen-hole course can be built, although many are built on smaller areas.

INSPECTION OF GOLF COURSES

A part of our service is to make personal inspections of golf courses and advise with you on the ground. Frequently we can arrange to do this without cost to you—we suggest that you write us.

The greens at the Arcola Country Club were the result of periodic reseeding with European Agrostis, or South German Mixed Bent. The 1923 New Jersey State Championship was held at Arcola. Seeds supplied by the Stumpp & Walter Co.

At the Shoreacres Country Club, Lake Bluff, Ill., the Twelfth Hole, 135 Yards. Grass seed supplied by the Stumpp & Walter Co.

Figure 7-17: The humor in this cartoon arises from the fact that there is no need to worry about trampling plastic grass; this is why artificial turf should be considered in unique green situations.

ronmental prohibitions against pesticide and fertilizer use, microclimatic limitations, and the inability of turfgrasses to take the anticipated abuse (see Figure 7-17). Although greens of bare soil or a surface devoid of vegetation can provide an interesting golf experience, there is something special about playing on a uniform, fast, green surface, even if it is artificial.

Plastic or other synthetic materials were relatively new after World War II, but by the mid 1950s, they had become part of everyday life because they were desirable, cheap, and could be easily molded or shaped. The concept of plastic grass, which never needs mowing, watering, or pest control treatments, was appealing, especially in areas where it was difficult to grow native grass anyway, such as in sports stadiums. The first highly published use of artificial turf, as it was called, was in 1965 in the Houston Astrodome, and it was called "AstroTurf™." The advantages were obvious; it didn't look too fake, wouldn't wear out, always looked fresh, and although the cost was high, it was justifiable. Monsanto Industries Co. invented AstroTurf, filed for a patent on December 25, 1965 and was issued U.S. Patent #3332828 on July 25, 1967. Later, as AstroTurf became more widely used on sports fields (see Figure 7-18), indoors and out, it was found that the artificial turf was less forgiving than natural turf, and that more injuries were occurring to highly paid athletes. So began a search for a softer plastic grass that was just as tough, and that search continues today.

It didn't take long for someone to propose artificial turf for golf courses, and I believe that the first one built was a par 3 course in Tennessee. It didn't last long, because the plastic grass wouldn't hold an approach shot, it melted when a cigarette was placed or dropped on it, chewing gum spots were hard to get out, and the ultraviolet light of sun caused the color to wash out, making greens look more like yellows. It seemed that artificial turf had little or no use in golf except as durable hitting mats for driving ranges. These mats made acceptable tees but lousy greens because they were too firm.

At this point, it would be well to discuss how artificial turf is normally installed. The earliest attempt was to use a one-half to three-quarter inch long synthetic turf fiber with a thin one-sixteenth of an inch backing, glued to a hard, stable surface like asphalt. This surface was not very forgiving and many new sport injuries started to appear, ranging from rug burn to concussion. The next attempt in the early 1970s was to use compacted sand as the base, but it was too loose and would distort under traffic. An improvement was the spraying of an elastic polymer onto the sand subsurface, allowing it to soak in about one-tenth of an inch and solidify, then apply the carpet of grass. Still, artificial turf was not the equivalent of natural grass, so the use of a pad between the sub-surface (sand and polymer, asphalt, cement, compacted stone and dust, etc.) and the turf was tried. This system finally resulted in a surface that was acceptable for most athletic events, especially when athletes used shoes designed to grip the synthetic turf surface. However, even new injuries to athletes began to appear, such as "turf toe," pulled knee and shoulder strains, and "stingers." Consequently, improvements to artificial turf continue even today in an attempt

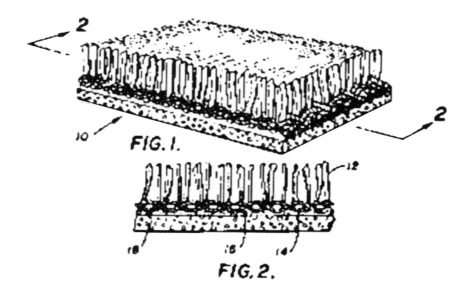

Figure 7-18: Artificial turf or synthetic grass has almost a 40-year history of being used for athletic playing surfaces, golf greens and tees. James M. Faria and Robert T. Wright of Monsanto Industries co-invented Astroturf (U.S. Patent #3332828). A patent for Astroturf was filed on December 25, 1965, and issued by the USPTO on July 25, 1967.

to match the safety aspects of natural grass. Over the past 30 years, many stadiums and athletic fields have switched back and forth between natural grass and synthetic turf in an ongoing search for a surface that is forgiving, yet is all-weather, needs little maintenance, and is extremely durable. The list of sports that have these needs includes golf, which has its own requirements for artificial turf, especially for greens.

HISTORY OF ARTIFICIAL TURF FOR GOLF

Quoting a 1971 patent application for Monsanto Chemical Company for a golf green fabric, "[S]ince the ball response on a synthetic golf green must of necessity simulate the response on natural sod, there must be some provision for absorbing the energy in the manner that natural sod does." There are actually discussions about the "coefficient of restitution" or C.O.R. of the grass blades to an incoming golf ball, as well as a "coefficient of putting friction" or C.O.P.F. In other words, all sorts of engineers were looking at all sorts of measurements and characteristics of artificial turf in their efforts to simulate a natural grass putting surface. First the turf had to "hold" an incoming shot, and then it had to putt true and fast. Getting the synthetic turf to do one or the other was not difficult; getting it to do both was an enormous challenge. These problems would take a couple more decades to solve, before golfers would acknowledge synthetic turf as acceptable, for remember, natural grass surfaces were being improved at the same time. At this writing, there are still differences between plastic and real golf green turf, but that gap is closing, and in many instances, artificial turf should be the clear choice. A look at the evolution of artificial turf for golf course putting greens can show why.

It took a far-sighted pro golfer from Louisiana by the name of Fredrick T. Haas, Jr., to lead the way (see Figure 7-19). On August 23, 1977 Freddy, as his friends called him, received a patent for "Mod Sod™," which is a grass carpet with a pile or "leaves" ranging from one-half inch to one and one-half inch long, that is filled with sand, cork, and vermiculite almost to its entire depth by top-dressing and brushing. Fred's system of filling the carpet with resilient materials is a clear advance to solving the problem of shock absorption, but it is still not the same as natural turf.

In the early 1980s, several companies in the United Kingdom were offering artificial turf soccer fields of sand-filled carpet but also with a rubber pad underneath. Although somewhat popular, these fields proved to be too abrasive and looked more like sand than turf.

About the same time in the United States, Omniturf solved some earlier problems by doubling the pile height of the carpet, and although an improvement for stadiums, the new system doesn't do much for golf. The longer these sand-filled systems are in place, the more compact they become. Drainage

Figure 7-19: Professional golfer Fred Haas, Jr., gets a patent for "Mod Sod™" which is the first artificial turf surface that permits golf and tennis balls to rebound as they might on natural turf.

slows down as well, and the surface tips become so damaged that adding new sand becomes very difficult.

Fred Haas, Jr.'s 1977 patent was mostly aimed for use in tennis courts, where the firmness is not as big a problem as for golf greens, so in his 1983 patent, he added an under pad for greater shock absorbance. This pad can be from one-quarter inch to one and one-quarter inches thick, and the density of the foam can range from about 3.5 to 12.0 pounds per cubic foot. This is a definite improvement for golf use.

A couple of other innovations came along in the late 1980s, including the use of rounded sand particles for the fill material to reduce or eliminate the chance for compaction, and the addition of crumb rubber for added resilience. Minor things, like coloring the sand green for better appearances, improved UV resistance, finer crumb rubber, and better adhesives to bond the synthetic materials together have further improved artificial turf golf greens.

The author's first experience building such a green was in the early 1980s at the direction of Fred Haas, Jr. The green was built to extreme slopes, ranging from zero to ten degrees slope to test the flexibility limits of the material, as well as the wearability of such slopes. After 20 years, the green naturally shows signs of wear but is still functional. Realistically, I would suggest the useful life is six to eight years of normal conditions and use, at which time the artificial turf should be refreshed or replaced. One material manufacturer (ASTRO-PLAY™, phone 512-259-0080) claims an improved life expectancy of their synthetic turf because they build in a Thatch Zone™ of pure rubber at the bottom of the fabric above the backing. Even if the surface gets firm, overall it remains a resilient turf.

In the mid-1990s, we built another green at the offices of Hurdzan/Fry Golf Course Design. It was an entertainment center for guests as well as a test plot we could observe daily and a demonstration area to help clients see the fun and wisdom in artificial turf (see Figure 7-20, color insert). Our green gets the most minimal of maintenance; we generally use a half-distance golf ball (made by POINTFIVE LTD.™ of Loveland, OH, phone 513-248-0356) for safety, and it plays very well. Consequently we can speak with authority about plastic grass. Recently, during a very wet spring and summer, the green was invaded by mosses, especially in the shaded areas. These can be controlled with a variety of methods, from spraying with Dawn Ultra dish soap to vigorous brushing to sprinkling with baking soda.

The design of an artificial turf golf green should follow all of the design criteria mentioned earlier for natural grass greens, as well as following the specific manufacturer's recommendations. There is no need to make the green as large as a natural grass green for it will not wear out. I believe that, for a backyard green or a pitch and putt, 1,000 to 1,500 square feet is a nice size (see Figure 7-21). The installed cost of such a green would range from $10 to $20 per square foot. Although it is possible to move the cup or hole on some products, I would recommend designing in three or four permanent hole locations of an eight-foot radius with 1.5 to 2 percent slopes around them, and then separating those target areas with valleys or ridges, which can go up to 6 or 8 percent slope. You may choose to use one hole at a time, filling the others with a hole plug. If the site for a course was very small, then you could build three greens, with three holes each, and three tees and come up with a minicourse of 9 to 27 holes. Bunkers, bumps, and valleys built into the green surrounds would give each hole a personality.

The sub-base of the green or tee to be covered with artificial turf should be stable and compact. Various installers recommend various bases, such as asphalt, concrete, compacted stone, and compacted soil, some with a polymer topcoat and others with separate pads of glue-down type. There are lots of vendors for synthetic grass, and although most of the material comes out of only a couple of factories in Dalton, GA, there are few but subtle differences. As with so many things, the best choice is the vendor that can give the best service, most experience, and a competitive price. It is not a simple task to decide what is best for a given situation and location, for it requires asking lots of questions and listening to the answers, or getting claims and guarantees down on paper.

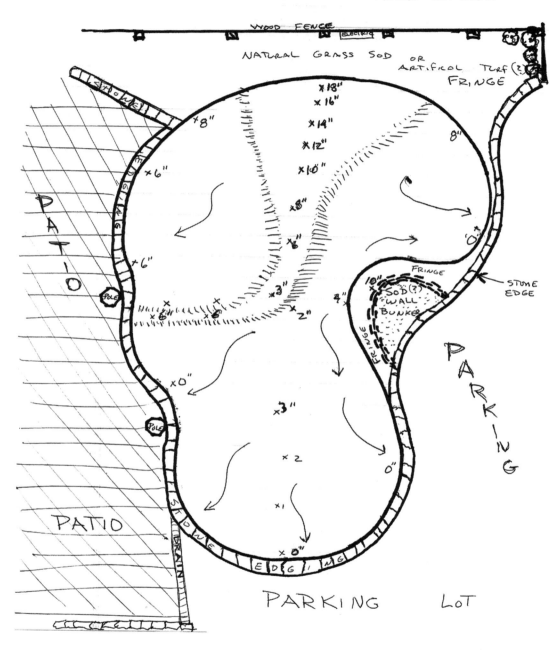

Figure 7-21: Planning for an artificial turf green should follow all of the thought processes used for natural turf greens, but it can be made smaller because of increased wearability. This simple drawing was done for the green at Hurdzan/Fry offices.

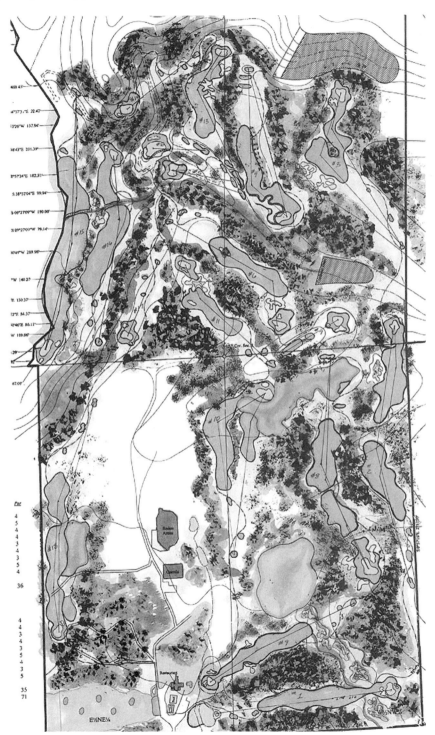

Figure 7-22: The first complete, full-size, artificial turf golf course is to be completed in 2004 in Colorado because there was no water to irrigate natural turf.

Because the initial cost of artificial turf greens can be three to five times higher per square foot than a natural grass green, it makes sense to build smaller greens that are fair targets for the length of shot being played. Even for a full size golf course, greens in the size range of 4,000 to 5,000 square feet would be large and expensive.

ARTIFICIAL TURF GOLF COURSE

Recently, a Colorado businessman proposed an entire golf course—tees, greens, and fairways—to be covered in artificial turf, the first in the world (see Figures 7-22 and 7-23). The motivation was a lack of an irrigation source, as well as a desire to virtually eliminate traditional practices of water, fertilization, pesticide applications, mowing, and aerifying. Instead of an annual maintenance budget of perhaps $750,000 for a real turf golf course, his projected annual maintenance cost was between $100,000 and $150,000. The total estimated construction cost for the required 1.4 million square feet is between $9 million and $14 million, and green fees should be in the $60 range. If the golf course gets completed, it will be a hallmark project in the use of synthetic turf for golf courses. The idea is sound and makes great sense, but golfers are the real test. Will they want to play on artificial turf? How important is natural turf to the game? Pitch and putt par 3s and putting greens of plastic grass are one thing; an entire golf course of it should prove interesting.

The critical reactions are that the uniformity of the turf would be visually striking and provide a vivid contrast to the natural surroundings. However, it is possible that initial awe could turn to boredom after a few hours. Then there is the question about the temperature of the artificial playing surface versus the natural cooling effect that comes from tran-

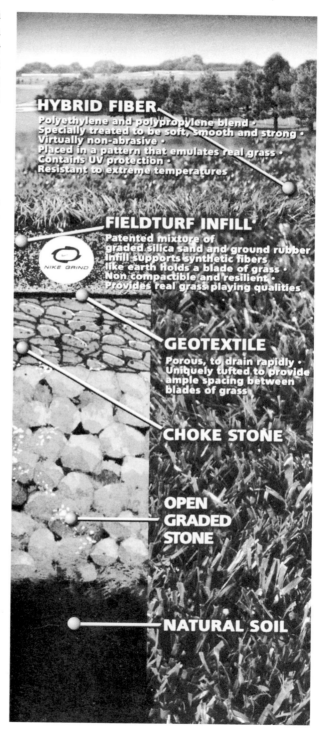

Figure 7-23: Cross section of Tour Turf™ material being used on Colorado golf course. (Courtesy of Tour Turf)

spiring live turf. Playing golf on a full size hole should be interesting as well, for the ball should bounce and roll further on the synthetic turf as opposed to natural grass, which could be either a plus or a minus. In areas of high rainfall or snow melt, the artificial surfaces should be expected to surface drain more rapidly than a natural grass area of similar slope would. Consequently, receiving points of this surface drainage may have to be enlarged to receive this extra water. Lastly, many will be watching the turf as it begins to age a bit to observe what unforeseen problems may develop. Taken all together, this is a bold experiment, but it will no doubt help to establish and improve artificial turf position and acceptance on golf courses.

Legal Liabilities of Golf Green Construction

DISCLAIMER

As soon as I use either of the words *legal* or *liabilities*, or heaven forbid, use them together, I feel compelled to give this disclaimer. I am not an attorney, I have no legal training, I do not profess to be a technician of the law in any way, so any legal question you have should be discussed with an attorney familiar with laws in your area. I am only a golf course architect who has served as an expert witness in many states on many golf course–related subjects, who, through professional practice and involvement as an expert witness, has learned the generalized meaning and implication of legal liabilities. On top of that, I consider myself to be blessed with a fair amount of common sense, which is very important in matters of liability, if not law.

PROOF OF LIABILITY

In a nutshell, proof of liability or negligence is based upon one's duty to protect or preserve something; violating that duty, knowingly or unknowingly, if it results in a loss or injury to a second party, leaves you liable. Ignorance of your obligation to protect or preserve doesn't give you relief, if a prudent person in your same position could have, or should have, foreseen the injury or damage caused by your neglect of duty. This is a grossly oversimplified definition of negligence and liability, and proof of these in a court of law can be exceedingly difficult, but I hope you get the idea.

Now that I have told you what I don't know, please allow me to tell you what I do know about liabilities in golf green construction. For discussion purposes, I group these topics into categories of:

1. Design
2. Environment
3. Construction
4. Maintenance

Some things might overlap between categories and I trust you will recognize the ones I don't point out.

Intuitively, prudent foreseeability of one's obligation or duty to protect and preserve will vary with one's individual training, experience, and position in life. Since we are talking about a golf green, the various groupings of people who might come in contact with it might be:

1. Owners of the facility
2. Management of the facility
3. Staff (superintendent, greenkeepers, golf staff, etc.)
4. Designer
5. Builder
6. Golfer
7. Nongolfing visitor

Clearly, all of these groups would have different obligations or duties based upon their backgrounds (see Figure 8-1). To keep this from getting too complicated and confusing, I will use a hypothetical example of constructing a new green and try to show how each phase of its development might relate to one or more of these groups of people.

Figure 8-1: Each person has a different duty to protect and foresee a danger based upon his or her individual education, training, experience, or position in life.

Figure 8-2: Hiring an unqualified consultant could be seen as a failure in one's duty to protect. Investigate qualifications and do not rely on reputation or how they look.

SELECTING COMPETENT CONSULTANTS

The first step in building a new green(s) should be the selection of a consultant, presumably a golf course architect, to guide the design and construction process. Right away potential liabilities may begin, for what if the selected consultant is unqualified and makes some decisions out of ignorance or inexperience that later result in legal action (see Figure 8-2)? It could be argued that not knowing the qualifications of your designer is not a defense and that the act of selecting an unproven consultant violated a duty to protect or preserve that was the owner's responsibility. If this seems farfetched, consider how you would feel if your child were injured in a school bus accident and you found out that the school board had hired an unqualified or unstable driver. Most people believe that the "boss" has a responsibility to hire qualified "workers." More about this later.

ANALYZING A SITE

After selecting a qualified consultant for the job, you should select a few possible sites for the new green and have a site assessment done. This means researching the site for:

1. Environmental impacts
2. Legal restrictions (rights-of-way, easements, property boundaries, etc.)
3. Archaeological significance
4. Engineering qualities (stability, soils and rock, percolation, etc.)
5. Golfing and safety implications
6. Economic feasibility

Many of these assessments may seem simple, and they probably are, until a problem develops; then efforts are made to attach blame for implied negligence. The responsibility begins with the design consultant who is assessing and recommending the various sites, and it is expected that, by the nature of his or her qualifications, such a consultant would have the skills to *prudently foresee* any problem. If he or she does not see the problem and later that problem results in a loss or injury, the resulting liability may be covered under a professional practice insurance policy the consultant carries for such "errors and omissions." If, however, a consultant does suspect a problem, he or she will usually refer it back to the owner to get another consultant to appropriately address the concern. The owner still bears the final responsibility for the site selection, so again it is in the owner's best interest to get qualified information. An example of this situation might be that wetland areas are suspected, but proper procedures for wetland issues are not followed, before or during construction, and wetland violations are discovered after the fact. In extreme cases, such violations may transcend negligence to become criminal misconduct and can carry fines and jail time for ignoring one's responsibility. My point is that the owner and consultants must be sensitive to these potential liabilities, and address, not ignore, them.

COMMUNICATING THE DESIGN INTENT

After the green site has been selected, assessed, and approved, the design consultant should conceptually communicate to the owner what the green will look like and how it will fit on the site (see Figure 8-3). Various methods of communicating the design intent in order of their descending specificity include:

1. Large scale (1 inch = 10 feet or 1 inch = 20 feet) plan view drawings with contour lines, or spot elevations, or cross sections, or a combination of these
2. Small scale (1 inch = 30 feet or larger) plan view drawings with contour lines, or spot elevations, or cross sections, or a combination of these
3. Nonscaled plan views with elevations
4. Panoramic sketches with elevations

Figure 8-3: Communicating a green design to the owner/client can take many forms, from drawings to models or, as shown, an explanation on the site.

5. Panoramic sketches
6. Verbal descriptions and hand waving
7. Designer's grunts and gestures

The potential liability here is that the designer doesn't communicate well with the owner, and the owner doesn't like the finished product and won't pay the bill. As a golf course architect, I make sure the client approves the design before it is built, which shifts the liability to him or her, and I give the client an opportunity to change the design in the field in the rough grade stage for the same reason.

The sorts of issues I want the owner or owner's representative to approve are:

1. Location and clearing of vegetation
2. Size of putting surface
3. Shape and undulations
4. Elevation
5. Pitch and drainage
6. Bunkers and green surrounds
7. Identified safety issues
8. Possible construction impacts

CONSTRUCTION: IN-HOUSE OR OUTSIDE CONTRACTOR?

At last, a green design and details are completed and approved by the owner, and it is ready for construction. If the construction is done by the owner's workforce (usually a superintendent and crew), then the owner assumes all liabilities associated with the construction, from Environmental Protection Agency (EPA) requirements to Occupational Safety and Health Administration (OSHA) regulations, as well as performance characteristics of the completed green. Since contractors only hope for about 15 percent profit on each project, many owners and superintendents don't feel the risks justify the savings. If the owner's workforce does the construction, the design consultant's duty to ensure the design is properly constructed rests with the agreement with the owner. If the designer is expected to approve every construction step, his or her liability exposure is much greater than if the owner is only paying the designer to observe the process. Again, the owner assumes the responsibility, unless he or she delegates it to others through mutually agreed-upon verbal or written contracts.

The golf course superintendent is normally an employee of the owner and is thus the owner's agent. This means the superintendent should be protected from personal liability by the owner, a long as the superintendent is acting legally, ethically, and morally within the guidelines and authority given to him by the owner—or within the guidelines and authority that should be expected of the superintendent given his or her training and experience in the position. If the superintendent acts without authority or in an imprudent way, such as knowing of or approving a wetland violation, that superintendent could be found negligent and solely accountable. Likewise, the superintendent's crew is acting as the superintendent's agents and he or she may have to take responsibility for their negligence.

If the green is to be built by an outside contractor, the liabilities shift. Now the consultant has a greater duty to define exactly where the contractor's work starts, stops, and what takes place between those end points. If the designer is not specific, and a problem develops, the contractor could take legal action against the designer or owner or both. So the more clearly detailed the contractor's obligations are, the more responsibility he or she assumes. This is where knowledge and experience of the professional golf course architect becomes critical. It is assumed that the designer sets the standard of workmanship and interprets and observes the work in relation to that standard. The designer is expected to be acting solely in the owner's best interest.

BID DOCUMENTS

The preferred method of communicating with a contractor is called "bid documents," or "plans and specs" (see Figure 8-4). These drawings and written descriptions should perfectly complement one another so all conceivable items are covered, and there should be provision for mutually resolving any misunderstandings or situations that might not be anticipated. This process is often referred to as "the method of professional practice," which seeks to assign responsibility before conflicts arise.

If the designer has a construction company as part of his or her business operation that is doing the work, the designer assumes more liability than if an independent contractor is used. The relationship of the designer to the con-

Figure 8-4: Plans and specifications are the usual method for defining the exact scope and quality of a proposed construction project.

tractor should be fully disclosed to the owner, for now the owner is assuming additional liability because the normal checks and balances of designer versus contractor relationship is being obviated: a classic example of the fox guarding the hen house.

Somewhere in the design process the decision will be made as to the type of interior green construction or rootzone concept to be used. It is assumed that the owner or owner's representative will be presented with the optional methods available, such as USGA, USGA modified, California, topsoil, and so on, and that the owner will direct the designer as to which method to use. If the owner is never given this option, it could be argued that the designer acted capriciously and thus assumes some responsibility for the method chosen. The point I am making is that any method can fail, and when it does and when correcting that failure involves major expenditures, invariably lawsuits arise. Such an example happened a few years back in Breckenridge, CO.

THINGS GO WRONG

In Breckenridge, the golf course was built to supposedly rigidly enforced USGA specifications, but the greens failed within six months with percolation rates of two inches per hour and less. The town initially sued the contractor for supplying faulty materials, but he was exonerated at arbitration hearings, along with the sand supplier. Suit was then filed against the architect for improper quality control, despite his having fulfilled the most rigid and extensive testing requirements ever observed for that time period. The court found against the designer with an award greater than his fee. The point is that simply specifying the method to be used does not shift the liability to the builder or supplier, nor does it guarantee against failures and negligence lawsuits.

Similarly, when a designer specifies a performance characteristic for a rootzone, the owner has a right to expect that characteristic or to be compensated for lack thereof. If it is specified that a green will have a saturated hydraulic conductivity (Ksat) of 12 inches per hour, and a year later it is 6 inches per hour, is this grounds for a claim? Not if the owner was clearly apprised that the 12 inch per hour performance spec was for mix only, compacted in a certain way, with no turf cover or root mass, tested in a lab, before placement. A few years back, some testing labs and blending companies *guaranteed* the rootzone blend against defects. I thought this was a risky offer, for although most blending companies field test the rootzone mix several times per day as part of their service, and will provide a summary report of those test results, there is lots of variability in testing methods. All this means is that on a specified day, under specified conditions, using specific methods, a specific result was found — it does not guarantee performance into the future. In fact, a single sample could be taken from a rootzone blend, divided and sent to three separate, accredited

Figure 8-5: Rootzone materials that were properly blended can change physical properties while sitting in the pile, especially if amended with organic materials.

labs, and each lab might get different performance data (Ksat), none of which agree with the blender's test result.

I personally avoid performance specifications, for too many things can happen to change performance of a green over time. These include breakdown of organic matter, contamination during handling or storage, chemical aggregation, biological disorders, irrigation water effects, topdressing influences, anaerobic conditions, and so on. When greens fail performance specs, lawsuits are considered. This is a sensitive issue that can become a source of liability. Let me cite another example.

A golf course was being built in southern California to USGA standards, and the 8,000 or 9,000 tons of 85:15 (sand:peat) mix was blended by a professional soil blender who field checked the Ksat rate every hour to insure it stayed in the 12 to 14 inches per hour range. A few months later as the mix, which was sitting in a big pile, was being moved to the green wells, it was discovered that the perc rate was less than 2 inches per hour due to anaerobic decomposition of the organic matter (Figure 8-5). The owner expected 12 inches per hour, so he wasn't going to pay anyone. The sand supplier, peat supplier, and blender all said they did not cause the problem and they wanted to be paid. This had the makings of a huge suit when the problem somehow disappeared. (I suspect the performance standard was compromised and the lower perc rate material used to save an enormous problem.) But you see the potential liability and difficulty of determining who was to blame? No one did anything wrong, but the owner wasn't getting what he was promised, and he rightly refused to pay anyone's bill. Like the bumper sticker says, "Stuff happens."

Another problem has been that the same sample, sent to three different test labs, would most likely come back with three different test results. Most of this was due to nonuniform testing equipment and protocol, not the skill or integrity of the various labs. Needless to say, those of us who depended on these tests were confused and would simply select one lab or another on the basis of who we trusted most. Recently, efforts have been made to standardize testing labs, but this is just starting. This problem is discussed more in depth in Chapter 6, on how to read a soil test report.

The summary point is that things can go wrong in the research, design, and contract document phases of green construction, things that should not be ignored and that can cost lots of money to correct. No one person can be held accountable or exonerated for all such problems, so often it takes a lawsuit to settle the issue, but a solid method of practice is an excellent defense.

The next area for consideration is the actual construction of the green, where different exposures to liability may exist.

These generally fall into the following categories:

1. Site conditions
2. Construction operations and workmanship
3. Faulty materials
4. Improper maintenance

SITE CONDITIONS

The list of site condition problems is probably endless, for just when one thinks one has seen it all, new problems pop up. The most common sources of site condition problems are too soft a subsoil or base, groundwater surfacing, hard rock layers which require jackhammering or blasting, or trees and vegetation (see Figures 8-6 and 8-7 in color insert). Rather than reviewing these individually, let me just say that the base of the green must be solid, must have no shallow groundwater problem, must allow for excavation and grading of the green interior subgrade, and must not have any roots from bordering vegetation intruding into the rootzone.

Generally, solving these unseen problems is the responsibility of the owner or his or her appropriate consultant and not the contractor, unless the contractor did not properly execute the work according to agreed-upon plans and specifications. However, since these are common problems, provisions are made in the bid documents to handle these situations, and it is usually as an extra payment to the contractor for any extra efforts that must be made to complete the work. This extra is normally paid as direct cost plus fifteen percent more profit, overhead, and so on.

Some of the more unusual site conditions have included having wrong property lines and hence building on another's property, discovering natural gas wells seeping under and into the green cavity, or finding the green site was an ancient peat bog that has started to slowly sink under the weight of the root-zone mix. Such problems are solved either by selecting a new green site, or by innovating an engineering solution, such as using geotextiles, geogrids, or geomembranes under the green. The worst green sites are old landfills where one should be prepared for settling of the ground as the underlying materials decompose or compact, along with volatile and phytotoxic gas seepage, and leachate that looks like it is from another planet.

The liability of such siting problems would again be the designer's if he or she were aware of these problems during initial design phases. If these were discovered after initial mapping and design, the responsibility would go back to the owner or to the owner's appropriate consultant who was charged with identifying such potential problem areas. The contractor should rely on having normal site conditions unless he or she is expressly warned to check for such conditions before beginning work. Also, a good set of plans and specs include provisions for protecting and compensating the contractor.

CONSTRUCTION OPERATIONS AND WORKMANSHIP

It is assumed that a person or contractor offering to do the work has the proper experience, training, equipment, and work force to professionally execute the work. It is wrong to assume the contractor is qualified, however, so don't assume. It is normally the consultant or golf course architect who may recommend to the owner about who is or is not qualified, based upon an investigation into the contractor's past performance. But it is the owner's responsibility to fully investigate the contractor, for the contractor will be solely the owner's responsibility, not the consultant's. It is the owner who enters into a legal agreement to pay the contractor for services rendered, not the consultant, even though the contractor may have been hired on the advice of the consultant. So, if you get a bad contractor, whose is the liability problem? The answer is the owner's.

What kind of problems can occur during the construction that might result in a liability and/or lawsuit? They can start with preparing the base of the green site and normally have to do with compacting the fill. If undisturbed ground has a value of 100 percent proctor, as it is called, and roadways require 95 percent while dams must have at least 92 percent, then a green should have at least

90 percent. This can be achieved by building on soil that is undisturbed, such as a green cut down into a site, or by compacting each lift or layer of soil as it is brought into a built-up green (see Figure 8-8, color insert). A normal specification calls for lifts or layers of perhaps 6 to 8 inches, depending on soil type, which are compacted by rolling or wheel tracking before the next lift goes down. Bulldozers don't compact; they float across the surface on wide tracks, so bulldozers cannot compact most fill material. However, if fill material is being brought in by rubber-tired scrapers, or pans, or earthmovers, whatever you wish to call them, and the scrapers drive back and forth over the fill, then it will usually be compacted. Care must be taken that the fill is not too wet or too dry, because moisture control is important to get good compaction. Most disturbed soils will settle 10 to 15 percent of their depth. This means that a 48-inch fill will settle about 5 inches over time to 100 percent proctor. Mechanical compaction compresses this time. Failure to compact means subgrades, and thus final grades, will settle out sometime later—perhaps after the green is in play, leaving small depressed areas, called "bird baths," that hold water, complicate maintenance, and drive superintendents nuts. When the construction goal is for 1.5 to 2 percent slopes, it only takes a small amount of settling to result in a birdbath.

The worst case of noncompaction I ever saw was on a golf course built of clay soils by big scrapers. As these powerful earthmovers were pulled and pushed through the soil, the cutting blade caused the clay to come out as long ribbons, like wood chips off a sharp knife. These huge waves or chips of clay were hauled to the green site and dumped, in deep lifts of two to three feet, and leveled by a bulldozer that simply cut the tops off the "chips," often creating air pockets. Then one spring, a couple of years later, I got a call from the course owner, who said that while he recognized that I had nothing to do with his course, he would like my help with a little problem he had on his greens. It seems these trapped air pockets were starting to settle out, and that spring, a member was putting when he suddenly sank to his waist on the green. Soon other sinkholes of various depths and sizes were appearing. The golf course owner finally ended up rebuilding his greens, this time using a contractor who understood that good construction begins from the bottom or base up.

Once the base or subgrade of the green is in place and approved by the golf course architect and owner's representative, then tile patterns are laid out with wire flags, stakes, paint, or chalk lines. These too, should be approved by the architect or owner's representative before installation, for the single most common, although not fatal, mistake in green construction is improperly placed tile line patterns. The problem is not in the uniform spacing (15 to 21 feet between tile centerlines), but rather that the tile is not *perpendicular* to the surface grade of the green. Tile patterns do not need to be pretty and uniform; they need to be functional. Put tile where it is needed regardless of how haphazard the final pattern looks. Ideally, someone from either the owner or contractor's staff should be made responsible to photograph the green cavity with the tile installed, prior to adding any other layers. These photos should all be taken from out in front of the green, and from 10 to 12 feet above the ground. These photos serve as a permanent record to help the golf course superintendent if he suspects a tile drainage problem, and they protect the contractor by showing how the work was done to the associated specifications.

Naturally, the contractor continues to be responsible for protecting the drainage systems, which means keeping them free of damage, silting, settling, debris accumulation, and the like (see Figure 8-9, color insert). Unfortunately, improper tile installation may be the source of future drainage or turf problems, but since it is buried, it is very difficult to evaluate and hence difficult to place liability. Having photographs helps sort it all out.

FAULTY MATERIALS

There is some liability, however, associated with the choice of envelope around the tile. The purpose of the envelope around the tile is to keep the tile functional, *not* to act as a filter. The best envelope is one-quarter to three-eighths of an inch of pea stone surrounding the tile, which will texturally separate it from the fine-textured particles of rootzone above it, allowing for migrating soil particles to drop out or bridge before they reach the tile, and giving multiple free passageways for water to reach the tile. So where could there be any liability there?

First, if the wrong envelope material is chosen. The proper size material for a golf green is usually one-quarter to three-eighths of an inch pea stone, but whether that size is appropriate in a particular instance should ultimately be determined by an accredited rootzone-testing lab to assure compatibility between rootzone and gravel. If one selects a material of improper size, then not only may this allow for more rootzone to filter down, it could also impede the conductivity of water to the tile by establishing an exaggerated textural discontinuity. In my opinion, using ½-inch or larger stone as a tile envelope is courting possible failure or reduced drainage and perhaps liability, although some research in Britain seems to disprove this. I recommend erring on the side of safety, or smaller rather than larger gravel, unless there are no alternatives, and then the owner should approve this change in writing, which would shift the responsibility for any later failure to him or her. Without such approval, whoever chooses the wrong gravel must assume the responsibility.

Secondly, the envelope material must be physically stable. Not all stone or stone chips are stable, and they can sometimes become soft and break down under certain conditions, such as certain drainage water. I have seen two examples where stone chips that were used as the envelope material had become so soft after two to three years, you could squeeze them between your fingers and they would turn to an almost clay-like consistency. Sooner or later these tile drains will fail, and the person who chose the material may have a liability problem.

In my opinion, using a geotextile cover on a tile that is not bedded in 100 percent fine sand is also courting failure due to the possibility of filter caking on the geotextile. Manufacturers even warn consultants that geotextile coverings on tile are for very specialized situations, such as in areas of 100 percent sand soils such as near lake beds, in blow sand regions, or in places where chances of silt or clay migrating in the profile are almost nonexistent. There is a huge difference between keeping tile clean and keeping it functioning. A tile can hold a lot of silt before it clogs, but it takes only a micro-layer of the same material on geotextile to filter cake and become impervious to drainage water. Specifying a geotextile cover over tile is chancing a liability, unless soil laboratory tests indicate otherwise. This same logic applies to putting geotextile under rootzones—don't do it. Geotextiles have no place in green construction, except under certain very specialized conditions, and then with a geotextile that is guaranteed by its manufacturer to not allow filter caking.

Some superintendents are experimenting with bedding tile with geotextile covering with sand as the envelope, and not the pea gravel. As long as no silt or clay can possibly reach the sock, this system will be functional, but why risk any liability when one-quarter to three-eighths of an inch of pea stone is a proven method?

Assuming the tile is properly installed, the next chance for liability is the selection, perhaps blending, and placing of the rootzone mix (see Figure 8-10, color insert). Sometimes I believe we try to make things more complicated than necessary or required. This is not rocket science; it is soil science, which makes the margin for error much, much wider. I have seen just about every kind of sand possible, blended with any one or more of every kind of rootzone amendment, and they all work, but why risk it if there is sufficient budget to use lab-selected materials that meet some standard test and performance criteria? Trust an accredited laboratory that specializes in evaluation of rootzone materials for golf greens. Although this will not eliminate all liabilities, it certainly reduces your risk. On the other hand, to ignore verified lab results and choose a material that does not meet the specifications is a risk that should not be taken unless authorized in writing by the owner.

About 20 years ago I had a client who was building a cheap—yes, cheap—golf course. This client could get bank run sand from his site for $0.50 per ton. The particle analysis showed this sand to be rather uniformly coarse with a percolation rate in excess of 120 inches per hour. I strongly advised against using this material and reminded the client that there were probably laws that prevented me from helping him commit soil science suicide. He said it was his golf course, his money, and his risk—so he built it. His source of organic amendment was five- to seven-year-old oak sawdust he got free for the hauling. I continued to expressly warn him to spread no more than two inches of sawdust over the "sand" before rotovating them together to a depth of 10 inches. He, of course, put 4 to 6 inches on and blended it in with a rototiller. But he did do it very uniformly. Predictably, in order to grow grass on this mess, he had to use excessive amounts of water, to the point that when the sprinklers shut off, you could hear the water being sucked down through the sand. It also required massive amounts of nitrogen by today's standard, which was tied up by the organisms decomposing the sawdust as well as leaching like crazy. Three years later, he could manage the greens normally, and for the past 20 years, the golf course has enjoyed the reputation as the best putting surfaces in the area. Now, as back then, I thought that this was an environmentally and scientifically irresponsible thing to do, but he didn't know any better, and he made it work. But it would have been his responsibility if it failed.

ROOTZONE SELECTION

The point is that one should use the best information available at the time *and* common sense. A good superintendent only needs a predictable rootzone and he or she will learn to manage the conditions, even though they may be far from the theoretical ideal. Rootzones don't have to meet any national standard or performance spec but they should resist compaction, allow for good air and water drainage, and be as uniform within a green as physically possible. If there is any liability in rootzone material selection or blending, it arises from promising more than can be delivered.

No one wants to accept full and sole responsibility for the rootzone, so the initial step is to find the best material available for the construction budget allowance. If the budget allows for a thoroughly tested, custom top mix of $35 per ton (I have seen it quoted at $140 per ton when long-distance hauling was involved), then I would strongly suggest using it. If the budget only allows for $12 per ton, then test what's available as carefully as the custom stuff, and be prepared to adjust the grow-in and maintenance program as necessary to compensate for any less than ideal performance characteristics. I am convinced that most sands will grow grass with some problems, but to have the fewest problems use the most predicable sand, which is one of uniform particle size. The California method suggests that at least 50 to 70 percent of the particles be between 0.25 mm and 0.50 mm, and 90 percent between 0.1 mm and 1.00 mm. The narrower the range of particle sizes, the more predictable the sand performance. If I were to err on the range of particles, I would rather have the sand be too coarse than too fine. In my opinion, there is greater liability with a fine sand than a coarse one, because on droughty sand, you can just irrigate more until it becomes more manageable with age, but on poorly drained sand, there is no relief. Any time one must depart from the ideal, the owner or owner's representative should be involved in the decision making and be properly apprised of the pros and cons of the decision. If possible, the owner should be asked to sign a letter acknowledging the change with a clear warning of its consequences. If that is done, the owner now accepts the liability of the decision, instead of the person who must do the work or who is searching for a suitable alternative.

Choosing organic amendments is even more hazardous than selecting sand, for sand is a fairly stable product while organic matter can and will decompose at some unknown rate to some unknown product. Few labs can test organic matter and offer a prediction of how long it will perform as tested. This can only be approximated by using such measurements as carbon-to-nitrogen ratio, content of cellulose, lignin and ash, percentage of silt and clay found in the organic, and its current state of decomposition. Selecting the organic amendment is the most difficult part of the rootzone process, and therefore the most likely source of liability. Since no one can accurately predict this part of the rootzone, it should be made clear to all parties that no guarantees are made, only that every effort will be made to protect the owner's interest. The greatest liability comes with using composts, which can vary markedly from batch to batch.

BLENDING

Mixing or blending should be done as uniformly as possible to produce the most consistently performing rootzone. However, it is pure speculation what are allowable tolerances of error and whether the blend must be within 0.5 or 5 percent of the recommended amount. I have seen very poor mixes produce acceptable putting surfaces and very precise mixes that fail. Off-site mixing is always preferred over on-site mixing, but I don't see any liability in on-site mixing if that is all the budget will allow. Again, the most important thing is for the owner to understand that compromises are being made in his best interest based on budget.

In fact, I don't see any liability in building 100 percent topsoil greens if that is all the budget will allow and if the owner understands the pros and cons. I grew up maintaining greens made of yellow clay that you could have made pottery out of, and by managing our conditions, we always had great greens. In fact, most great old golf courses have soil greens, including Oakmont, which has the fastest greens in golf.

However, mixing soil into a sand/organic rootzone blend can be a source of liability unless a lab recommends it. The problem with any rootzone, fumigated or not, is the lack or imbalance of soil organisms, which can allow some strange first-year diseases. Many researchers have seen excellent results achieved by mixing in about 5 to 10 percent soil that has been thoroughly tested into the rootzone mix. I think that conceptually this makes great sense, and back in the 1960s, a 6–2–2 (sand–soil–peat) blend was the norm. The danger or liability is if the soil silt and clay fraction migrates and accumulates to slow down or block the internal drainage system. In the 1970s, we got away from blending in soil for this reason, and now we are going back to it. I am in favor of it if it doesn't change the performance characteristics of the rootzone and if the intended mix is verified by an accredited lab.

Similar to the problem of mixing in topsoil is the problem of adding any amendment that might decompose or move and thus alter the performance of the sand. In the late 1940s and early 1950s, calcine clay was the rage, but over time we found that it softened with age and became a clay layer that sealed off the lower profiles of the green. Now more than ever, people are selling soil amendments—overselling them perhaps. I encourage experimentation, but don't risk your job over it by assuming the liability. Involve the owner and have him or her agree with the concept or product; get that agreement in writing if possible.

Another approach to the lack of balanced soil organism activity in new greens is the concept of inoculating the rootzone with soil organisms. Again, the concept is very sound, and many consultants recommend supplements of biological organisms with excellent results. I would not hesitate to try this technique, for I see no liability involved unless you promise something that can't be delivered. Cost-to-benefit ratio analysis should be done with any and all such products to put a dollar value on each, as well as to establish some limits of liability.

PLACING ROOTZONE

Once the proper rootzone material has been selected, and perhaps blended, then it is a matter of placing the materials within the green well. Installing a gravel blanket, ideally, can be done by dumping the gravel on the edge of the green cavity and pushing it out, or one can drive between tile lines (not over them) and dump the gravel on the compacted green base for spreading. Gravel can be spread by hand with rakes, by a small bulldozer, or by a bobcat with a track attachment on the wheels. Care must be taken not to crush the tile, contaminate the gravel, or get an uneven blanket. However, if some smart-aleck architect is going to change the grades within the putting surface from what is built into the subgrade, the gravel blanket application should be his or her last chance. Varying the depth of gravel is no big deal, whereas varying the intermediate or topmix layer is. The only liability in placing gravel is the contractor's for improper workmanship.

Likewise, it is the contractor's responsibility to properly install the intermediate and topmix in very precise and uniform layers. If the intermediate layer is used, it can only be spread uniformly using grade stakes and by hand-raking, in my opinion. If the contractor wishes to use any other method I would ask for a demonstration first, and I would inspect the work for uniformity of the gravel layer below and the intermediate layer on top. Chances are the only way to do it properly is by dumping the intermediate material on the edge of the green wall and spreading by hand while working off four-foot by eight-foot plywood sheets. Unless otherwise specified, contractors are free to use any method they wish to execute the work, but they must also accept responsibility for any failure caused by the deviation of method.

QUALITY CONTROL

Random samples of rootzone material should be taken periodically during delivery of every 500 to 1,000 tons of rootzone or sand to the green site and sent to an accredited lab to be checked at least for particle size consistency. This can be done in the field by drying a small sample and putting it through standard screens. Some blending companies provide this service and even measure the infiltration rate on a periodic basis, although this testing lacks the accuracy and sophistication of lab protocols. A field expedient method is to place a fixed amount (one level cup) in a standard vessel (a one-quart mason jar), mix it thoroughly with a separating solution (water), and allow it to settle for a standard time (five minutes, two hours, or 24 hours), then visually compare various samples by placing them side-by-side. If there is any variation between the layering of particles, then immediately do a screen analysis. There is some responsibility—and hence liability—to insure that what was ordered is what is delivered, and that liability is shared by the contractor and the supplier. It is not uncommon for the sand or rootzone mix at the beginning of the delivery to be different from that at the end of the process. Quality control testing by an accredited laboratory is the only safe procedure. The goal is to minimize such differences, or at least make sure there is consistency within each green. On several occasions I have had the contractor remove sand or rootzone mix from a green well if I believed it was not close enough to the proper quality or would perform substantially differently than other greens. Grade stakes at 10- to 15-foot intervals should be used to insure that the rootzone mix is spread to a uniform depth. If no grade stakes are used and there are problems of uniform depth of rootzone, the contractor has a liability.

After the rootzone is in place, it is usually irrigated and wheel tracked with a tractor to compact it. Once compacted, the rootzone can be fine graded and smoothed with a riding sand trap rake or garden tractor, or can be hand raked. If the designer changes grades of the putting surface by rearranging topmix and the green fails because of that, the designer has a liability problem. Rootzone materials should be uniform in depth. The tolerances of deviation from what is specified is not known, but I would guess it is plus or minus one inch.

CHECKING FINAL GRADES

At this point, the topmix is compacted and fine graded, ready for the interior green slopes to be checked by the contractor with a surveying instrument. A contractor who doesn't verify the putting surface slopes and fails to get approval by the owner or architect to skip this step may have a liability problem if the greens are later found to be too steep or if they don't surface drain. You would have to be a fool to rely on your eye to check slopes that are supposed to be within the final range of one and one-half to two percent. But I see it done all the time, often with disastrous results. Either the greens don't surface drain well or they are too steep to skillfully putt when the turf is shaved down. If the contractor gets approval of these final grades, the liability shifts to the owner or architect, depending upon who gave the OK. As a designer, I always want the owner's representative to have final approval.

Next is the preplant phase of construction, where the irrigation system is again tested for function, and planting bed preparation takes place. First, all stones, clods, or debris are removed and soil amendments are applied to the topmix as preplant applications. Here is where so little is known about achieving a properly balanced nutritional and biologically optimum rootzone that mistakes are made but there is no liability. This is because proof of negligence requires the person directing the work to have known the right answer and not to have used it. In this case, no one knows the right answer so we all guess, particularly when it comes down to such things as humic acid levels, cytokinins, vitamins, micronutrients and their ratios to each other, and so on. We do OK with the macro nutrients (N–P–K–Mg–Ca–Su–Fe, etc.) by using a complete fertilizer package. Over the years, golf course architects, turfgrass agronomists, and superintendents have developed a preplant application program that tries to address a broad spectrum of turf needs. Generally, this includes a micronutrient package of one kind or another. Unless that package can be shown to be phytotoxic, there should be no liabilities involved. The exception may be when there was a specific limitation regarding a particular material for environmental reasons, and someone ignores this limitation. Then there is not only negligence but also perhaps even criminal intent, and most certainly liability for whoever authorized the material's use.

Figure 8-11: Selection of turf varieties rests with the owner and consultant, but the contractor is responsible to properly plant and/or establish them as per contract.

SELECTING AND PLANTING TURF

Back in the old days, when our choices of turfgrasses for greens were Tifdrawf or Tifgreen, Bermuda grass, or creeping bents such as Toronto, Cohansey, Arlington, Velvet, and a few others, all of which were vegetatively propagated, deciding what to plant was not a big problem. If greens were seeded, then South German bentgrass was used. Then we were blessed with a seeded variety called Penncross, which solved all of our problems for about 50 years. Today, the choices of bent grasses are incredibly broad as plant breeders continue to select and produce cultivars with varying strengths and weaknesses in various climates under various maintenance regimes (see Figure 8-11). Again, so little is known about this ever widening array of choices that to honestly choose the wrong variety for a project probably carries no liability. I would suggest that, in my opinion, there might be some negligence in planting Toronto bentgrass (C-15), which has extreme susceptibility to a bacterial wilt condition called C-15 Decline, or planting Tifdrawf too far north. Otherwise, anyone who does a reasonable amount of homework should be able to avoid negligence in choosing the planting material. This also applies to planting rates and planting seasons. However, there can be extreme liability for not specifying seed of the highest practical quality, for seed lots can be severely contaminated with unwanted plant species. Of course, the seed supplier would be liable, as would the contractor if he or she were to use seed that did not meet the designer's specifications.

IMPROPER MAINTENANCE

Assuming the construction workmanship was properly done, most of the liability associated with improper maintenance falls to the owner or the owner's representative (superintendent), unless the golf course is contracted out to a management company. If, however, the construction or design can be shown to be faulty, then the liability shifts back to the contractor or designer. But for discussion purposes, let us assume that the superintendent inherits a properly designed and built green.

The sources of liability could be an environmental incident, an employee accident, or a golf related problem (see Figure 8-12, color insert). Environmental incidents might range from groundwater pollution through excessive or improper fertilizer or pesticide misapplications to improper irrigation with either potable or effluent water. In truth, there is not much chance of any real liability as long as you follow the applicable regulations, and as long as you are acting legally, morally, and ethically.

I do know of one case in which the superintendent was accused of negligence for not properly applying a weed grass preventer. The club owner said he lost thousands of dollars in green fees because his greens had *Poa annua* and goose grass in them, and he spent tens of thousand of dollars correcting the situation. Both the owner and superintendent were devastated, and both were losers in this situation, for they shared the liability.

Employee liability can result from improper training on a piece of maintenance equipment, through requiring unsafe maintenance practices, or through failing to enforce safety standards and regulations. I have recently heard of several incidents involving green rollers and employees losing control on slopes and being seriously injured. Similarly, requiring hand maintenance on steep slopes without providing reasonable safety equipment can be a source of liability. But here again, with some training and common sense, there should be no liability.

Golfer type accidents or incidents can range from allergic reaction to maintenance products to golf-ball-related injuries. With a reasonable number of warnings posted to alert golfers to potential threats, liability against owners or staff should be very slight. However, if owners, management, or staff are aware of any defect or possible defect, they should immediately take corrective action. Such possibilities may include golf balls landing dangerously near anticipated play areas, steps in disrepair or without handrails, unmarked or unguarded steep slopes, and so on. This is all common sense stuff beyond the scope of liabilities of green construction.

Nongolfers present an entirely new set of problems, for they may not recognize dangers of the golf course that the rest of us instinctively do. Nongolfers don't pose any special liability problems to golf greens other than careless damage they might cause by improper footwear or walking on putting surfaces. Of course, any premeditated damage could be considered criminal and not negligent. I would also recommend that you warn nongolfers about such hazards as flying golf balls, routine pesticide applications, steep grades, or any other potential threat to their well-being.

Common sense and prudent precautions remain the best defense against all liability charges.

CHAPTER 9

Postscript: My Personal Experiences Building Golf Greens and the Future of Greens

Throughout this book, and particularly in this chapter, I present my personal opinions and bias based upon over 45 years of staying current with evolving research, open-minded experimentation and observation, and common sense in building greens in North America, Japan, and Australia, often for low budgets, using locally available materials. I call it the "real world."

THE VALUE OF PATIENCE AND OBSERVATION

As a preface, I would like to recall a story attributed to the famous paleoanthropologist Dr. Louis S. B. Leakey. In 1903, Louis Leakey was one of the first white children born in Africa to missionary parents. Louis grew up more African than English, as his playmates and teachers were African tribesmen. He, of course, grew to international fame as a result of his findings of fossil evidence of the ancestors of man in Olduvai Gorge. In an interview, Louis was once asked what he considered to be his most valued lessons in life. To paraphrase his answer, he said he had learned them as a young boy hunting with the

African tribesmen and the lessons were patience and observation. To be successful, the hunter must learn to read the landscape and look for telltale signs like a broken spider web, a crushed leaf, dew on a leaf, and so on, and then have the patience to understand their relevance. I am certain that Dr. Leakey would not approve of my capacity for patience, but I believe he would approve of how he inspired me to be observant about natural systems, especially about golf courses and golf greens.

BE OPEN-MINDED

I also believe that the admonition "Don't believe everything you learned in school," is often appropriate. Formal education is only as good as the person who is teaching and how well the student interpreted the teaching points, and for most of us that translates into "not very much." I have great admiration for teachers, but knowledge is constantly evolving as new discoveries are made, and this is especially apparent to me when I review my son's current college textbooks on subjects that I thought I had mastered, like biochemistry, and I see how much I don't know. Remember how dogmatic some people were about the importance of the perched water table? The point is to be open-minded about all things. Another old cliché is: "The more you know, the more you see that you know nothing about." I have found this is true for me even when observing golf greens, and I would like to share some of what I have seen.

Since my first experience constructing greens in 1957, I have seen greens built the following ways:

1. Original 1960 USGA Spec and all subsequent revisions
2. California method
3. Push-up greens
4. Plain old coarse river sand
5. Native soils of all types
6. Silica sand or calcareous sand in combination with:

   - Native peat
   - Peat humus
   - Peat moss
   - Sphagnum peat
   - Humus
   - Irish peat
   - Composted sawdust
     - Hardwood
     - Softwood
     - Aged
     - With household wastes

- ○ Young or green
- ○ With sewage sludge
- Spent mushroom soil
- Spent worm soil
- Tea leaves
- Coffee grounds
- Coconut coir
- Leaf mold
- Ground tobacco stems
- Seaweed
- Chopped pine straw
- Ground peanut hulls
- Ground cotton seed hulls
- Rice hulls
- Processed manure
  - ○ Chicken
  - ○ Turkey
  - ○ Horse
  - ○ Human
  - ○ Cow
- Calcined clay
- Porous ceramics
- Perlite
- Vermiculite
- Polyacrylamide gels
- Clay tile
- Plastic tile (rigid and flexible)
- Flat tile
- No tile
- Fine gravel
- Coarse gravel
- Cinders

And probably a few other things I have forgotten about. In addition, I have seeded, sodded, sprigged, and stolonized about every type of bent or Bermuda suitable for greens.

Surprisingly, all of these attempts ultimately produced acceptable putting green turf. In some cases it may have taken the superintendents a while to figure out how to do it, but they always found a way to make the greens work. Many of these greens were not built to prove any kind of theory or as some abstract research; rather they were built because we simply did not know any better and that was all we had to work with. My intent is not to recommend or condemn any of these methods or products but, rather, to suggest that there can be many ways to build golf greens within limited budgets using locally available, and often free, materials.

At this point, if you heard a loud and persistent gasp, it probably came from agronomists and university researchers around the world who are trying to focus on finding the most correct way(s) to build greens. I support them and their science, but unfortunately they often do not understand the budget constraints under which many golf courses are built, constraints that simply do not allow for "correct" methods. That, again, is real world.

METHOD TO MINIMIZE RISKS

However, as has been stressed in other chapters, this need to be flexible doesn't amount to license to do whatever one wants. Rather, it suggests that there is a process or method that should be considered if only local materials are available and when compromises to sound science must be made. Simply put, that procedure is:

1. Identify and analyze irrigation water source
2. Send samples of locally available materials to an accredited testing lab sympathetic to helping you succeed
3. Visit other existing golf courses in the area and speak with superintendents about successes and failures of using these locally available materials
4. Establish a test plot(s) of most probable materials, and subject it to normal stresses
5. Decide upon the level of risk you will take.

This is nothing more than a commonsense approach and observations. That use of common sense and observational attitude must continue throughout the construction process and beyond into long-term maintenance.

With that said, allow me to share a few more memorable experiences I have had with golf green construction.

MY FIRST 100 PERCENT SAND GREEN

One of my earliest experiences was with the 100 percent sand greens I helped build at my mentor's (Jack Kidwell's) old golf course (Beacon Light in Columbus, OH, see Figure 9-1, color insert). This golf course was originally built during the Great Depression in the early 1930s, and greens were built out of native Ohio clay—yellow clay, brown clay, gray clay, and so on. Some greens had a little bit of square, clay tile under them with cinder backfill, but most greens were just pushed-up clay with lots of surface drainage. After returning from the Second World War, Jack began to slowly remodel the golf course as time and money allowed. In the mid-1950s, he attended a turf conference, where he heard about the virtues of 100 percent sand greens, and so each fall, those of us on the greenkeeping crew would rebuild a green or two. For the first two years, I hated those 100 percent sand greens, which were built with concrete or coarse sand. They needed more water and fertilizer, they grew so much grass you had to empty the mower carrier about every two or three passes, and they got dollar spot like crazy. When moving holes, you could remove the top four to six inches with the first bite of the cup setter, then you had to dig the rest of the sand out with your hand. When young, the greens all putted badly and got really scuffed up by metal spikes. But I will concede that they did drain well, so one could be a little less precise with irrigation and not worry about problems with scald or wet wilt during protracted rainy periods, problems we encountered on the clay greens. The sand greens came out of winter quickly, and they grew lots of grass. Soon I loved those greens, for they became the easiest to take care of and the most forgiving of severe weather and golfer wear, and they needed only light topdressing. But when I started at Ohio State University in 1961 as one of the first turfgrass science majors, I was taught that 100 percent sand was the wrong way to build a green and that it was imperative to blend in organic matter. This becomes more important later in this story.

The old clay greens could only be hand watered or they would get too soft in places. In addition, you had to be vigilant for isolated dry spots, and wet and/or humid weather could be disastrous, for brown patch and pythium were always out there trying to surprise us.

My first experience with aerification was with a Turferator, which actually drilled holes into the hard clay surfaces. After using it, you had to try to clean up the stuff that came out of the holes by letting it dry and then sweeping it up. Finally, you had to refill the holes with topdressing that was mixed by hand, spread with a scoop shovel, and dragged in by hand by pulling a steel drag. The first hollow-tine machine for aerification seemed like a gift from the great greenkeeper in the sky, but on the clay greens, the tines would clog up, sometimes after only a few feet of operation. This meant stopping the machine, removing the tine, cleaning it thoroughly, replacing it, and then going only a few more feet before stopping again. Once we started aerifying the high sand greens, the hollow tine machine was awesome, giving me yet another reason to like 100 percent sand greens.

I was fortunate at the age of 14 or 15 of having the opportunity to go to superintendent meetings with Jack, where I could meet the "old timers" and hear their stories. I remember one old guy telling me that he got so disgusted cleaning out those hollow tines on his aerifier that he welded the tines shut. We all thought he was nuts, for in those days no one thought that solid tine aerification would do anything but compact the subsoil of the green. Decades later research showed how wrong we were and how right he was, and now solid-tine aerification is common.

We also tried to keep *Poa annua* out of our new Penncross greens by using arsenate of lead or tricalicium arsenate, whichever was cheaper. The theory was that the bentgrass had a higher level of tolerance for arsenic than did the *Poa,* so the goal was to *slowly* find that threshold level that disadvantaged the *Poa* but not the bent. This was really tricky stuff, for those materials move very slowly in the soil, especially clay soils. Apply a little too much and the whole green might die, or would be so weakened that when the hot, humid weather came, the green would be extra stressed out. Even today those old greens may contain levels of these chemicals that would be considered toxic wastes by today's standards. Again, what we believed to be the "best management practices" of that day could land us in jail today for environmental misjudgment.

In those days, we also routinely applied materials like mercury, cadmium, and other heavy metals, plus chlordane, DDT, and 2-4-5, T, or Agent Orange. We were not environmental terrorists, we just didn't know any better, for Rachel Carson had not yet written *Silent Spring* (Boston: Houghton Mifflin, 1962) and the fate of pesticides was of no concern. Today, to paraphrase an old cigarette ad, "We've come a long way, baby!"

Because we had no money back then, we often just added onto existing greens by installing tile drainage, and then bringing in good soil and trying to mix in a bunch of sand. Fortunately, this usually worked, but it was just pure luck, for we heard about others who did the same and only produced a low-grade concrete rootzone. By the late 1960s and early 1970s, we were all getting smarter because of the USGA agronomists and many trained turf specialists and researchers we had to advise and educate us. That was during the period before sending samples to testing labs became fashionable and when everyone tried everything, and in all different combinations. Almost every conceivable material was tried and incorporated in many different ways. We tried to blend materials with scoop shovels, mixing bins, old cement mixers, paddle pans (self-loading earthmovers), disks, rototillers, rotovators, rototerras, front end loaders, bull dozers, hammer mills, elevators, and just about anything else that could move sand, soil and organic matter. A common ratio was 1–1–1 (sand–soil–peat) and over the years the blend got progressively sandier until most golf course architects settled on 8–1–1 or 8–0–2 blends. Materials were mixed on-site in the green cavity, off-site, which meant somewhere else on the property, or at the sand pit, or the materials were laid down in thick layers of four to six inches on a big flat field and driven over with mixing machines until we heard that famous American saying, "That's good enough," at which time the stuff was pushed up into a pile, maybe put through a soil shredder, loaded in trucks, wagon, or pans, and hauled out to the greens. Pretty unscientific stuff, but that was how it was done from the mid-1920s to the mid-1970s.

ADDING SAND APPENDAGES TO A CLAY GREEN

During this period of free-spirited thinking, we had just replaced an old soil green with a high sand green at a well-known Cleveland, OH, club, when the golf course superintendent said the club would like to make some of the greens larger. I said, "OK, let's find some places for some temporary greens and start getting them ready." The superintendent asked why we needed temporary greens. I replied, "So when we close the green for rebuilding, the members won't have to skip that hole, and they'll have a full 18-hole round." Then he said something to the effect that they could just use the green they had, and we would rope off the new construction. So I asked, "Charlie, how do you rebuild a green without closing it?" His answer was that he hadn't said "Rebuild," he'd said, "Enlarge." I asked, "Do you mean build the new part out of soil like the old part?" His answer was, "No, we'll build them out of a sand-peat mix (80–20), like we did the new green." I thought, boy, do I have an education job to do on this guy! So I patiently began to explain all of the scientific reasons that I learned in school about why you cannot add a sand appendage onto a soil green without creating major maintenance problems.

"Come with me," he said, and we went out on a nice big green out on the course. "OK, Dr. Architect, tell me what you see about this green." I was determined to answer his question, but I finally gave up and told him all I could see was a nice big green. "Well, half of it is native soil, and the other half is an 80–20 mix." I couldn't believe it, so we stopped a greenkeeper with a cup setter, and we started cutting cups, and sure enough it was as he said. But I wasn't giving up, and so I told him it must be a maintenance nightmare.

"Mike," he said, "one station controls all the sprinklers on this green, so everything gets watered the same. We mow it with the same mower, topdress it with the same topdressing, fertilize and treat it with the same rates of pesticides. We aerify and verticut it all at once. And we added this half while the other half was in play."

"Yeah, Charlie," I said, with what little defiance I could still muster, "but I'll bet it plays differently between halves." At that point, we asked a member who was playing alone on a practice round to go out to the fairway and hit shots into each half of the green, and we would measure how the ball performed once it landed. There was no difference in playability. Now I was convinced, and we added sand-based appendages to those old soil greens, and they worked out just fine. Years later we did that at several other clubs that had low budgets, and all of them did well.

As new associates came to work for me, I would relate that story, and none ever believed me until I took them to one of those courses; we walked out on a nice big green, and I would say, "OK, Mr. Architect, tell me what you see." They, too, became believers when we pulled cores to show part of the green was soil and other parts were sand. I am not advocating doing this, for I still think that it won't work in every case, but I came to believe in a concept that everyone else seemed to say wouldn't work.

LEARNING ABOUT SEAWEED

I was taught many other valuable lessons by superintendents, especially older ones who were great observers of natural systems and had the courage to experiment. They also were innovators because they had to be — they had no budget to work with. Another such lesson was on the value of seaweed. Growing up managing turf in the Midwest, I was never exposed to seaweed type materials, nor was I ever taught anything about them. So I only knew that there were lots of different kinds of seaweeds, they decomposed quickly and completely, and they usually contained minerals not normally found in other organic sources like peat, humus, or compost. Now this was also during a period of time when ureaformaldydes were fairly new and were thought to be the final answer in fertilizer formulation. Why use a stinking, fairly expensive, and unorthodox growth stimulant, when you could use a clean, long-lasting, high-nutrient plant food?

Well, we were in the process of designing and building a very low budget project in Canada, and had planned to use a locally available peat source mined not far from the project, haul it in bulk to each green, spread it two inches deep, and rotovate it into the top eight inches. This was a common, cheap way to get an 80–20 mix, and if grade stakes were used to accurately control the depth of sand and organic, the resulting mix was pretty uniform. Of course, the university people, who mix small batches of stuff in washtubs or kid's wading pools, thought our methods were pretty crude, and we thought theirs was pretty labor intensive, impractical, and expensive.

Anyway, it was a very rainy summer, so peat could not be mined, and the owner would not pay for baled peat, which went up dramatically in price because of the shortage of bulk peat caused by the rain. In fact, it rained well into the fall, and the next spring was wet, too. The result was no peat to blend into the sand, which had already been placed in the green cavity. So the choices were either to pay for a high priced organic or to leave it out all together.

Remember, I said this was a cheap project and the rain had already cost both the owner and contractor money in lost efficiency and in not having the golf course to open, so they both wanted to skip the peat. I related my stories of building high sand greens as a kid and how well they had worked, but almost every university and agronomist was convinced that not to add organics to a rootzone was just plain stupid. As you may imagine, despite dire warnings about how the greens would fail, we all decided to seed the greens to pure sand but using those new whiz-bang, synthetic slow-release fertilizers that were the rage. The seed germinated with no problem and was growing in fairly well, so we were all relieved to have succeeded where others had predicted failure. Then the grass just went dormant and wouldn't respond to any of the many fertilizers that we tried to use to stimulate its growth.

The superintendent who had been hired was an old Dutchman—named John Arrons, I think—a quiet but observant man who had been around golf courses most of his long life. One day, as we were all standing around, perplexed at why the grass wasn't growing, John asked if he could put some seaweed on the greens. At that point, we were all desperate enough that we agreed to try it on a couple of greens, and within days, the grass woke up. It was almost like magic. The question then was, what is there about seaweed, applied at rates even as low as ten pounds per thousand square feet, that is important to plant growth? It certainly was not the nutrient value, nor the organic content, nor some microbial stimulant, but whatever it was, it had supplied that little something that was missing.

When you have such success, you learn to keep doing it and figure out why it works later. About this same time, a new company was formed in Michigan, Emerald Isle, to sell turf care products made from seaweed. Of course, there was a lot of skepticism about how beneficial these products might be, and most superintendents were slow to adopt them. But old John had taught me that there is something wonderful in seaweed, so we embraced that product quickly, and we were never disappointed. As time went on, I came to believe that the special factor in seaweed is cytokinin, a growth-stimulating hormone for roots, or some alginic acid. We tried other kinds of seaweed, but none worked quite as well as this stuff that came out of the Irish or North Sea and was cold water-treated. Today Sand-Aid® still remains a critical part of building any high sand green. It is applied at 80 pounds per thousand square feet on top of the root-zone, and it is lightly raked by hand into the top inch or so, just before seeding. The material works so well that, from experience, I can almost visually tell the rate at which the material went down by observing the speed, color, and density of the germinating seed and seedling growth.

CALCIUM-TO-MAGNESIUM RATIO IS CRITICAL

Yet another experience I referenced in an earlier chapter that is worth mentioning was a grow-in of high sand greens on a cheap golf course. The owner built the greens out of bank run sand that came out of a creek that ran through the property, and he amended it with sawdust that wasn't very old. The result, of course, was that the sawdust had a carbon-to-nitrogen ratio of about 150:1 or greater, so much of the applied nitrogen was tied up by the organisms trying to break down the sawdust. It was a warm, wet fall, so applications of ammonium nitrate at one pound of nitrogen per thousand square feet per week were used, but the grass still stayed yellow. Nothing seemed to be able to stimulate this turf. The superintendent and I had weeks of soil tests to look at, we recalibrated the spreader, tried different nitrogen sources, and still—yellow turf.

When all else fails, read the book. So we got out old Burt Musser's 1950 book on *Turfgrass Management* and O. J. Noer's booklet on turf culture, and saw that the recommended ratio of calcium to magnesium should be below 20:1, and ideally between 10:1 and 7:1. We checked our soil test results and saw the ratio was 70:1. Immediately, we went to a local drug store, bought them out of Epsom Salts (magnesium sulfate), and made an application to a test area at the rate of ten pounds per thousand square feet. The results were spectacular, and in two to three days, the test strip was dark green and growing. Another lesson learned. *Now* I know that the reason for these results is that the center of the chlorophyll molecule is magnesium, and without it the plant simply cannot metabolize and use other nutrients like nitrogen. This taught me the extreme importance of finding the right balance between growth-promoting factors, which was, again, something I must have missed in school.

BALANCE IS MORE IMPORTANT THAN QUANTITY

I learned that it is not the amount of any individual fertilizer that is important; rather, it is the balance between all nutrients that the plant uses that is important. There is lots of talk about the physical aspects of rootzones but little about how to balance those micronutrients that are so essential. Generally, the superintendent figures it out by applying multiples of micronutrient packages, but it can be a painful and slow process. There is a branch of agriculture called "hydroponics," which deals with growing plants without soil, usually in aqueous solutions that contain a prescribed balance of nutrition for the particular plant or crop. Plants are grown on glass beads, marbles, silica sand, or some other inert material so plant roots can anchor to them, and the solution is aerated from the bottom to supply sufficient oxygen for the root growth. One nutrient solution commonly used in hydroponics is Hoagland Solution, which was developed in 1950 by D. R. Hoagland and D. I. Armon at the California Agricultural Experiment Station. Hoagland Solution contains the correct amounts and ratio of nutrients for optimum plant growth. Assuming a high-sand golf green is nothing more than a form of hydroponics helps set a mental image of how to fertilize establishing putting green turf with the minimum amount of wasted nutrient. Rather than use the rather expensive Hoagland Solution, I worked with a formulator of organic fertilizers to prepare a blend of dry materials that would mirror the proportions found in Hoagland's. The result contained everything that is in Hoagland's and in about the same proportion. However, the system involved putting down eight different products in five or six separate applications, and this was labor intensive for contractors. Some agronomists called it a "witches' brew," and they thought it was unnecessary and wasteful, and one university researcher even set out to prove it. Basically, he and his students built "greens" in children's wading pools so they could capture and measure all of the leakage from these newly seeded "greens." They used the most commonly recommended preplant methods and my witches' brew, and surprise, surprise, the "green" that grew in fastest, with the least amount of leachate, was the one using the witches' brew along with proper irrigation. Vindication. Although the results of this study have never been released, fewer people are knocking it.

On one project, a superintendent didn't believe in the witches' brew, because in his estimation, it was too salty, so he left a few things out on a couple of the greens. For over a year I struggled to find out why those greens were so far behind the others, and on every visit he assured me that he had treated the slow greens exactly like the healthy ones. When I found out he had deceived me, I actively worked to get him replaced, and when the new superintendent came in and followed my recommended program, the greens flourished.

Today we have asked a formulator to produce a new witches' brew that the formulator calls Architect's Blend. It is composed of the following:

> Product specifications—Architect's Blend 4–1–2 with 5 percent total phosphorus, 0.7 percent iron, 5.5 calcium, 1.0 percent magnesium, and 0.5 percent manganese.

> Methex 40 provides 13 percent of the total nitrogen, with the remaining 87 percent provided by slowly available natural protein/amino acid nitrogen forms.

> Nutrients are derived from kelp, alfalfa, fish, feather, and crab meals, seaplant extract, Methex 40, rock phosphate, sunflower fly ash, and iron, magnesium, and manganese sulfates.

> Also contains vitamins, mycorrhizae, sugars, and beneficial bacteria.

> At the rate of 150 pounds per 1000 square feet, Architect's Blend provides a total of 5.9 pounds N, 2.5 pounds available P_2O_5, and 3.1 K_2O. In a straight sand root zone, this application incorporated into the top three inches provides approximately 0.7 percent preplant organic matter.

For more information about Architect's Blend call George Seaver at Ocean Organic Corporation (phone number: 207-832-4305). I add this information because this is a product that has worked well for us and there isn't much practical information on how to maximize the grow-in potential of new greens. This works as well with Bermuda grass as well as bentgrass. Without question, we will continue to try to find our own best management practices for golf greens, but the keys to success will remain to be observant and open-minded.

CATION EXCHANGE CAPACITY IS OVEREMPHASIZED

Another area that is misunderstood is the overemphasis placed on cation exchange capacity (CEC) in new rootzones. CEC is expressed as milliequivalents per unit of mass or volume, typically milliequivalents per milligram or milliliter. A milliequivalent is defined as a milligram of hydrogen per 100 grams of soil, or the amount of any ion that will displace it. Simplistically I think of CEC as a magnet that can hold so many paper clips (equal to 1 milliequivalent each). A ten-milliequivalent magnet can hold ten paper clips, or perhaps five nails at two milliequivalent. As you know, any element with a positive charge is called a cation, as opposed to one with a negative charge called an anion. With regard to pH, the basic cations and positive charges are calcium (+2), magnesium (+2), potassium (+1), and sodium (+1); acidic cations are hydrogen (+1) and aluminum (+3). On the face of it, having these elements held in an exchangeable form for plants to use would seem like a good idea, and it is. However, it is all a matter of proportion.

So if one simplistically thinks of CEC as a measure of a magnet's strength and cations as paper clips, then it is easy to visualize that the magnet has a limited capacity for paper clips it can hold. So no matter how many paper clips there are, or cations, once the capacity to hold them is used up, then they will simply not be retained. The CEC for sand-based rootzones is so low to begin with that when a CEC of two, for example, is converted to pounds per acre it doesn't amount to much, and any excess nutrient will be permitted to leach through nearly as freely as if there were no CEC.

Using the magnet example, the next concept is that not all paper clips are the same. Some are carbon steel, others are alloy steel or plastic coated steel, some are large, some small, and so on. The point is that, like paper clips, different cations are attracted and held by the magnet at different force levels. This activity is determined by their charge and size with the general order of bonding strength of exchangeable cations as follows:

$$H^+ \rightarrow Al^{+3} \rightarrow Ca^{+2} \rightarrow Mg^{+2} \rightarrow NH^{+4} \rightarrow K^+ \rightarrow Na^+$$

Strongest bond $\longrightarrow$ Weakest bond

This means that, all things being equal, those cations of the strongest bonds can replace those of weaker bonds on an exchange site. Just as a magnet can exert greater attraction for paper clips of different sizes and material composition, cations are preferentially attracted and held by negatively changed sites on rootzone mediums. However, even the strongest of these bonds can be broken by, and the cation replaced by, the mere acts of dilution and equilibrium of the soil solution. For example, hydrogen is a strongly held cation that generally results in an acidic soil solution, but by applying a calcium source, such as lime, enough calcium can displace enough hydrogen to alter the pH to more basic in reaction. Likewise, if irrigation water is high in sodium, the concentration of sodium cations can dilute and displace other more tightly bound cations, and over a long enough period can produce a sodic soil that is generally not friendly to normal plant growth. Consequently, having a high CEC is not always a marked benefit to plant growth. Remember, I said this is a simplistic explanation.

So what? Generally, I do not believe that extra effort to obtain any CEC in a rootzone medium is necessary, or in some cases even desirable. The logic is that the only real desirable cations the greenkeeper wants to retain are calcium, magnesium, and potassium, and perhaps ammonium (NH_4), but these nutrients must compete with the less or undesirable cations of hydrogen, aluminum or sodium for a site. If there are rich sources of the "bad" cations, such as the aforementioned problem with poor quality irrigation water, it makes no sense to retain or even encourage retaining them. Chances are the greenkeeper is going to have to spoon-feed the turf anyway during early growth phases, simply because the volume of irrigation water required to keep the surface of a sand-based rootzone moist is going to leach out any desirable nutrients or cations. As the turf begins to establish a root system and, hopefully, a mat layer, organic matter will naturally begin to accumulate in the rootzone, ultimately providing a cation exchange capacity when a lower volume of irrigation water is required, whether we want it or not.

With sand-based rootzone properly blended with organic matter, the best CEC that one can normally measure is about 2.0, which, figuratively speaking, is a very high for a green but still a relatively small magnet.

Simplistically (if I did all the math correctly), one milliequivalent of potassium equals about 18 pounds per thousand square feet, while one milliequivalent of calcium and magnesium equal about 9 and 6 pounds, respectively. So even with a very high milliequivalent of two, the amount of nutrient is small compared to what can be easily added through fertilization. The added benefit is that, when these nutrients are applied, they can be applied in a proper balance and at a rate, location, and form the plant can absorb and metabolize with greatest efficiency.

Of course, the folks selling soil amendments list as one of their benefits increasing cation exchange capacity, and without question they do that over pure sand. However, the question becomes the cost-to-benefit ratio. Does it make any sense to spend $200,000 in amending a rootzone to save $200 in fertilizer?

I trust you understand my point that having CEC is not necessary for growing turfgrasses if proper fertility is provided, that to raise the CEC can be expensive, that the amount of increase in CEC and hence cations held in a sand-based rootzone is small on a per unit basis, that organic matter will naturally develop in the soil that will raise the CEC, and that if water quality is poor, then a higher CEC can be a determinant to long-term turfgrass management.

I have also heard folks argue that having a source of CEC will help retain applied pesticides, but, again, remember that it is a relatively small magnet and will only retain positively charged ions. So the theory is correct but practically of little real value, and most of the pesticides we use today are either contact or systemic or a combination thereof, so very few ever reach the mat layer, let alone the root system. Someone needs to research this area so we can all decide on the basis of facts, not conjecture.

I believe that there are small advantages to adding certain soil amendments but that they are neither critical nor essential for success and that it should all come down to cost-to-benefit ratios, measured in dollars.

I apologize if I have offended or embarrassed anyone other than myself. I do not claim to have any more right answers than anyone else who has made the same patient observations of golf greens and how they grow in the real world that I have. Being a lifelong learner, I also know that what I believe today I may not believe tomorrow, if there is an overwhelming reason why I should not. But since "truths" are slow to reveal themselves, my strongest admonition is to remember the values of patience, observation, and open-mindedness.

THE FUTURE OF GOLF GREENS

If there is any truth that, by studying the past and living in the present, one can predict the future, then I guess I am as qualified as anyone to venture a peep into the future, and with about the same authority. So for what it's worth, here is the future of golf greens according to Mike.

IMPROVED GRASSES

I guess this one is pretty much a given, but how they will improve may not be. It is pretty much agreed that it is going to take a cataclysmic event to roll back green speeds, so the trend will be toward even finer bladed, more densely textured putting green surfaces. The logical progression seems to be improved *Poa annua* cultivars, then a new generation of velvet bents, and then nonturf coverings, perhaps of mosses. The maximum practical speed might be 16 feet on a USGA stimpmeter. This is important to the greenkeeper of the future (GOTF) because it will require altering his or her thinking, practices, and machines to topdress, aerify, fertilize, mow, and even water. Each new generation of putting green surfaces will bring new reactions to the stresses associated with ultrafast greens. These will include new diseases, pests, and mechanical problems. There is a physical limit to how low we can cut and still maintain turf, although I have seen even Bermuda greens mowed daily at 0.080 inches—less than one-twelfth of an inch! When one considers that left alone that same plant has evolved and developed to grow to a natural height of 12 inches or more, or 100 times higher than it has been mowed, something has to give. We all seem to understand that, if you ran a car motor wide open at 8,000 rpms for hours on end, it would break. Yet golfers somehow think we can mow grass at ridiculously low heights, a practice that stresses the physical and physiological limits of the plant just as much as racing an engine stresses mechanical parts, and yet expect the plant to never "break" or die. That is why I predict that a whole family of nongrass plants will emerge as putting surfaces, and mosses seem likely candidates.

ARTIFICIAL TURF

The other alternative is artificial turf, or artificial turf combined with natural grass, or some sort of surface geogrid to protect and support a turf species but at a more sustainable height of cut while still producing fast greens. In any case, I believe that there is a bright future for synthetic turf, especially where there are expected to be continuing restrictions placed on the use of water, pesticides, fertilizers, fossil fuel, and even noise pollution. Nowhere in the rules of golf does it say it must be played on green, natural grass, and, in fact, golf is sometimes more fun and memorable when not played on lush turf. The lure of the game isn't the setting, although there are few places more beautiful and serene than a golf course, for the magical hook of golf is in the game itself, no matter what the playing surface may be.

Even if artificial turf does become popular for golf courses, the GOTFs will still be as important then as they are today, for even artificial turf will require daily management. I can say this with some authority, for I have purposely let the artificial turf green at our office go through a period of neglect and have observed what happened. Mother Nature seems always to want to reclaim her space, and so an interesting ecological succession began to take place on that green. First were the pioneer plants, in the form of algae, that were quite happy in the more shaded and damp portions of the green. Then I noticed that ants, little red ants, began to populate the higher, drier parts of the green, and burrow into the sandy filler material. Along the collar of the green, the bluegrass began to creep in and the rhizomes actually began to grow into the carpet. Weeds such as dandelions and thistles would happily live in the green if I, and others, didn't have the compulsion to pull them out whenever they got too big. But the big invaders seemed to be the mosses, which started with a small expeditionary force to establish a beachhead in the most shaded areas and which have been advancing toward the center at several feet per year. I have not counterattacked yet with my baking soda or Dawn Ultra™ dish soap, but I intend by actually setting up some small test plots to measure the efficacy of whatever pesticide substitute is suggested.

I believe that, if we did nothing to that little green, within two to three years we would have not only normal field weeds proliferating but also small shrubs and early succession trees. In fact, if we were not vigilant with our blacktop parking lot and cement walks, Mother Nature would reclaim those as hers, too. So GOTFs may be as essential on nonturf golf courses as they are now, or even more so.

FERTILIZERS AND BIOSTIMULANTS

Fertilizers and biostimulant materials and application methods will continue to evolve, for science and industry are just at the frontier of knowing how, when, why, and with what to nutritionally sustain plants. Some believe the future is in foliar feeding with material capable of being absorbed through the cuticle, directly into the plant tissue, and then being systemically translocated. Since the site of most metabolic activity is within the cell, the GOTF will need to better understand molecular biology. The key will be finding and maintaining the right balance of essential elements or precursors. Tissue-testing equipment and spectrophotometers and gas chromatographs may be standard pieces of greenkeeping equipment.

Others believe that foliar feeding is shifting the competitive edge to weakly rooted or nonrooted plants such as *Poa annua,* algae, and mosses. They believe that by only providing nutrition deep in the rootzone will turf species keep the upper hand. The mechanism for fertilizing them might be air- or water-injected encapsulated fertilizer placed deeper into the rootzone. Another avenue would be root feeding at construction with poly-coated material that can last for years at a metered rate. Then, too, once subirrigation becomes more common, fertilizing would be by "subfertigation."

SUBIRRIGATION

Speaking of subirrigation, I believe that it is inevitable that some form will be developed and become widely used on golf greens, and perhaps golf courses. I say greens for sure, for I am certain that water usage and the quality of that water are going to become more and more important. Even now many citizens see golf courses as luxury consumers of water, even effluent water that can be used for agriculture, and as the population grows and greater demands are placed on water, golf courses will be given low priority. (Although it sounds silly now, if water usage reaches crisis proportions, it may be that each citizen would be rationed or allocated so much water for personal use, and if you were a member of a golf club, you would have to transfer some of your water allocation to it for irrigation.) However, subirrigation would not only be very efficient and may allow for potable water to be used, it would also be more discrete and not be as "in your face," so to speak, as golf course irrigation is now.

In the near future, however, I believe it is predictable that water for golf course irrigation is going to go down in purity, or in other words, water quality will decrease. This means golf courses may only be allowed to use water that is considered unsuitable for other uses. Typically, this means water higher in salt, heavy metals, suspended biomaterial, and perhaps other local impurities such as boron or silicates. This translates into finding turf cultivars with higher salt tolerances, managing soil salts, and understanding the impact of such water on soil and commonly used fertilizers and pesticides. It may be that water to be used for chemical applications will have to be bought, or processed to remove confounding materials that might mute or misdirect the intent of the application. The cumulative effect on equipment and people will have to be studied and allowed for in the future. One can only speculate what long-term effects lower quality water will have, but there will be quite a few of them and they should be planned for accordingly. Vacuum-assisted drainage seems to have a bright future.

NONLETHAL PEST CONTROLS

One doesn't have to be too sharp to see that pesticide use is a public hot button, and the more nonlethal the means of pest control strategies, the better. One current example is the United States Environmental Protection Agency's (EPA's) attempt to get rid of all organophostate pesticides, including nematocides. For those who have seen what a nematode infestation can do to a golf green, not having good control is pretty scary. One alternative pest control strategy being looked at is to pump the rootzone full of a nonlethal gas, such as carbon dioxide or nitrogen oxide, that would kill the oxygen-breathing nematodes, but not the turf or people on the turf. Then the rootzone would be flushed with air to restimulate the plant roots. There have been minor successes with this approach, and this is yet another reason why having a green built to allow for rootzone gas exchange makes good sense.

MANAGING SOIL AIR

In fact, the futuristic idea of emphasizing managing soil air over our current thinking of managing soil water also seems inevitable. As we learn more about optimizing the growth potential of plants, managing rootzone gases will move from being a novelty to being a necessity. Of course, in rootzones there are either solids, gases, or liquids, and it is the balance of the gases and liquids that will most concern the GOTF. At present, several companies are offering affordable and accurate soil gas analyzers, and one even offers permanent sensors that can be placed into the rootzone profile and automatically control pumps to either vacuum or force air under a green to preset oxygen and/or moisture levels. To gain the full benefit of this equipment, the rootzone profile, including the tile system, gravel, and topmix, should be selected to support this concept. There is no way to simply retrofit an old green with such equipment and expect it to be as efficient as one designed and built to maximize it.

THE UPSIDE DOWN GREEN

It may even be that in the future that green profiles will be built upside down, with the coarsest materials on top and finer materials on the bottom. In such a design, poor-quality water would drain quickly, being pulled down by gravity, capillarity, and vacuum, more fresh air would be brought into the upper rootzone; there would be greater aerobic microbial activity to control organic matter buildup; and root systems would have to go deeper to reach capillary water. This would be the first revolutionary idea in green construction in the last 100 years, and one that is the child born of the mother necessity.

AIR HEADS

Clearly, air above and below the putting surface is something that the GOTF can and will manage more than now. Today it is common to see fans around greens, especially in more southern climates, where they can help overcome summer stress of turfgrass. But fans are loud and annoying, they affect incoming golf shots, and running the electric lines to run them out to each green is expensive. Plus they are inefficient for the most part. What if, instead of a big old fan sounding like a prop-driven airplane doing a thrust test before takeoff, there was a barely visible silent alternative that was more effective and efficient? Well, there isn't one—yet! Although I have proposed the following idea to the big three irrigation company engineers and salespeople, all I get in response is rolling of eyes. My idea would be something called air heads, like pop-up sprinkler heads, placed around the green and connected to a high-pressure air line—an irrigation system that sprays air. (I even suggested coloring the heads blonde to distinguish them from sprinkler heads and calling them air heads, but my yellow-haired wife thought that might be a little politically incorrect.) These air heads could be controlled like sprinkler heads and, when on, would blow a stream of air out across the putting surface in a much quieter and more uniform fashion than fans. They could be connected to time-delayed motion sensors that would turn the system off when golfers were on the green, and back on again when they left, so the green would be in moving air all day and night. I also envision quick couplers for air hoses to blow off dew, leaves, clippings, topdressing, and so on. And better yet would be to have those hoses in a pit with retractors, with a valve to switch between air and water, so one hose could do either job—or better yet, mix them to form a light mist to cool the air above the greens—or make snow in the winter to protect against winter desiccation. So I believe in the future that installing air systems will be as common as installing irrigation is today, at least for putting greens.

THE NEW AGE GREEN

Along the same lines of providing a futuristic rootzone is one called "The New Age Green," which is the brainchild of one of the original 1960s contributors to the USGA method, Leon Howard. Mr. Howard's original 1950s test plot work formed most of the recommendations that Dr. Ferguson and others edited into the presented form. Leon has continued his interest and activity in green construction for over 50 years, and now believes he is reaching a much improved green construction method for the new age, fine textured grasses. From years of experimentation and observation, he believes he has developed a system for the regeneration of micronutrients and fertility that may be as important as the physical properties of the rootzone mix. He says it maintains a better balance of air and water in the rootzone, as well as advances in amendments and nutrition. Some of the first golf course greens to be built by Howard's new method are going in in Tennessee, or in the middle of the transition zone, which should be a good test. To learn more about the continued advance that Leon Howard is making, he can be reached at the New Mix Lab, at phone 325-388-2174. Other researchers working closely with Leon Howard, such as David Doherty, are reevaluating the requirement for a standard 12-inch-deep rootzone and believe that an 8-inch-deep profile using 6-inch-tall cups may work well on lower-budget projects.

GLOBAL POSITIONING SYSTEMS/GEOGRAPHIC INFORMATION SYSTEMS

Over the past couple of years, the concept of global positioning systems/geographic information systems (GPS/GIS) has gained in sophistication and availability, and has become part of golf. Currently, it is used with yardage systems in golf carts or to lay out golf features instead of conventional surveying, or even to control functions on some pieces of maintenance equipment. However, in the future, the power of GPS/GIS systems will be as common and essential as walkie-talkies and computers on golf courses. On golf greens in particular, I see the ability to pinpoint a location on the ground as a tool to allow mapping of small zones that should best be managed individually. For example, suppose one area of a green is more prone to infestation of a particular pest, say dollar spot, than the rest of the green. That susceptible area could be mapped to create historic files so that over a number of days, weeks, months, and years a greenkeeper could measure the exact area and assess the damage and record the treatment; then the computer tech on staff (that position would be new, too, but will probably exist not too far into the future) could create a graphic or map to show the efficacy of the treatment. At some point, the concentration of the treatment could be precisely and automatically matched to the area and severity of the infestation, using a GPS/GIS controlled proportioner pump on the sprayer. Even now I see forward-thinking superintendents mapping areas of snow mold infection by location, type, and severity so they can precisely apply controls only where needed and in the precise rate. Such zonal maintenance capability could reduce required maintenance inputs, which would save time and money, and lessen environmental impact.

PESTICIDES

As science and technology better master gene printing, pests will be identified, not by the symptoms they cause, but rather by their DNA, and perhaps well in advance of an infection, so that an appropriate control can be applied. These future pesticides will be more targeted, safer, and more effective. One could write a book about the future of genetics and biochemical interactions, but that is way beyond my limited expertise.

INORGANIC AMENDMENTS

In the future, I believe that there will be strong justification for inorganic amendments in green rootzones. A century ago cinders were placed under greens to discourage earthworms as well as help drainage. It is not unthinkable that an inorganic product could be infused with a chemical that, when incorporated into a rootzone, released a micro amount of material sufficient to control threshold populations of certain pests. These would not necessarily be lethal materials, but perhaps something like an anti-pheromone for insects or worms, especially nematodes. It is possible these would be nothing more than resin sinks that can be charged up with a particular chemical on a long-term periodic basis to control root pathogens or other critters like mole crickets.

Inorganic amendments may also find greater utility and justification as water quality decreases and causes certain imbalances. Instead of cation exchange capacity, there may be a shift to anion exchange capacity, or to CEC and AEC together, to support a particular management program.

My point is that greens in the future may be radically different from those we have now at the start of this millennium, and one should be open-minded to the possibility. However, what will always remain the same is that the golf course superintendents and/or greenkeepers must find the best balance of chemical, biological, physical, and microclimatic factors for a golf green, to produce an acceptable playing surface to satisfy golfers who are, after all, paying the bills. It will become a more complex and intellectual search, and, as a result, the esteem and recognition of the greenkeeper will rise to new high levels.

Therefore, greens and greenkeepers should not be compared. Rather, they should be appreciated. Good greens are expected...great greens should be appreciated...and perfect greens cherished, for they are as fragile and changeable as life itself.

INDEX